This is the first in a series of studies on competition and monopoly in American industry financed by a grant from the Merrill Foundation for the Advancement of Financial Knowledge. The series has been planned to include a number of studies focusing on the effectiveness of competition in particular industrial markets accompanied by certain investigations into the effect on competition of various elements of market structure and business practice common to many industries. Although each volume is an independent study representing only the views of its author, all are expected to contribute to the central objective of the whole project: an evaluation of monopoly policy in the United States.

COMPETITION IN THE

COMPETITION IN THE RAYON INDUSTRY

JESSE W. MARKHAM

Assistant Professor of Economics
Vanderbilt University

HARVARD UNIVERSITY PRESS · CAMBRIDGE

1952

Distributed in Great Britain by
Geoffrey Cumberlege, Oxford University Press, London

LIBRARY OF CONGRESS CATALOG CARD NUMBER: 52–5035

Printed in the United States of America

TO PENELOPE AND MY MOTHER

PREFACE

This study, in substantially its present form but under the title "Price and Output Behavior in the Domestic Rayon Industry," was accepted in 1948 in partial fulfillment of the requirements for the Ph.D. Degree at Harvard University. The intervening two years I have devoted to collecting and analyzing additional data to verify some of the tentative conclusions reached in the original study, to strengthening the analysis, and to improving the style and presentation. In the process, several of the chapters have been materially expanded but the scope of the study has remained about the same.

Although I had, as a callow youth, spent three years in the production and accounting departments of one of the large rayon companies, my interest in the economics of the rayon industry was first aroused while studying economic theory at Harvard University under the late Professor Joseph A. Schumpeter. Professor Schumpeter had closely observed the bonanza days of the rayon industry in Europe and in the United States and frequently employed the industry as illustrative of his perennial gale of creative destruction. In a footnote (p. 90) in his *Capitalism, Socialism and Democracy* he suggests that, although the industry has never come close to conforming to all the conditions of theoretically perfect competition, there is little reason to conclude that society is any worse off for its not having done so. In the final chapter of this study, entitled "The Workability of Competition in the Domestic Rayon Industry," I have tried to give an answer to the question Professor Schumpeter raised by applying several definitions of workable competition to the rayon industry, including one that he, perhaps unwittingly, suggested; namely, an industry may be said to be workably competitive if public policy measures can produce no changes in the industry that would obviously make society better off. Since a generally agreed-upon definition of workable competition has not yet emerged from the writings of those who are presently concerned with the concept, I have employed this definition as a provisional standard in judging the extent to which competition in the rayon industry has been workable. However, because value judgments must inevitably play some part in framing such a definition, it is probably superfluous to state that I cherish no expectations that all economists who read the study will agree with my conclusions. I do hope, however, that I have provided something of interest to those who are students of economic theory and its relevance to framing public policy toward industry.

More than to any other individual, I am indebted to Professor Edward S. Mason, George F. Baker Professor of Economics at Harvard University, for aid in carrying the project through successive stages to its final form. He has read the manuscript at several stages of its development and has given me the benefit of his very valuable comments and criticisms. Moreover, his classroom lectures and seminar discussions have greatly influenced my thinking upon the sort of problems treated in this book. I, however, am entirely responsible for the views expressed.

I also owe much to Professors George W. Stocking, Carl Kaysen, and Myron W. Watkins, and to Dr. Sidney S. Alexander, Dr. Corwin D. Edwards, and Mr. Stanley B. Hunt, Director of the Textile Economics Bureau, for having read and commented upon all or part of the manuscript. I am particularly indebted to Professors Stocking and Kaysen for their extremely helpful suggestions and their time spent in consultations with me. My debt to Mr. Hunt for the use of statistical data compiled by the Textile Economics Bureau is acknowledged in numerous places throughout the study. I am also grateful to Mr. J. W. Ward, a graduate student in the American Civilization Department at the University of Minnesota, for his criticism of ideas and expression. My debts to the writings of others, particularly those of Professors Edward H. Chamberlin and George J. Stigler, are acknowledged throughout the study.

I have naturally benefited much from consultations and correspondence with various officials of companies engaged in producing and in using rayon. Some of them have gone to considerable trouble and expense to compile and make available to me data that could not possibly have been obtained elsewhere. The industrial engineers and cost accountants of one multi-plant firm undertook the task of computing the statistical relationships between unit costs and size of plant and unit costs and per cent of capacity operations. Because they preferred that I do so, the names of companies and individuals have not been mentioned in my acknowledgments of their assistance. My discussion of the extent to which rayon competes with natural fibers owes much to the information furnished me by Mr. M. K. Horne, Jr. of the National Cotton Council of America and Professor Daniel Vandermuelen of Claremont College. Both of these gentlemen made available to me their unpublished manuscripts concerned with intertextile competition and helpfully suggested other sources of data.

Finally, a research grant from the Institute for Research and Training in the Social Sciences at Vanderbilt University enabled me to consult sources of information that otherwise would have had to remain unexplored, and the typing services furnished by the Institute were essential to preparing the manuscript for publication. To Professor George W. Stocking, Director of the Institute, who arranged for the financial and typing assistance and for a teaching schedule that permitted continuing research on the project, I shall be forever grateful.

A good preface should probably contain a sufficiently full description of the study to allow the reader to decide whether or not he is interested in its contents. Since a complete description appears in the introductory chapter, I shall try here, in a few concise sentences, to convey to the reader only the general nature of the problem investigated. Since theoretical models of oligopolistic markets yield, according to the assumptions made, price and output solutions that range from those which would be expected under perfectly competitive conditions to those which would be expected under conditions of pure monopoly, empirical studies can help us single out those assumptions which seem to hold the highest degree of relevancy to the problem. The domestic rayon yarn industry, for reasons set forth in the introductory chapter, is a good candidate for a case study of an oligopolistic market.

In this connection, the reader may be interested in the metamorphosis of the title of the study. The first chapter written was concerned with the relationship among firms with respect to price determination. After making an analysis of list-price behavior, I was prepared to call the study "Monopolistic Aspects of the Rayon Market." As the study progressed, however, evidence of intertextile competition and of deviations from list prices during periods of depression appeared so strong that the original tentative title was dropped in favor of the present one. If only from a tactical point of view, the presence of competition is probably more difficult to establish with finality than the presence of monopoly. The discovery of a single monopoly restraint in an industry prevents it from being classified among the highly competitive ones, whereas the discovery of a large number of competitive forces does not prove the absence of monopoly. Nevertheless, I have selected the present title because I believe conditions in the rayon industry to have more nearly conformed with the precepts of competition than with those of monopoly. I therefore believe it to be more descriptive than one implicative of fairly strong monopoly forces.

J. W. M.

Nashville, Tennessee
November 1950

CONTENTS

APPENDICES

CHARTS

ILLUSTRATIONS

TABLES

1

INTRODUCTION
to the Problem

To those who believe that price theory can be tested and implemented by empirical price studies, the domestic rayon industry offers itself as fertile ground for a case study. Until the middle thirties, rayon output more closely approximated homogeneity than does the output of most large industries in the American economy. From 1911 to 1920 all rayon produced in the United States was 150-denier viscose yarn; the entire output was accounted for by a single firm. Although new production processes, new types of yarn, and new commodities such as staple fiber have been gradually introduced as the number of firms has increased, the bulk of the domestic rayon yarn output can still be conveniently reduced to its 150-denier equivalent, or 150-denier yarn can, for purposes of price and output analysis, be viewed as representative of all rayon.

Moreover, the structure of the rayon industry falls within the definitional framework of an oligopoly. The number of rayon producers has never exceeded twenty; virtually the entire domestic output has been in the hands of eight producers. Two firms still account for one-half of total output and one firm alone still accounts for approximately one-third of total output. All sellers produce yarns of similar denier and filament count and, until 1947, quoted identical prices for any given denier. Although some differences in grading among producers have undoubtedly existed, by and large uniformity of products made possible through chemical control has made for a homogeneous product among producers employing the same process. Hence, the domestic rayon industry has been, until recently, an oligopoly with little product differentiation. Since much recent literature acclaims the ubiquity of oligopoly in the industrial sector of the American economy and the concentration of productive capacity in the hands of few sellers in many industries, case studies of price and output behavior (when a meaningful construction can be placed upon the terms "price" and "output") in industries characterized by these features should be of considerable interest.

The distinguishing feature of an oligopolistic industry is the possibility of a number of alternative relationships between a firm and its rivals — a possibility not admissible in the areas of either perfect competition or monopoly as ordinarily defined since no single "rival" can influence price or output in a perfectly competitive industry and a perfect monopolist has no rivals. Current economic literature contains explanatory hypotheses which yield, depending upon the assumptions made, solutions to oligopolistic markets ranging all the way from a perfectly competitive to a monopoly price. Since such a wide range of possible solutions leaves so much in doubt, the chief contribution made by this study is that portion which concerns itself with the relationship among sellers. Although a close examination of a single market can produce little for purposes of generalization, a large number of such studies might clear up much of the haze that surrounds markets in which sellers are few.

The relationships among sellers in the rayon industry produce neither a perfectly competitive nor a monopoly price but a price which probably varies between the two over the course of the business cycle. Although an analysis of published price lists reveals evidence of strong price leadership, deviations from published prices lead *de facto* prices toward the competitive level during a depression and difficulties of entry permit sellers to charge more than the competitive price in a market revival. Even if it could be assumed that the price leader has acted as though the remaining sellers would follow any price revision he would make in either direction, however, the arbitrary power which the price leader has had over rayon prices has been severely limited by the prices of closely competing products. Within fairly narrow limits, declining natural fiber yarn prices unaccompanied by rayon price reductions lead to a substitution of cotton, silk, and wool for rayon. Since natural fiber prices are usually regarded as highly competitive, it follows that prices geared closely to them partake of some of their competitive aspects. Hence, the rayon industry is at once an oligopoly and a segment of a larger, very highly competitive, market. The latter feature of the industry severely limits the use of any potential monopoly power inherent in the former.

There are several reasons why some *modus operandi* such as the tacit acceptance of a price leader should have developed in the rayon industry: (1) Rayon was introduced and developed in the United States by subsidiaries of European firms; hence, domestic sellers were, until recently, loosely associated with each other through European cartels. (2) Early consumer resistance to a synthetic substitute for silk and cotton, attributable in part to adverse publicity, provided rayon producers with a common enemy. By the late twenties they had jointly launched several organizations and associations for purposes of advertising, chemical research, and promulgation of information of interest to the industry. Such common interests could not be best served by complete arms' length competition. (3) The home offices of the two largest sellers are located close to each other in Wilmington, Delaware, and the principal sales office or home office of practically every domestic producer is located in New York City; whether by accident, by design, or for economic reasons, such proximity enables each to keep in touch with the activities of all. (4) Structurally, the rayon industry was, until about 1930, similar to those industries likely to be characterized by price leadership of the dominant firm type.

Having accepted the evidence that the price leader's price is representative of prices throughout the industry, the remaining chapters constitute a case study of that often discussed but as yet rather poorly defined economic virus, the administered price. It had been hoped at the outset that considerably more attention could be paid to the differences among firms with respect to costs and to output policy over the business cycle. Output and cost data for individual firms, however, particularly the latter, are closely guarded by most producers. Sufficient evidence is available to show that large producers bear more than their proportionate share of output curtailment during periods of depressed rayon markets, but large producers have occasionally secured some coöperation from small and medium-size producers on production policy. For example, during the 1932 rayon market crisis, large producers stressed the need for "production leadership" as well as price leadership. Most firm cost data available are limited to the few largest producers, one of which generously submitted in index form the relationship between unit costs and size of plant (the company is a multi-plant firm) and the relationship between unit costs and per cent of capacity operated for one of its plants. These two curves, which approximate the envelope curve and short-run cost curve of economic theory, were helpful in explaining much of the historic price and output behavior of the industry and the differences in price and output behavior between large and small firms. In view of the possibilities that (1) the cost curve of a single-plant firm may not be the same as that of an identical plant when operated by a multi-plant firm, and (2) that cost curves computed at an instant of time may lose some of their relevance when applied to time periods a few years removed, the curves may have been given more general application than can be justified on strict theoretical grounds.

Lack of both absolute tools of measurement and comparable administered industrial prices with which the price of rayon could be contrasted led to a decision against special treatment of the question of price flexibility. The movement of rayon price with respect to various orders of economic fluctuations and to such variables as costs, output, and competing commodity prices is central to the entire study. But measurement of the flexibility of particular prices in some absolute sense must await the development of more meaningful standards.

Most of the time series which appear in the pages that follow have been taken up through 1948. It should be emphasized that, although rayon was a fairly homogeneous commodity at any given instant of time over most of the period covered in this study, rayon yarn has undergone remarkable changes since it was first produced on a commercial scale in this country in 1911. Prior to World War I rayon was, at best, regarded as an inferior substitute for silk; by the outbreak of World War II rayon had practically displaced silk in the production of many style fabrics and had made serious inroads in a number of cotton fabric markets. It is impossible, of course, to take into direct account the secular improvement in quality. Moreover, in the early thirties over 90 per cent of the output of the industry was in the form of viscose textile yarns. By 1948 only 66 per cent of total rayon output was produced by the viscose process, of which over one-third was in the form of heavy industrial yarns such as automobile tire yarns, and nearly one-fourth was staple fiber. Both tire yarn and staple fiber are relatively new products which differ considerably from textile yarns. By 1948 one-third of the output of the rayon industry was produced by the acetate process either in the form of textile yarns or staple fiber, whereas in 1930 less than 10 per cent was produced by the acetate process. Hence, much of what has been said about the homogeneity of rayon is less applicable to the past ten or twelve years than to the period 1911–1938. Although treated separately where possible, tire yarns, staple fiber, and acetate yarns have, for certain purposes of analysis, been viewed simply as viscose yarn output; i.e., the assumption is sometimes made that the rayon industry and the viscose rayon industry are the same. Such an assumption, while it does not appreciably impair the analysis as a whole, is much less valid for the more recent years than for the period 1911–1938.

2

DEVELOPMENT AND STRUCTURE of the Rayon Yarn Industry in the United States

The meteoric rise of the rayon industry to a position of significance in the American economy has few parallels in our industrial history. In the brief span of 40 years, annual rayon production has increased from 36 thousand pounds to over one billion pounds. In 1923 the rayon industry was of so little importance that it was inauspiciously included among "industries not elsewhere classified" in the *Census of Manufactures;* by 1947 the annual output of the industry had reached a value of slightly less than three-quarters of a billion dollars.[1] Increases in employment, though not quite so striking, were significant: Between 1925 and 1947, the number of wage earners employed by rayon producers increased from 19,128 to about 60,000; over the same period, wage-earner payrolls increased from 23 million dollars to 150 million dollars.[2]

Expanding from a single plant built at Marcus Hook, Pennsylvania, in 1910, the industry now consists of 16 companies that operate 31 plants located in 15 states, not including the plants of two new companies that have recently announced plans to enter the industry. Four large firms own and operate over two-thirds of all plants and employ over three-fourths of all wage earners in the industry.

[1] 1947 *Census of Manufactures,* rayon and allied products section.

[2] United States Department of Labor, *Wages in the Rayon Industry,* Bulletin no. 806 of the Bureau of Labor Statistics (Washington, May 1944), and 1947 *Census of Manufactures.*

The phenomenal success of rayon in the United States is usually attributed to a rapid secular decline in price (from $5.00 per pound in 1919 to $0.54 per pound in 1941) made possible by an unusually high rate of technological progress and the perfection of mass-production techniques.[3] Effective tariff protection, brilliant marketing strategy, and product improvement through chemical research, however, have also been important factors.

A. Historical Background of the European and American Rayon Industry[4]

The technology of rayon production is one of the few mass-production techniques wherein European scientists and industrialists have set the pace. Indeed, all the four major processes employed in commercial production of rayon were introduced and perfected in Europe and, until 1929, the rayon industry in the United States was composed chiefly of subsidiaries of established European firms. Even producers in this country not bound by financial ties to a European parent were, until about 1935, dependent upon European technical assistance. Consequently, some discussion of the development of the rayon industry both here and abroad is essential to an understanding of the American market. A detailed treatment of the technical aspects of rayon production, however, lies beyond the scope of this study.

As early as 1664, Dr. Robert Hook, an eminent British scientist, foresaw the possibility of producing silk artificially,[5] and later predicted fortunes for those who could successfully produce it commercially.[6] In 1754 René Réaumur, a French naturalist and physicist, stated that there was no reason why the work of the silkworm

[3] United States Department of Labor, *Bulletin* no. 806, p. 2.

[4] The history of the rayon industry and a more complete description of the major processes used may be found in the following sources: Mois H. Avram, *The Rayon Industry* (2nd ed.; New York: D. Van Nostrand, 1929); Joseph Foltzer, *Artificial Silk and Its Manufacture*, translated from the French by T. Woodhouse (London: I. Pitman, 1924); Edward Wheeler, *The Manufacture of Artificial Silk, with Special Reference to the Viscose Process* (New York: D. Van Nostrand, 1931); United States Tariff Commission, *The Rayon Industry* (Washington, 1944); E. W. K. Schwarz and H. R. Mauersberger, *Rayon and Synthetic Yarn Handbook* (New York: Rayon Publishing Co., 1934; 2nd ed., 1936); E. W. K. Schwarz and H. R. Mauersberger, *Rayon and Staple Fiber Handbook* (New York: Rayon Publishing Co., 1939); and various historical articles in the *Rayon Journal*, *Rayon Organon*, and *Textile World*.

[5] Until 1926, rayon was called "artificial silk." The term "rayon" met with general acceptance in this country after the Federal Trade Commission, on October 31, 1925, accepted it "as meaning and properly designating the artificial silk products, the basis and chief ingredient of which is cellulose." Avram, *The Rayon Industry*, p. 227.

[6] Avram, p. 2, quoting *Micrographia*.

could not be duplicated in the laboratory;[7] yet a century passed before practical experimentation began, and another half-century elapsed before rayon was successfully produced on a commercial scale.

Early development of rayon yarns began after F. G. Keller, a Saxon weaver, discovered a mechanical process for producing wood pulp. Soon afterward, Louis Schawabe, of Manchester, England, and George Audemars, a Lausanne chemist, independently produced rayon filaments by forcing chemical solutions into coagulating baths.[8] In 1885, Sir Joseph Swan, a co-worker of Edison's, after eight years of experimentation, produced rayon, denitrated it to remove its inflammability, and exhibited some fabrics in London. Lack of knowledge of manufacturing techniques and of the potentialities of the rayon market probably accounts for the failure of early experimenters to attempt commercial production.

The Nitrocellulose Process. The work of Count Hilaire de Chardonnet, a pupil of Pasteur, culminated all the efforts of his predecessors and won for him by general acclaim the title "father of the rayon industry." [9] After he obtained his first French patent on November 11, 1884, Chardonnet exhibited rayon at the great Paris Exhibition in 1889. Capitalists were sufficiently impressed to provide funds for the first artificial silk factory at Besançon, Chardonnet's birthplace. Two years of operation under the nitrocellulose process overcame many of the technical problems connected with large-scale production and rendering the filaments non-inflammable. The process, later employed in Belgium and the United States by the Tubize Company, was rendered obsolete by the twenties with the perfection of the viscose process, and its use was discontinued in the United States when Tubize employees walked out of the Hopewell, Virginia plant on strike in 1934.

The Viscose Process. The chemistry underlying the viscose process was discovered through experiments conducted by Charles F. Cross and E. J. Bevan of Great Britain, who obtained patents on the process in 1892. Eight years of use in the manufacture of incandescent lamps, linen and curtain fabrics, doorhandles, valve wheels, cellulose film, and artificial leather improved the process considerably and, in 1900, viscose yarn was exhibited in Paris. The discovery

[7] Avram, p. 2, quoting Réaumur's *Memoires pour Servir à l'Histoire des Insectes.*
[8] Avram, p. 2.
[9] Avram, p. 3.

of the centrifugal spinning pot by C. F. Topham in 1902 also solved many of the manufacturing difficulties.

The Cross and Bevan patents were taken over by Courtaulds, Ltd., which, in 1904, began commercial production along with Vereinigte Glanzstoff Fabriken A. G. and a group of French, Belgian, and Swiss manufacturers. In 1910 Samuel A. Salvage, a yarn agent for Courtaulds in America, persuaded his company to erect a viscose yarn plant at Marcus Hook, Pennsylvania. Salvage's foresight, coupled with exclusive American rights to the Cross and Bevan patents, led to the establishment of the Viscose Company, the largest producer of rayon in the world for over twenty years. The company changed its name to the American Viscose Corporation in 1937.

Like all rayon plants, viscose yarn plants are sharply divided into chemical and textile operations. The latter are quite comparable to the familiar operations employed in the production of various types of natural fiber yarns. The chemical operations, however, are a distinctive feature of rayon and other synthetic yarn production. In all three processes currently used in the United States, chemical departments perform two principal operations: producing the solution from cellulose, and transforming the solution into rayon yarn. In the viscose process the blending of sheets of wood pulp or cotton linters (purified linters) is the initial step in the first operation. A predetermined number of sheets (totaling approximately 250 pounds on the average) of known weight are sorted from the different batches of stock in order to insure uniformity and even running quality in the finished yarn. The blended sheets are steeped for several hours in a strong caustic soda solution which dissolves the soda-soluble hemi-cellulose leaving only the resistant alpha-cellulose. Hydraulic presses then squeeze out the excess caustic soda liquid, which is drained off and recovered for future use, leaving the sheets (or alkali cellulose) three times their original dry weight. A disintegrating machine or shredder reduces the sheets to white fluffy crumbs which are discharged into aging cans and stored at a constant temperature for fifty hours. The mature crumbs of alkali cellulose are then placed in rotating drums and mixed with a measured amount of carbon bisulphide. Within a few hours the agitation reduces the pulp to an orange-colored, spongy mass called "cellulose xanthate." The xanthate is conveyed to a mixer provided with powerful paddle stirrers where it is dissolved in water or a weak solution of caustic soda to form the spinning solution. The dissolving process requires about six hours.[10] The viscose solution, a mixture having about the consistency and appearance of molasses, is drawn into tanks where successive meshes of a series of filter presses remove all foreign matter and undissolved cellulose xanthate. The filtered solution is then stored in vats for several days to age or ripen to the proper stage of viscosity and deaerated with vacuum pumps to extract air bubbles. Filtration and aging is completed in about 100 hours.

The second operation, consisting of spinning[11] the rayon yarn, is accomplished by pumping the ripened viscose solution through a candle-like filter, to which is attached a spinnerette submerged in a coagulating bath. The spinnerette face, usually made of platinum, has a multitude of nearly invisible orifices through which the viscose is forced. The size and number of orifices determine the denier and filament count of the finished rayon yarn. The coagulating bath contains sulphuric acid, a salt (usually sodium sulphate), and glucose to prevent salt crystallization. As the jets of viscose from the spinnerette orifices enter the bath, the acid in the bath neutralizes the caustic soda in the viscose solution, breaks down the xanthate, and precipitates the regenerated cellulose. The coagulated and neutralized filaments have sufficient strength to undergo the winding operation without breakage. Two methods of taking the thread from the bath are currently employed: (1) A bobbin system, in which the filaments are wound parallel, without twisting, on a perforated metal cyclinder; the twist is then imparted to the yarn in a subsequent throwing operation; and (2) a centrifugal or Topham box method, which gives the wet yarn a twist of about two and one-half to four turns per inch as the coagulated filaments are carried vertically over a Godet wheel and dropped through a funnel into a spinning pot. The pot revolves at a rate of from 3000 to 10,000 revolutions per minute depending upon the desired twist. For low-twist yarns the latter method is more economical since it eliminates the subsequent throwing room operation. The bobbin method must be employed for all high-twist yarns. Improved strength in rayon over time, however, has virtually eliminated the necessity of a high-

[10] If delustered yarns are desired, pigments are introduced at this stage.

[11] Actually, the formation of the thread. No spinning is involved but the term has long been used in the industry to describe this operation.

twist to protect the filaments, thereby bringing the centrifugal box method into more general use.

After several baths and a washing and bleaching process, rayon yarn is handled in much the same manner as any other yarn. Currently it is put up in skeins, cones, cops, beams, or spools according to customers' specifications. Viscose yarns destined for knitting mills are not usually bleached at the rayon plant since this can be performed easily at the mill after the yarn has been knitted into fabric. After the creeling, winding, and spooling operations, the yarn is graded according to breakages, loose filaments, discolorations, etc., by highly trained inspectors into first, second, and inferior grades of yarn. There is pressure upon viscose producers to grade yarns and sell their imperfect product as second grade or inferior yarn since their only alternative is to sell it as waste. This is not true of the acetate process, where imperfect yarns may be used as a purified raw material and again carried through the chemical process.

Raw materials consumed in the production of one pound of rayon under the viscose process are about 1.2 pounds of wood pulp or cotton linters, 1.8 pounds of sulphuric acid, 1.4 pounds of caustic soda, 0.5 pounds of glucose, 0.4 pounds of carbon bisulphide, 0.4 pounds of other chemicals, and approximately 175.0 gallons of water.[12] The tremendous purified water requirements, about 7 billion gallons per year for the large viscose yarn plants and about 40 billion gallons for the large acetate yarn plants, are an important factor in rayon plant location decisions.

The Cuprammonium Process. L. H. Despaisses, a French chemist, announced the first alternative method to the nitrocellulose process in 1890,[13] after other scientists, notably Schweizer (1857) and Weston (1882), had laid the basic groundwork through successful experimentation with the principle in the laboratory, and later in manufacturing incandescent electric lamp filaments. After Dr. H. Pauly had modified and improved the cuprammonium process in Germany, capitalists in the Mulhouse region organized the Glanzstoff Fabriken, A. G. at Elberfeld in 1898, and a year later constructed a plant at Oberbruch. Glanzstoff soon abandoned the cuprammonium for the viscose process, but Dr. E. Elsaesser of Germany subsequently perfected the cuprammonium process and

[12] Schwarz and Mauersberger, *Rayon and Synthetic Yarn Handbook*, p. 70.
[13] Avram, p. 7.

put it on a commercial basis by making it possible to produce filaments finer than silk. It has been used by J. P. Bemberg, A. G. in Germany since 1918, and in the United States by the American Bemberg Corporation, a subsidiary of the German company, since 1928.

Technically, the process is quite similar to the viscose process; however, the following differences should be mentioned: Cuprammonium yarns can be made only from cotton linters, whereas viscose yarns may be produced from either wood pulp or cotton linters, or both. The alkali crumbs are immersed in a copper sulphate solution instead of carbon bisulphide and are later dissolved in a solution of ammonia. An important variation from the viscose process also occurs in the spinning operation. When the solution passes through the spinnerette orifices, jets of the solution pass into a glass funnel where diffusion and absorption of the ammonia in the liquid bath induces coagulation. The filaments then pass through an additional acid bath where the copper residue is extracted. Because coagulation takes place less rapidly in the cuprammonium than in the viscose process, the thread may be stretched to almost any desired degree of fineness. For this reason, producers that employ the process specialize in very fine denier yarns. The cost of production is higher under the cuprammonium than under the viscose process and a price differential has always existed between cuprammonium and viscose yarns. Since 1928, the first year cuprammonium yarn was produced in the United States, the differential has decreased but has not entirely disappeared. The textile department operations are similar to those of the viscose process.

The Cellulose Acetate Process. Although experimentation in the acetate process also began in Europe, cellulose acetate yarn was first produced successfully on a commercial scale in the United States. The cellulose acetate chemical had been prepared by Naudin and Schutzenberger as early as 1865 but no progress was made until 1894, at which time it was discovered that zinc chloride or sulphuric acid could be used as a catalytic agent to speed up its formation. Subsequent research by Cross and Bevan led to their patent in 1899, the first obtained for the technical application of acetate.

The first real impetus to the acetate process came during World War I when it was discovered that cellulose acetate "dope," a protective chemical dressing, could be used on airplane wings. By this time the Dreyfus brothers, Camille and Henri, had successfully produced acetate fibers and toilet articles in their laboratory in Switzerland. Upon the invitation of the British Government, the Dreyfus brothers established a "dope" plant at Spondon, England, to service the R.A.F. Later, at Cumberland, Maryland, a plant was constructed to service the United States Air Corps. When the war ended, demand for "dope" was reduced to practically zero. The British Cellulose and Chemical Manufacturing Company (now Celanese Corporation) was formed in 1918 and the former "dope" plants were converted to manufacture textile filaments and yarns. The yarn, which the company has always sold under the trade name "Celanese" [14] rather than the generic name rayon, was successfully produced in 1924 in the Cumberland plant after the Dreyfus brothers had bought the patent rights to produce acetate yarn in the United States from the Lustron Company.

Until intricate acid recovery systems were devised, the acetate process was not widely used. In 1924, acetate yarns were priced considerably above viscose yarns of identical denier and filament count. By 1937, however, the introduction of better acid recovery methods, particularly for acetone recovery, had decreased production costs to where acetate yarns could be priced comparably to viscose yarns.

Primary acetate is produced by treating purified bleached cotton linters from five to eight hours with a mixture of equal parts acetic acid and glacial acetic acid. A catalyst, usually sulphuric acid, is used to hasten the acetylation of the cellulose. The resulting primary acetate is not suitable for the manufacture of synthetic yarns because it is impervious to moistures and dyestuffs and soluble only in such industrially impractical solvents as chloroform. Hence, it must be placed in huge storage vessels and diluted with acetic acid and water and allowed to ripen until chemical tests show that the proper degree of solubility has been attained. The solution (now secondary acetate) is run off into large vats of cold water equipped with rotating paddles that induce precipitation of fine white flakes. These are transferred to washing tanks to settle and the clear liquid is piped to a recovery plant where the acetic acid is salvaged for re-use. After several baths the flakes are dried and pressed into

[14] Acetate rayon producers have recently approved the word "estron" as a new generic term for fibers made from cellulose esters. References to the rayon industry throughout this study, however, include the viscose, acetate, and cuprammonium processes unless otherwise stated.

blocks or bales which are transferred to the spinning department.[15] From this stage of production the viscose and acetate processes are quite similar in principle. The stock is blended from several batches and conditioned to a fixed moisture content to make the spinning solution. It is then dissolved in a proper amount of acetone in heavy closed mixing vessels where it is constantly stirred. From the mixers the solution passes into a blending tank where the thick, very viscous, almost colorless liquid is filtered several times, deaerated, and stored in large supply tanks from where it is piped to the spinning machines.

In spinning acetate yarns, coagulation is induced by immersion in warm air instead of a liquid bath; however, the same spinnerette principle is employed as in the viscose process. Warm air evaporates the acetone, leaving coagulated filaments which are passed over a guide and collected on a motor-driven spindle carrying a bobbin. The yarn is ready at this stage to be put up in spools, cones, cops, or other types of packaging as desired by the fabricating mills. No additional washing and bleaching operation is necessary.

The raw materials required to produce one pound of rayon yarn under the acetate process are 0.70 pounds of cotton linters, 0.07 pounds of sulphuric acid, 2.40 pounds each of acetic anhydride and glacial acetic acid, 4.00 pounds of acetone, and about 1000.00 gallons of water.[16]

B. Development of the Rayon Yarn Industry in the United States

The history of the rayon yarn industry in the United States may be divided into two phases: (1) The period of introduction by established European firms and American firms under European technical direction; and (2) the gradual breaking away from European ownership and control. The first phase began in 1910 with the establishment of American Viscose Corporation's plant at Marcus Hook, Pennsylvania, then a wholly owned subsidiary of Courtaulds, Ltd., and continued through 1928.[17] The second phase commenced

[15] Acetate flakes are usually produced in a separate building located some distance from the spinning department. There is no precise counterpart for this stage of production in the viscose process.

[16] Schwarz and Mauersberger, *Rayon and Synthetic Yarn Handbook*, p. 84.

[17] Foreign-owned and foreign-controlled subsidiaries continued building new plants and adding to their old plants until World War II, but the introductory period may be considered as virtually completed by 1928 when American Enka Corporation was organized with a plant at Asheville, North Carolina, as a subsidiary of A. K. U. (Allgemeene Kunstzijde Unie) of Arnhem, Holland, and when American Chatillon Cor-

when Du Pont bought out all foreign holdings in the old Du Pont Fibersilk Company in 1929 and was virtually completed during World War II when Courtaulds sold its interests in the American Viscose Corporation to a group of American banking firms on April 16, 1941, and the Office of Alien Property acquired the plants of American Enka, American Bemberg, and North American from the Netherlands Government.[18]

Prior to the establishment of the plant at Marcus Hook, several attempts had been made to produce rayon in the United States but none became successful business ventures. When Cross and Bevan discovered their viscose process in 1892, they communicated their findings to Dr. Arthur D. Little of Boston. Subsequently, with a group of intimate friends, he experimented with the production of viscose molding, sheets, and solutions, but did not attempt production of yarn until 1900. In that year Dr. Little and his associates set up the Cellulose Products Company, after an extensive study of European viscose yarn plants. The company held options on the American rights to the Cross and Bevan process. The venture collapsed in a year due to a lack of funds.

A few months later, in 1901, the General Artificial Silk Company was started in Philadelphia. Rights to the Cross and Bevan viscose solution patent were obtained from the Cellulose Products Company on a royalty basis, and title to the Stearn and Topham spinning patent was obtained from the inventors. Promoters of the General Artificial Silk Company found that it took far more than the originally estimated capital to produce rayon on a commercial scale. After three attempts at refinancing, the company was sold at a receiver's sale in 1904 to Silas W. Pettit, chief stockholder of the company, for $25,000. Pettit continued the venture under the name of the Genasco Company after he purchased the Stearn and Topham spinning rights for an additional $25,000. In four years of operations, production reached a peak of 600 pounds per day, but the venture was financially unsuccessful until Pettit's death in 1909.

Upon the death of Pettit, Samuel A. Salvage, an aggressive,

---

poration was established by joint American and foreign capital to exercise the American rights of the Ruth-Aldo acetate process and, later, the viscose process of Italian Chatillon Corporation.

[18] Since their acquisition the American Enka Corporation has been released from government control and controlling interest in the properties of American Bemberg and the North American Rayon Corporation has been sold to Beaunit Mills, Incorporated. See *Moody's Manual*, 1949.

forward-looking representative of Courtaulds in the United States, persuaded his company to purchase the patent rights from Pettit's heirs and commence producing on a commercial scale at Marcus Hook in 1910. Annual output of the company increased from 362,544 pounds in 1911 to over 225 million pounds by the outbreak of World War II. An array of staggering figures evidences the almost unparalleled success of Salvage's venture. Starting with an initial investment by Courtaulds of only $930,000, the company has financed its rapid expansion completely out of earnings. In twenty-four years the company's aggregate net profits amounted to $354,000,000, or 38,000 per cent of original investment. Dividends of $237,000,000, or about 25,500 per cent of investment, were paid to Courtaulds. The ratio of net profits to its sales of about $1,025,000,000 was 35 per cent.[19] *Fortune* has commented, "American Viscose, modest, secretive, and unknown, is one of the industrial miracles of our times, a phenomenon comparable to Standard Oil, or the automobile empire of Henry Ford." [20] The company now operates plants at Marcus Hook, Meadville, and Lewiston, Pennsylvania, Nitro and Parkersburg, West Virginia, and Roanoke, Radford, and Front Royal, Virginia. Total annual capacity (after completion of plants currently under construction) is estimated at nearly 400 million pounds. The company produces viscose and acetate rayon yarn and staple fiber.

The expiration of the Viscose Company's Cross and Bevan patents, the development and improvement of other processes, the growing general acceptance of rayon, and the high cost of silk (twenty dollars per pound in 1919) led to rapid expansion in the domestic rayon industry in the twenties. In 1920 the Du Pont Fibersilk Company was founded jointly by E. I. du Pont de Nemours and Company and the Comptoir des Textiles Artificiels of France, with the construction of a plant at Buffalo, New York. Du Pont purchased the French interests in 1929 but continued to maintain cross-patent agreements with them and with other European firms. Du Pont is the second largest producer of rayon in the United States, currently operating plants at Buffalo, New York, Richmond and Waynesboro, Virginia, and Old Hickory, Tennessee.

In the same year the Tubize Artificial Silk Company of America was organized as an outgrowth of the Fabrique de Soie Artificielle

[19] See Clair Wilcox, *Competition and Monopoly in American Industry*, Temporary National Economic Committee, Monograph no. 21 (Washington, 1940), pp. 204–205.

[20] *Fortune*, July 1937, pp. 40, 106.

de Tubize of Belgium. The venture was financed by American capital but was operated under the Belgian Company's patent rights to the Chardonnet Process. Tubize started its first plant at Hopewell, Virginia, with an initial capacity of eight million pounds per year. On March 12, 1930, Tubize merged with the American Chatillon Corporation. After about three years of persistent rumors that Tubize Chatillon was negotiating a merger with the Industrial Rayon Corporation, it finally consummated a merger with Celanese, February 8, 1946.

The Industrial Fibre Corporation of America, a subsidiary of Snia Viscosa of Italy, commenced operations in 1920, in Cleveland, Ohio. The company merged with American Borvisk Company in 1924 to form the Industrial Rayon Corporation. The initial size of the first operating unit cannot be exactly determined, but the operating capacity of its Cleveland plant was two million pounds per year in 1924. Foreign stockholdings in Industrial Rayon have gradually been purchased by American interests.

Although organized in 1918, the Celanese Corporation of America (formerly American Cellulose and Chemical Manufacturing Company, Ltd. of British Celanese) did not begin rayon production in the United States until 1925. The company employs the Dreyfus patents for the acetate process. Commencing with an installed capacity of three million pounds per year, Celanese has been one of the "big three" rayon producers since 1933. After its merger with Tubize in 1946, which had merged with American Chatillon Corporation in 1930, the company's capacity was probably not much below that of Du Pont.

The three-year period 1927–1929 saw another great influx of European-owned subsidiaries and a rapid expansion in plant capacity of those companies already established in the United States. Organized in 1925 as a result of an agreement between J. P. Bemberg and Company of Barmen, Germany, and the Vereinigte Glanzstoff Fabriken, A. G. of Elberfeld, the American Bemberg Corporation introduced the cuprammonium process in the United States when it began production at its plant in Johnson City, Tennessee, in October 1927. Initial installed capacity was 2.5 million pounds per year. By the end of 1928 another plant had been constructed on the same site increasing the company's total annual capacity to 5.5 million pounds. The American Glanzstoff Corporation, a branch of Vereinigte Glanzstoff Fabriken, commenced production in 1928 on the same plant site occupied by American Bemberg Corporation. Initial capacity was 5 million pounds of viscose yarn per year. The two corporations have always operated under joint management. The American Enka Corporation, a branch of the N. V. Nederlandche Kunstyigdefabrick "Enka," was incorporated in 1928 and began production at its plant in Asheville, North Carolina, in 1929. Initial installed capacity was 5 million pounds per year. The formation of the Algemeene Kunstzijde Unie (General Rayon Union) in 1929 by Dutch and German rayon interests virtually threw the American Bemberg Corporation, American Glanzstoff Corporation, and American Enka Corporation under single management. As previously stated, the properties of these three corporations were acquired by the Office of Alien Property at the outbreak of World War II. American Enka has since been released for operation and a controlling interest in the properties of American Bemberg and North American was recently sold to Beaunit Mills.

While these European giants were establishing branches in the United States, some smaller domestic companies were being organized with American capital but usually under the direction of foreign technical staffs and backed by large textile mills which wanted direct control of their supply of rayon yarn.

The Hartford Rayon Corporation (formerly the Belamose Corporation) began production in January 1925. The company had been organized jointly by American and Belgian interests in 1920 with plans for an initial capacity of approximately one million pounds per year.

On June 26, 1926, the Delaware Rayon Corporation was formed with an operating plant at New Castle, Delaware, to produce viscose yarns under a process owned by the French Allegre-Mondon Company. The French Company also furnished the technical staff. When plant construction began, Allegre-Mondon Company commented that the corporation "was really a branch of the French Company." [21] The corporation soon erected another plant at New Bedford, Massachusetts that was in production by 1929.

The Acme Rayon Corporation was organized in 1920 and commenced production in its Cleveland plant in 1925. Although the company has had an uphill struggle from its inception, having closed down for protracted periods of time on several occasions, it produced yarn under special price ceilings during the war. It was

[21] *Rayon Journal,* March 30, 1927, p. 10.

recently reported "to have closed down for an indefinite period." [22]

The Cupra Rayon Company, Inc. was organized by the Atlas Powder Company in 1924 to produce rayon by the cuprammonium process. The uncompleted plant was sold to the Napon Company in 1925. The company never got into full commercial production. Installed capacity was one thousand pounds of yarn per day but peak output, reached in 1928, was never over 25 per cent of capacity. In the spring of 1931 the company went into receivership and was liquidated.[23]

In 1925 the Skenandoa Rayon Corporation was organized and acquired the properties of the Skenandoa Cotton Company at Utica, New York. Arrangements were made with the Strasbourg interests of France for technical advice and aid. The company began commercial production in 1928 with an initial installed capacity of slightly over one million pounds per year. For the first few years the plant's entire output was taken by the parent cotton company.

Three other cotton companies, Manville Jenckes (Woonsocket Rayon Company) at Pawtucket, Rhode Island, Amoskeag Mills at Manchester, New Hampshire, and Burlington Mills at Burlington, North Carolina, commenced producing rayon in their own plants for cotton mill consumption in 1930. All three rayon plants were small and produced only for their parent cotton mills. Burlington Mills' rayon plant was not in operation on September 26, 1931,[24] and has not been listed among rayon-producing plants since that date. Also, by September 26, 1931, the Amoskeag Rayon Company had been converted into a knitting and weaving laboratory.[25] Neither plant reached the scale of production of a million pounds per year. The Woonsocket Rayon Corporation, starting in 1930 with an installed capacity of almost two million pounds per year, has gradually increased output to approximately three and one-half million pounds per year. The company operated for about ten years under the name of Synthetic Yarns, Inc., but in January 1948 again adopted its former name.[26]

In 1928 the Roseland Corporation commenced production on a scale slightly beyond the laboratory stage in its Paterson, New Jersey plant. This is the only year the company was listed as a rayon pro-

[22] *Rayon Organon,* April 1949, p. 51.
[23] *Rayon Journal,* April 1931, p. 111.
[24] *Textile World,* Annual Rayon Review Number, September 26, 1931.
[25] *Textile World,* September 26, 1931.
[26] *Rayon Organon,* January 1948, p. 2.

ducer. The fate of the enterprise is not known but it apparently failed before reaching production on a commercial scale.

In the same year the Furness Corporation began production on a laboratory scale in its plant at Gloucester City, New Jersey. The corporation has undergone four financial reorganizations and has been in operation only a fraction of its life. Plant facilities recently have been moved to Brooklyn, Connecticut, where a resumption of operations is planned.

In 1930 the Hampton Company began rayon production in its East Hampton, Massachusetts plant with an initial installed capacity of about one million pounds per year. By 1938 capacity had increased by one-half million pounds. The company was not listed among the active rayon yarn producers in the United States in the April 1947 issue of the *Rayon Organon.*

In 1931 the Tennessee Eastman Corporation, a wholly owned subsidiary of Eastman Kodak Corporation, commenced commercial production of acetate yarns in its plant at Kingsport, Tennessee, after several years of experimentation. Initial installed capacity was about one million pounds per year, but the plant had been designed for rapid expansion of output. By 1938 installed capacity had been increased to 24 million pounds per year and current capacity is believed to be approximately 51 million pounds per year. The company handles virtually none of its sales directly but sells through A. M. Tenney Associates, Inc. of New York. There were no new entrants to the rayon yarn industry after the formation of the Tennessee Eastman Corporation until 1948.

C. Composition and Structure of the Domestic Yarn Market

The foregoing historical sketch of the development of the rayon industry indicates in a general way the prerequisites to financial success. Intricate manufacturing processes and the complicated plant installations require access to industrial "know-how" and highly experienced technical staffs. Moreover, since fixed charges are relatively large regardless of size of plant, initial installed capacity should be large. Every profitable rayon venture in the United States began operations with a large plant backed by large reservoirs of capital, and fulfilled one of the following conditions: (1) It has been organized as an outright subsidiary of a successful European firm which furnished the capital, experienced technical staffs and top management, and process patent rights; for example, American Bemberg Corporation, North American Rayon Corporation, American Enka Corporation, Celanese Corporation, and American Viscose Corporation; or (2) it has been launched jointly by American and European firms with European interests furnishing most of the technical staff, top management, and process patents; for example, Du Pont Fibersilk Corporation, Tubize Corporation, and Industrial Rayon Corporation; or (3) it has been organized by American financial interests, but only after relations with a European producer had been established for the purpose of obtaining technical information and managerial assistance; for example, Skenandoa Rayon Corporation, Delaware Rayon Corporation and its affiliate, the New Bedford Rayon Company, Woonsocket Rayon Corporation, and the Belamose Rayon Corporation.

Three producers, Tennessee Eastman Corporation, Cuprammonium Rayon Corporation, and Acme Rayon Corporation, do not clearly fall into any of the above three groups, but since Tennessee Eastman is a subsidiary of Eastman Kodak, it presumably had European technical advice at its disposal. Acme and Cuprammonium, neither of which was organized with direct connections to European technology, have experienced several protracted periods of inactivity and the latter has undergone four financial reorganizations. Significantly, both companies, along with those rayon companies that have completely failed, entered the industry on a small scale of production and with small capital reserves.

History has not only demonstrated that producing units must be planned on a large scale at the outset in order to be financially successful,[27] but also that the most successful producers have been the huge corporations with initial vast pools of capital to tide them over the period of organization, plant construction, and the first few years of unprofitable operations. This point has been adequately illustrated by the success of such firms as Du Pont, Courtaulds (American Viscose), Dutch Enka (American Enka), Allgemeene Kunstzijde Unie (North American and American Bemberg), Celanese, Eastman Kodak (Tennessee Eastman), and others.

Hence, the required capital, experienced management, trained technical staffs, and access to "know-how" make the cost of entry to the rayon industry extremely high. They largely explain why only about two dozen firms have ever attempted production, of which

[27] This point is strongly emphasized by engineering firms that specialize in rayon plant construction. See specifications of Lockwood Greene Engineers, Inc., Chap. 3.

only sixteen[28] have survived and currently constitute the supply side of the domestic rayon yarn market. Ten of these firms had expanded capacity to reach an economical scale of operation by 1930. Since then, the new entrant has been confronted with the difficult task of emulating the performance of large entrenched producers in order to operate at a profit.

The Role of Patents. Closely associated with difficulties of entry is the role played by patents in the development of the domestic rayon yarn market. There are hundreds of patents that relate directly to the manufacture of rayon yarn and staple fiber or are indirectly related to rayon production through the chemical industries that furnish indispensable raw materials.[29] For this reason an exhaustive treatment of the role of patents must be by-passed in preference to a presentation of evidence that attempts to answer the question: If all other necessary conditions could have been fulfilled, to what extent would the potential rayon producer have been restricted from entry because of existing patent rights? The answer will differ somewhat among the three principal processes currently used.

From 1910 to 1918 the American Viscose Corporation enjoyed a complete monopoly in the production of viscose rayon in the United States by virtue of its exclusive rights to the Cross and Bevan, and Topham patents. In 1918 the patents became public property. Since that date patents probably have not been a decisive consideration in planning for viscose yarn production. Until recently, however, some special processes used in the production of viscose yarn and staple fiber were protected by patents; notably, the Tubize-owned Singmaster process[30] for producing dull and semi-dull lustered viscose and acetate yarn and the Furness continuous process, owned by Industrial Rayon Corporation, for producing viscose yarn. Tubize gradually made its process available to other producers. By 1936 the entire domestic rayon industry was licensed to produce delustered yarns under the Singmaster patents.[31] Presumably, any new firm to enter the industry would have been granted the same license privileges. Patent rights to the Furness continuous process were pur-

[28] Of the eighteen firms that currently operate in the United States, two entered the industry after World War II and had not commenced commercial production by the end of 1949. (See Appendix A.)

[29] See George W. Stocking and Myron W. Watkins, *Cartels in Action* (New York: Twentieth Century Fund, 1946), pp. 363–479, for a survey of international chemical alliances and patent agreements with references to the rayon industry.

[30] Patent rights expired in 1946.

[31] *Rayon Journal*, March 1936, p. 119.

chased by the Industrial Rayon Corporation in 1936. The company commenced using the process in its new Painesville plant in 1939.[32] At the present time Industrial does not license the process to other producers.

Lustron was the first company to acquire patent rights for acetate yarn production in the United States. The patent rights to Lustron's process were purchased by the Dreyfus brothers when they commenced constructing an acetate yarn plant in 1918 at Cumberland, Maryland. The Celanese Corporation, under the Dreyfus patents, was the sole producer of acetate rayon in the United States until 1929. In that year American Viscose and Du Pont entered the acetate yarn field, the former under the Courtaulds-owned Cross and Bevan acetate process patents and the latter under patent arrangements with I. G. Farben of Germany and Rhodiaseta of Italy. At about the same time, American Chatillon commenced acetate yarn production under the Ruth-Aldo patents. Two years later, Eastman Kodak, through its wholly owned subsidiary, the Tennessee Eastman Corporation, entered the acetate yarn field employing its own process.

In the cuprammonium field American Bemberg, operating under the patents of the parent German company, has been the sole successful producer. The Cuprammonium Rayon Corporation (which successively has operated under the names Furness Corporation, New Process Rayon Corporation, United States Rayon Corporation, and Cuprammonium Rayon Corporation) has produced cuprammonium yarn from time to time under the Furness patents, but to date has shown no evidence of financial success. Since the Furness process is generally held to be superior to the Bemberg process,[33] there is some evidence that other factors are more important in rayon production than ownership of patents. It is of some significance also that all of the four producers who followed Celanese into the acetate field commenced production between 1929 and 1931, several years before the Dreyfus patents expired.

The extent to which patents have limited the number of rayon producers in the United States is not clear but most of the available

[32] *Infra*, footnote 33.

[33] The Furness process is continuous, whereas the Bemberg process (and all other processes described in this chapter) is interrupted at several stages of production. The basic principle of the Furness process has been adapted to viscose yarn production by Industrial Rayon Corporation in its Painesville, Ohio plant. The process reduces the time required to convert raw materials into finished rayon yarn from eighty-five hours to six minutes. *Rayon Journal*, September 1939, p. 86.

evidence indicates that considerations other than patent rights have been the determining factors since 1918. In no case has production of the commodity been limited to a single patented process. If all other prerequisites for successful production have been met with, existing patents do not appear to limit appreciably the number of producers. For example, Tennessee Eastman devised its own process for acetate yarn production after it decided to enter the field. Also, the period of expansion marked by the formation of new firms came after the basic viscose process patent expired but before the expiration of patents for other processes. The period since 1930, by which time nearly all basic patents had become public property, has been marked by a complete absence of new entrants to the industry. Obviously, therefore, more significant factors than the legal monopolization of specific processes restrict entry to the rayon industry.

Geographical Distribution of Rayon Plants. Plant construction engineers, producers, and historians agree completely upon rayon plant-site requirements.[34] The principal site-determining factor is proximity to an abundant supply of flowing water. One million gallons of water per day are required per annual output of two million pounds of viscose yarn. Water requirements for acetate yarn production are approximately six times as great. In addition, an adequate drainage area must be located on or near the plant site to take care of the unneutralized waste water contaminated with caustics and acids. The site must be practically level with a minimum area of about fifty acres and located approximately one thousand feet above sea level.[35] It is necessary that at least one railroad siding be routed through the plant site. Other considerations are the cheapness and continuous availability of local power, the local labor supply, and freight rates on coal, other supplies, and finished rayon. With the above requirements satisfied, rayon plants locate close to their market outlets rather than near raw material sources.[36] This

[34] For a more thorough discussion of the plant-site requirements discussed here, see Mois Avram, *The Rayon Industry* (1929 ed.), pp. 355–356; United States Tariff Commission, *The Rayon Industry*, pp. 91–92; *Rayon, a New Influence in the Textile Industry*, Metropolitan Life Insurance Company (1928); Joseph Foltzer, *Artificial Silk and Its Manufacture*, pp. 206–208; *Financial News*, London, February 6, 1928; *Rayon Journal*, October 15, 1928, p. 36; January 1, 1929, pp. 36–52; September 1, 1929, pp. 7–38.

[35] The latter requirement has apparently played no part in plant location decisions when the use of power other than hydroelectric was contemplated; however, it is obvious that low river areas subject to floods are to be avoided.

[36] The chief sources of wood pulp have been Canada, the Pacific Northwest, and the Scandinavian countries. Until recently, oceanic freight to the nearest port of

is due primarily to business considerations other than transportation costs, such as ability to fill orders promptly, and so forth.[37]

These factors largely account for the concentration of rayon plants along the Allegheny Mountain region from Pennsylvania to Tennessee, the broad area which more nearly fulfills all the above requirements. The further concentration of rayon plants in the southern part of this region and elsewhere in the South has also been partially influenced by free or tax-free plant sites. The chief factors that led to the selection of southern plant sites, however, seem to have been abundant water supplies, adequate labor for which few other industries competed, and, most important, proximity to consuming markets. For example, when Du Pont constructed its large viscose plant on the old Amphill estate[38] near Richmond, Virginia in 1928, the following reasons were given for the site selection: The James River could furnish more than the seventeen million gallons of water per day that would be consumed; the labor supply was good; Richmond was a large railroad center, and, moreover, the Seaboard Railroad had offered to construct a spur line through the plant site; and the textile industry was then moving rapidly to the south — this made for lower freight costs and quicker service.[39] When Industrial Rayon selected Covington, Virginia as a plant site in the same year, natural resources, advantageous climate, good water supply, easy accessibility to markets, economical freight rates, favorable railroad facilities, adequate supply of competent labor, and splendid civic coöperation were listed as the determining factors.[40] In an article entitled "Rayon Production Centered in the South," the editor of the *Rayon Journal* listed ample supply of power, water, raw material,[41] and labor, and the shifting of the textile industry to the South as the principal considerations that determined the selection of southern plant sites by American Bemberg, American Enka, Tubize,

---

entry was borne by the seller; freight from port to plant was borne by the purchaser. During this period, inland plants such as the Du Pont plant at Old Hickory, Tennessee, and Industrial's plants at Cleveland and Painesville, Ohio, operated at a slight disadvantage. This was overcome when pulp plants in the Pacific Northwest commenced shipping pulp with minimum freight allowed from pulp mill to rayon plant.

[37] Cf. Glenn E. McLaughlin and Stefan Robock, *Why Industry Moves South*, NPA Committee of the South, report no. 3 (June 1949), pp. 45–46. The authors show that the synthetic fiber industry places great stress upon the ability to provide prompt service to customers.

[38] Because of stack fumes and the required acreage, rayon plants are usually constructed three or four miles from urban centers.

[39] *Rayon Journal*, January 1, 1929, pp. 36–52.

[40] *Rayon Journal*, September 1, 1929, pp. 7–38.

[41] Principally cotton linters for acetate and cuprammonium yarn production.

TABLE 1

Geographical Distribution of Rayon Plants by States and by Section for Selected Years, 1919, 1931, 1936, 1947, and 1949

	NUMBER OF PLANTS				
State	1919	1931	1936	1947	1949
Georgia	0	1	1	1	1
Tennessee	0	4	4	4	5
North Carolina	0	2	1	1	1
Virginia	1	5	4	6	6
West Virginia	0	1	1	2	2
Maryland	1[a]	1	1	1	1
Alabama	0	0	0	0	1
South Carolina	0	0	0	0	1
Total South	2	14	12	15	18
Delaware	0	1	1	1	1
Pennsylvania	1	3	3	3	3
Ohio	0	2	2[b]	3	3
New York	0	2	2	2	2
New Jersey	0	1[c]	1[c]	0	0
Total Mid-Atlantic and East Central	1	9	9	9	9
New Hampshire	0	1	0	0	0
Connecticut	0	1	1	2[c]	2
Rhode Island	0	1	1	1	1
Massachusetts	0	2	2	1	1
Total New England	0	5	4	4	4
Total United States	3	28	25	28	31

[a] Plant constructed but not producing.
[b] Includes one plant (Acme) inactive.
[c] The Cuprammonium Rayon Corporation. The company has undergone four financial reorganizations and has only been in operation occasionally. Plant equipment was moved from New Jersey to Brooklyn, Connecticut around 1946.

Du Pont, American Chatillon, American Viscose, and American Glanzstoff.[42]

The geographical distribution of rayon plants in selected years is shown in Table 1. The concentration of the industry in the South after 1920 is somewhat underestimated when the number of plants is used. For example, in 1931, 50 per cent of the plants were located in the South but these plants represented two-thirds of the total

[42] *Rayon Journal*, October 15, 1928, pp. 36–49, 63. Rayon sales in the South increased from 250,000 pounds to 6 million pounds between 1921 and 1927. Most present plant sites were selected during this period.

installed capacity in the United States. In 1936, the South had less than 50 per cent of the total number of plants but about 70 per cent of total installed capacity. At the end of 1949, 58 per cent of all rayon plants were located in the South but these plants accounted for over 70 per cent of the total productive capacity. About 50 per cent of total capacity is now located in the states of Virginia and Tennessee alone.

The Rayon Industry and Its Factor Markets. The fifteen companies actively engaged in the manufacture of rayon yarn and staple fiber in the United States at the close of the war employed approximately 55,000 workers, most of whom were concentrated in comparatively few occupations. There are fifty-eight representative occupations in the rayon industry but four-fifths of the total number of workers are classified in eighteen of them.[43] The general level of skill required in all job classifications is comparatively high. Wages for practically all workers employed in the industry have been determined by collective bargaining since around 1937. Out of twenty-eight plants operated by fifteen firms in 1944, twelve had collective-bargaining agreements with the Textile Workers of America (C.I.O.); three had agreements with the United Textile Workers (A.F. of L.); and three plants had agreements with both of these unions. Five plants had agreements with independent unions and five were unorganized.[44] Union agreements cover approximately 75 per cent of the industry's total work force, but actually influence the wage structure and level for the entire industry.[45]

The rayon industry has become an increasingly important consumer of certain basic raw materials and chemicals. In some markets the industry probably consumes a sufficiently significant percentage of total output to influence prices. In 1945 rayon producers purchased linters pulp equivalent to 458,000 bales of cotton linters, or 37 per cent of the total 1,250,000 bales produced in the United States during the 1944–45 cotton year.[46] Quantitatively, the rayon industry is a much larger consumer of wood pulp than of cotton linters, but

[43] *Wages in the Rayon Industry,* United States Bureau of Labor Statistics *Bulletin* no. 806, p. 3.

[44] *Wages in the Rayon Industry,* p. 3.

[45] Du Pont has always given its employees a better wage bargain than prevails in union plants; hence, its work force has had virtually no incentive to organize.

[46] Project V, "Production Studies of Synthetic Fibers and Paper," from *Hearings on Study of Agricultural and Economic Problems of the Cotton Belt before Special Subcommittee on Cotton of Committee on Agriculture,* House of Representatives, Eightieth Congress, First Session, July 7 and 8, 1947, p. 8. Hereafter referred to as *Hearings,* H. R., Project V.

probably exerts less influence upon wood-pulp prices. In 1945 rayon producers consumed 297,000 tons of wood pulp, which was equivalent to 2.7 per cent of the total consumption of wood pulp in the United States in all uses.[47] In 1945 the rayon industry consumed 495,000 tons of sulphuric acid, or 5.4 per cent of total domestic consumption, and 377,000 tons of caustic soda, or 20.6 per cent of total domestic consumption.[48] The industry also uses large quantities of carbon bisulphide, acetic anhydride, acetic acid, and small quantities of a number of other chemicals.

The relative importance of the rayon industry as a consumer of water, electrical energy, and fuel is impossible to estimate. Producers usually purify their own water in company-owned filter plants. They have also become increasingly independent of local power companies by constructing their own power plants. In 1925 rayon producers purchased 42 per cent of their total power consumed; in 1939 they purchased only 16 per cent.[49] In 1939 the fuel bill for the industry was slightly over 6 million dollars; it is estimated that fuel consumed cost slightly over 15 million dollars for 1945. The less important the industry becomes as a purchaser of water and power, the more important it will become as a purchaser of fuel.

The Demand Side of the Rayon Market. Although, at any given instant of time, rayon is a moderately homogeneous commodity for a single producer and among producers who use the same process, it has undergone rapid change since 1911. The evolution in the physical properties of rayon has been accompanied by an ever-widening market area and accounts for a substantial part of the tremendous increase in domestic consumption which took place between 1911 and 1949. Before the first World War, rayon was, at best, an inferior silk substitute. Consumption was confined largely to the manufacture of braids, trimmings, and other ornamental novelties not subjected to laundering or hard usage.[50] For several years rayon has been second only to cotton in textile fiber consumption and is currently consumed chiefly in the broad- and narrow-woven goods trades, tire fabric construction, the underwear, hosiery, and other

[47] Estimated in *Hearings*, H. R., Project V, quoting *Facts for Industry, Census of Pulp Mills and of Paper and Paperboard Mills*, United States Bureau of the Census (Washington, 1945).

[48] *Chemical and Metallurgical Engineering* (January 1946), pp. 99–101.

[49] 1939 *Census of Manufactures*, rayon and allied products section.

[50] United States Tariff Commission, *The Rayon Industry*, p. 161.

knit-goods industries, and in the manufacture of innumerable miscellaneous decorative articles.

In addition to the broadened market area brought about through improvements in the quality of yarn, the industry has invaded many new markets through the creation of new types of filament yarn and rayon staple fiber. The introduction of dull lustered viscose yarns in 1926 by American Viscose gave rayon several new market outlets, chiefly the nondecorative fabric markets such as hosiery and underwear. This market was further invaded when Tubize introduced its pigmented dull and semi-dull yarn in 1929 and American Viscose commenced production of dull acetate yarns in 1931. Also, early in 1937 Du Pont and American Viscose, in collaboration with the Goodyear Tire and Rubber Company, perfected "rayotwist," a high-strength, high-tenacity yarn suitable for heavy-duty tire fabric construction. Du Pont first offered the yarn for sale toward the end of 1937 under the trade-name "Cordura." Viscose tire yarns are currently produced by nearly all large viscose yarn companies.

Perhaps the most important single recent innovation in the rayon industry, however, is staple fiber. Whereas rayon yarn was originally introduced as a silk substitute, staple fiber was designed to compete with cotton and wool. Unlike continuous filament yarn, staple fiber is packaged in bales of short fibers similar to cotton and may be spun into "spun-rayon" thread on the cotton, wool, or silk spinning system. The increasing importance of staple fiber as a factor in total demand for rayon output is indicated by the fact that it accounted for only a fraction of 1 per cent of total rayon consumption in the United States from 1928 to 1931 whereas it currently accounts for slightly over 20 per cent of total rayon consumption. In addition to its own exclusive market, "spun-rayon" is blended with cotton, wool, and rayon filament yarn in the men's and women's clothing industry.

The absolute and relative importance of each of the principal domestic rayon yarn market outlets for the period 1925–1948 are shown in Table 2. The noticeable increase in the quantity of rayon used in the woven-goods industries since 1930 relative to the knit-goods industries reflects several developments that altered the nature of rayon and the relationship between rayon and other fibers. Since the weaving industry requires a higher grade yarn than the knitting industry, steady improvement in the quality of rayon yarn has rendered it increasingly more adaptable to the manufacture of rayon and mixed woven fabrics. Moreover, automobile tire yarn is included

TABLE 2

Distribution of Rayon Yarn Consumption by Trade, 1925–1948

(MILLIONS OF POUNDS AND PER CENT)

	KNIT-GOODS						WOVEN-GOODS							
	Hosiery		Other Knit		Total Knit		Broad Woven and Tire		Narrow Woven		Total Woven		Misc. Uses	
Year	lbs.	%	lbs.	%	lbs.	%	lbs.	%	lbs.	%	lbs.	%	lbs.	%
1925	10.7	20	10.5	20	21.2	40	26.1	50	2.9	5	29.0	55	2.6	5
1926	10.3	20	15.0	29	25.3	49	21.2	42	2.2	4	23.4	46	2.6	5
1927	16.7	20	28.9	34	45.6	54	31.5	37	3.3	4	34.8	41	4.6	5
1928	14.7	17	32.9	37	47.6	54	32.5	37	3.2	4	35.7	41	4.7	5
1929	18.8	16	43.7	37	62.5	53	45.4	39	3.1	3	48.5	42	5.4	5
1930	16.5	15	38.0	34	54.5	49	49.5	44	3.0	3	52.5	47	4.6	4
1931	21.1	14	48.7	31	69.8	45	75.6	49	4.0	2	79.6	51	6.2	4
1932	19.0	13	38.0	25	57.0	38	84.6	56	3.9	2	88.5	58	6.3	4
1933	17.0	8	41.3	20	58.3	28	141.3	67	5.5	2	146.8	69	5.9	3
1934	14.1	7	39.9	21	54.0	28	131.3	68	4.8	2	136.1	70	4.6	2
1935	14.7	6	47.9	19	62.6	25	179.5	71	5.2	2	184.7	73	5.4	2
1936	16.3	5	51.0	17	67.3	22	217.0	73	8.2	3	225.2	76	4.9	2
1937	12.6	5	38.9	15	51.5	19	202.5	76	7.4	3	209.9	79	4.8	2
1938	14.1	5	39.6	14	53.7	20	209.3	76	6.7	2	216.0	79	4.1	1
1939	16.2	4	49.9	14	66.1	18	278.6	77	9.1	3	287.7	80	5.8	2
1940	16.4	4	54.0	14	70.4	18	304.4	78	8.2	2	312.6	80	5.7	2
1941	26.3	6	57.9	13	84.2	19	349.2	77	10.2	2	359.4	79	8.8	2
1942	49.3	11	56.3	12	105.6	23	343.6	73	8.7	2	352.3	75	10.9	2
1943	49.2	10	56.1	11	105.3	21	360.4	73	10.4	2	370.8	75	18.1	4
1944	45.1	9	55.8	10	100.9	19	409.7	76	12.5	2	422.2	78	15.9	3
1945	35.4	6	57.1	9	92.5	15	483.2	81	14.1	2	497.3	83	12.6	2
1946	22.3	3	68.1	10	90.4	14	549.5	83	13.1	2	562.6	84	13.4	2
1947	18.4	3	72.6	10	91.0	13	608.1	83	12.7	2	620.8	85	17.2	2
1948	15.7	2	85.5	10	101.2	12	699.9	84	14.8	2	714.7	86	20.6	2

Source: *Rayon Organon*, Annual Supplements.

TABLE 3

Rayon and Cotton Yarn Used in Tire Cord and Fabric Production, 1937–1950

(IN MILLIONS OF POUNDS)

		Cotton		Rayon	
Year	Total Pounds	lbs.	%	lbs.	%
1937	260.9	260.0	99.7	0.9	0.3
1939	268.8	260.0	96.7	8.8	3.3
1943	295.5	240.0	81.2	55.6	18.8
1944	383.2	268.0	70.0	115.2	30.0
1945	463.4	276.0	59.5	187.4	40.5
1946	526.1	312.0	59.3	214.1	40.7
1947	575.0	345.0	60.0[a]	230.0	40.0
1948	556.0	307.0	55.2[a]	249.0	44.8
1949	395.0	113.0	28.6[a]	282.0	71.4
1950[b]	206.0	62.0	30.0[a]	144.0	70.0

Source: *Rayon Organon*, Annual Supplements.

[a] Includes nylon.

[b] First six months only.

in broad-woven goods. The increasing significance of rayon in tire fabric construction is evident from the data presented in Table 3. Whereas rayon accounted for only 0.3 per cent of total tire fabric in 1937, by 1950 rayon accounted for 70.0 per cent of total tire fabric construction and, if the present trend continues, will take over the entire market in the near future. These factors have tended to increase the relative importance of the weaving industry as a market outlet.

On the other hand, rayon has become less important in the manufacture of hosiery, a significant sector of the knitting industry. The era of inexpensive silk hosiery which began in the twenties and the introduction of nylon in 1939 have gradually driven rayon out of the full-fashioned and seamless hosiery industries. During the war, when silk stocks and nylon production were requisitioned by the Government for National Defense, rayon became the chief substitute for both fibers. Hence, over the four-year period 1942–1945, from 72 per cent to 99 per cent of the full-fashioned women's hosiery, and from 51 per cent to 57 per cent of the women's seamless hosiery, were produced from rayon.[51] With the lifting of wartime restrictions, however, it became evident that nylon would displace both rayon and silk in the women's hosiery field. By 1946 rayon accounted for only 28 per cent of the total production of full-fashioned hosiery and by 1947 rayon accounted for only 15 per cent.[52] The percentages were only slightly higher in the seamless hosiery industry. Also, rayon has become less important in the manufacture of men's hose. In 1939, 14.5 million dozen pairs of men's hose were made from rayon; by 1947 this figure had dropped to 9.0 million dozen.[53]

These shifts in the relative importance of major market outlets for rayon have resulted from steady improvements in standard yarns, the introduction of new types of yarn, particularly pigmented and tire yarns, and the introduction of nylon.

Competition Between Rayon and Natural Fibers. The consumption data for rayon, silk, cotton, and wool presented in Chart 1 show clearly that rayon has experienced the most rapid rate of increase in consumption. Hence, the relative share of rayon in the total fiber market has increased while the relative shares of all natural fibers

[51] Data supplied by the National Association of Hosiery Manufacturers, except 1947 from *Rayon Organon*.
[52] *Ibid.*
[53] *Ibid.*

Chart 1

Annual Rayon, Silk, Cotton, and Wool Consumption, 1912–1948

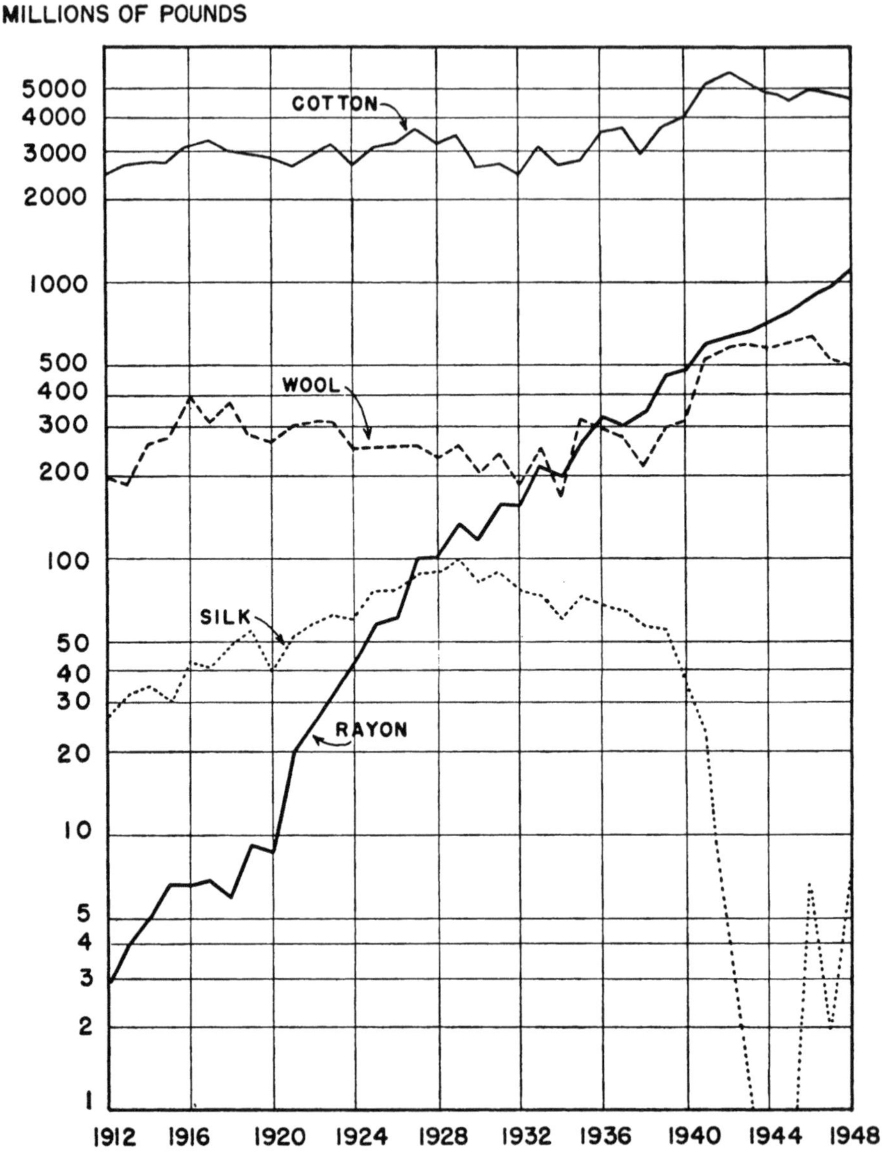

Note: Logarithmic Vertical Scale.
Source: *Rayon Organon.*

have decreased.[54] Since such percentage behavior would result wherever the consumption of one commodity included in the total consumption data for a group of commodities has experienced a noticeably more rapid rate of increase than any of the others, this does not necessarily imply a high degree of competition between rayon and natural fibers. It is certain that part of this percentage relationship is attributable to the fact that the rayon industry is a relatively new and rapidly expanding one, whereas the silk, cotton, and woolen industries are considerably more mature.

Even a cursory comparison of the consumption series, however, shows that much of the increased rayon consumption has been at the expense of silk. This is particularly true for the period after 1929. In 1929 silk consumption had reached an all-time high of 98 million pounds. By 1941 silk consumption had declined to 24.7 million pounds and, in uses other than hosiery manufacture, to less than 9.0 million pounds. The beginning of this decline is coincident with the introduction of cuprammonium and delustered viscose yarns and the rapid expansion in acetate yarn production. These three types of yarn are better substitutes for silk than the bright-lustered viscose yarns that accounted for over 95 per cent of total rayon output until 1927. Rayon had practically displaced silk in most of its major markets except the women's hosiery industry by 1941. Nylon, introduced by Du Pont in 1939, has heavily invaded this one remaining major market for silk.

In addition to the statistical evidence that rayon has been substituted for silk on a large scale, there are a priori reasons for assuming that a fairly high degree of competition has existed between the two fibers. Both are used heavily in the apparel fields where style and appearance are of paramount importance such as the manufacture of ladies' blouses, dresses, men's ties, sport shirts, and other outer garments. Both fibers are also used in knit-goods such as underwear and men's and women's hosiery.

The extent to which rayon consumption has increased at the expense of cotton and wool consumption is not so obvious. There are several reasons why this is difficult to determine; namely, rayon consumption, until recently, has been extremely small relative to cotton

[54] A number of textile market analysts have used this percentage relationship to demonstrate the *effect* rayon has had upon the consumption of other fibers. See United States Tariff Commission, *The Rayon Industry*, pp. 149–153; R. B. Evans, *Trends in the Consumption of Fibers, 1892–1939*, United States Dept. of Agriculture (Washington, 1940); and others.

consumption. A large percentage increase in rayon consumption at the expense of cotton, therefore, would have been hardly discernible in the cotton consumption series; and better heating conditions in the home, closed automobiles, and so forth, have probably influenced *per capita* wool consumption more than the new competition from rayon. Moreover, abnormal wartime demand for both wool and cotton so inflated the consumption data for these two fibers relative to those for rayon that their prewar consumption trends were noticeably interrupted. Cotton and wool consumption, for example, have fallen off since the end of the war, in spite of heavy postwar demands, whereas rayon consumption has continued on an uninterrupted upward trend.

Although quinquennial cotton consumption increased 100 per cent between 1896–1900 and 1915–1919, and only 12 per cent between 1915–1919 and 1935–1939, it is difficult to tell how much of this retardation in the rate of increase in cotton consumption was due to rayon competition. Cotton is used in many fields where durability, cheapness, and launderability rather than style and appearance are decisive factors. Examples are the manufacture of bags, tire fabric, work clothing, awnings, tents, sail cloth, sheets, pillowcases, and men's business shirts. Only in the tire fabric industry is it evident that rayon has greatly displaced cotton in the production of these non-style commodities. Since tire fabric production accounts for about 15 per cent of total cotton consumed in manufactures, however, competition in this field is not taken lightly by cotton growers.[55] Patently, the rapid increase in rayon consumption in the manufacture of broad- and narrow-woven goods since 1930 has brought rayon and cotton into closer competition with each other in these industries in recent years.

Of all the natural fibers, rayon competes with wool the least. Wool, as a fabric material, is desired chiefly for its warmth-giving qualities; these qualities are not characteristic of rayon. The area of competition between rayon and wool before the war was limited mainly to the cheaper grades of woolen and worsted suits, dresses,

[55] There was considerable controversy in Washington over the relative merits of cotton and rayon in tire fabric construction during the last war. The impact of rayon competition upon cotton falls almost completely upon the cotton grower. The cotton spinning and weaving mills, particularly since the advent of rayon staple fiber, spin and fabricate cotton or rayon or both. The mills, therefore, have benefited from rayon since they have had a wider range of choice. They have also benefited from the increase in total demand for textiles that has resulted from the introduction of rayon.

and topcoats, where, for a number of years, rayon has been blended with wool to reduce prices to the consumer. Since the war, however, the woolen industry has lost some of its spring and fall style-wear business such as light-weight woolen dresses, men's and women's suits, swim suits, and beach-wear, to rayon and nylon.

Hence, in framing their price policy, rayon producers have necessarily given silk prices considerable weight in their price equation since these two fibers have competed over a wide range of market areas. Some weight has obviously been given to cotton prices, particularly in the more recent years of "spun-rayon," rayon tire yarn, and mixed cotton and rayon woven-goods. The price of wool has probably been weighted the least since the area of competition between rayon and wool is fairly small.[56]

Rayon and the New Synthetic Yarns. Research in fields allied with rayon chemistry and manufacturing processes has led to the discovery of a large number of other synthetic fibers, principally the noncellulosic fibers of which nylon is by far the most important.

After more than a decade of fundamental research in organic chemistry, Du Pont discovered a new basic spinning material which, under the guidance of rayon technologists, was first used in the commercial production of textile nylon in 1939. The impact of nylon on the textile industry, except in the production of hosiery, had little opportunity to reveal itself before most of the output was requisitioned for war purposes. Since 1946, however, nylon filament yarn and staple fiber have been used in the production of all kinds of outerwear, shirts, underwear, nightwear, hosiery, apparel furnishings and accessories, household furnishings such as draperies, upholstery, and slip covers, automobile tires, seat covers, and upholstery, and other industrial and miscellaneous commodities. The annual output of nylon in the United States increased from 4 million pounds in 1939 to approximately 60 million pounds in 1950. As is evident from its end uses, nylon competes with virtually all fibers, particularly silk and rayon.

Other new synthetic fibers include such trade names as Vinyon,

[56] While testifying before the Federal Trade Commission, Mr. Scott, President of the Tubize Corporation, stated that silk and cotton prices very definitely affected the price of rayon. When asked whether the price of wool affected the price of rayon, he replied, "No, only very remotely, I think, in certain very limited fabrics. In a number of fabrics, it might be almost academic." Hearings of The Federal Trade Commission *v.* Viscose Company *et al.*, 1934–1936, Docket No. 2161, *Record*, pp. 422–423; Smith & Hulse, Washington, D. C., official reporters. Hereafter referred to as *Hearings, F. T. C.*

Saran, Vicara, Dynel, Velon, Permalon, Koroseal, Aralac, Saralon, and two fibers just introduced by Du Pont in 1950, orlon and dacron. Since most of these fibers are of such recent origin, the competition they offer to natural fibers and the more established synthetics is potential rather than real. Within the next decade, however, they are likely to bring about revolutionary changes in traditional fiber consumption patterns. Orlon and Dynel, for example, are expected to offer stiff competition to nylon and rayon and to the natural fibers for which these synthetics have already been substituted. Dacron, on the other hand, possesses many of the physical properties of wool and has the added advantage of being more durable, washable and mothproof. Hence, along with orlon, nylon, and rayon staple fiber, it will probably be substituted for wool in a fairly large number of end uses.

D. The Domestic Rayon Market and Foreign Trade

Encouraged by effective tariff protection, rapid expansion of domestic capacity after 1911 gradually eliminated foreign producers from the United States rayon yarn market. In 1911 rayon imports equaled 85.8 per cent of total domestic consumption; by 1931 imports had been reduced to 1.1 per cent of total domestic consumption. Since 1932 the United States has produced slightly more rayon than it has consumed but exports exceeded 1 per cent of total domestic production in only one year before the war. Rayon yarn imports since 1932 have been negligible (see Table 4). From 1928 until the interruption of foreign trade during the war, however, the United States imported over 50 per cent of all rayon staple fiber consumed. Since 1946 staple fiber imports have averaged annually about 15 per cent of total domestic consumption.[57]

Several factors have contributed to a closed rayon market in the United States. The industry has operated behind such high tariff walls that foreign producers would have had to produce and ship their yarn to the United States market at practically zero cost in order to absorb the tariff and meet domestic prices since 1931.[58] Hence, only a few million pounds of high-priced fine denier yarns (and some standard grades in a very tight rayon market) have reached the domestic market from abroad. Tariff barriers erected against the importation of staple fiber have not been quite so for-

[57] See Appendix D.

[58] Tariffs have ranged from $0.45 to $0.90 per pound, minimum. See Chap. 8.

TABLE 4

Imports and Exports of Rayon Yarn

ALL PROCESSES, 1911–1948

Year	IMPORTS Millions of Pounds	IMPORTS % of Total Consumption	EXPORTS Millions of Pounds	EXPORTS % of Total Production
1911	1.8	85.8	—	—
1912	1.8	62.2	—	—
1913	2.4	60.0	—	—
1914	2.7	53.0	—	—
1915	2.5	37.9	—	—
1916	0.9	13.6	—	—
1917	0.4	5.9	—	—
1918	0.2	3.3	—	—
1919	1.1	11.7	—	—
1920	1.5	17.7	—	—
1921	3.3	16.7	—	—
1922	2.1	8.5	—	—
1923	3.0	9.2	—	—
1924	1.9	4.5	—	—
1925	5.4	9.3	0.1	0.2
1926	9.3	15.4	0.4	0.6
1927	15.0	15.0	0.4	0.5
1928	12.1	12.1	0.2	0.2
1929	15.1	11.5	0.2	0.2
1930	6.3	5.3	0.3	0.2
1931	1.8	1.1	0.3	0.2
1932	0.2	0.1	0.7	0.5
1933	0.9	0.4	1.1	0.5
1934	0.1	0.1	2.5	1.2
1935	—[a]	—[a]	2.2	0.9
1936	0.3	0.1	1.8	0.6
1937	0.9	0.3	1.1	0.3
1938	0.3	0.1	1.4	0.5
1939	0.2	0.1	1.9	0.6
1940	—[a]	—[a]	1.4	0.4
1941	—[a]	—[a]	3.2	0.7
1942	—[a]	—[a]	5.5	1.1
1943	—[a]	—[a]	9.3	1.9
1944	0.0	0.0	16.8	3.0
1945	—[a]	—[a]	20.5	3.3
1946	0.1	—[a]	15.3	2.3
1947	0.3	—[a]	23.8	3.2
1948	9.8	1.2	14.9	1.7

Source: *Rayon Organon*, Annual Supplements.
[a] Negligible.

midable but, until recent years, staple fiber has constituted a very small percentage of total domestic rayon consumption. Since the war a greater proportion of total rayon output has been in the form of staple fiber (30 per cent in 1948). Domestic rayon producers, considerably disturbed over rising staple fiber imports, have already petitioned Congress for more favorable tariff protection.[59]

On the other hand, domestic producers' high costs of production (due largely to high wage rates) have prevented them from competing with Japan, Italy, Germany, France, and Great Britain in foreign markets. The bulk of the meager yarn exports from the United States has gone to Mexico, Canada, Cuba, and Central and South America, where lower transportation costs have offset higher production costs.

Protected by adequate tariffs and confronted with the greatest potential market in the world, it is not surprising that the rayon industry has grown more rapidly in the United States than in other countries. In the years 1910–1913, rayon output in the United States was only a fraction of that of either Germany or the United Kingdom and about two-thirds of that of France.[60] By 1919 the annual output of the domestic rayon industry had exceeded that of any other country. Except for a single year (1937), when the rayon yarn output of Japan exceeded that of the United States, domestic rayon yarn production has exceeded that of any other country for all the years 1919–1950. At the outbreak of World War II, annual domestic yarn production was about one-third of total annual world production and was several times that of either Germany, Japan, Italy, the United Kingdom, or France. If rayon staple fiber is included, however, the total annual rayon output of Germany exceeds that of the United States for all the years 1937–1943. The destruction of rayon plants and the disruption of operations in Germany and Japan which occurred in the closing stages of the war had reduced total annual rayon output in both countries to negligible quantities by the end of the war. Since 1945, the United States has accounted for from 55 per cent to 70 per cent of annual world output of rayon yarn and staple fiber combined.

The historical growth of the rayon industry in the United States, therefore, illustrates the arguments usually raised in defense of tariff protection for infant industries. Handicapped in its early stages by a

[59] The Textile Economics Bureau, Inc., in a report setting forth the extent to which staple fiber production was curtailed throughout the industry as of March 1949, stated, "These data were collected at the request of the Rayon Yarn Producers Group for use in a supplemental brief which was prepared to augment the Group's original bill of January, 1949, opposing the Italian request for a reduction in tariff duty rates on rayon staple imports into this country." *Rayon Organon,* April 1949, pp. 50–51.

[60] For rayon production by country for the years 1910–1948, see *Rayon Organon,* June 1949, p. 84.

late start and a technological lag, the industry has flourished behind tariff barriers which have effectively isolated the domestic market from the rest of the world. In the process, the results of rayon research, instead of flowing from Europe to the United States, had, by 1935, commenced to flow the other way. The question of what public policy toward tariffs on rayon imports should be, however, is reserved for the final chapter.

. . . . . .

By way of summary, thirty-one plants operated by sixteen firms make up the supply side of the rayon yarn market. All of the plants produce rayon yarn under one of the three processes discussed earlier in this chapter: the viscose, acetate, and cuprammonium processes. The highly specialized technology of the industry requires an unusually high degree of technical and managerial skill, heavy capital investment, and sufficient financial resources to operate for several years without making profits. Even the large, efficient producers have incurred heavy deficits their first few years of operations while they gradually converted their plants from experimental stations to fully operating units. The rapid growth of the industry, leaving in its wake a dearth of trained rayon technologists, and closely guarded production secrets have placed a high premium upon industrial "know-how." These features of the industry and the economies of scale to be discussed in the following chapter have served as the most important limitations to the total number of independent rayon producers in the United States, although patent rights have played a protective role in the initial stages of commercial production under each of the three major processes.

With respect to demand conditions that have confronted the rayon industry, several writers in the textile field have noted the relationship between the downward secular price movement and the sharp upward trend in rayon consumption and concluded that the demand curve for rayon is a highly elastic one; to wit: "The improvement in technology of yarn production and fabric construction, the steady reduction in prices over the last twenty years, and the accompanying steady increase in consumption, is an almost perfect example of elastic demand with increasing values and decreasing prices." [61] Such a demand curve, however, approximates neither the

[61] National Bureau of Economic Research, *Textile Markets* (New York, 1939), p. 53.

short-run nor long-run demand curve for a commodity as usually conceived. The difficulty involved in estimating the elasticity of the long-run demand schedule for rayon lies in the evolutionary character of the commodity under observation. The quality attributes of rayon have never remained static for a sufficiently long time interval to separate price effect from quality effect upon quantity consumed. Nevertheless, a few preliminary observations on the nature of demand for rayon would be useful.

In view of the foregoing history of the industry, it would be expected that the short-run demand schedule for rayon has gradually changed in slope and shifted to the right with the passage of time. In its initial stages of development, rayon had few alternative uses. In the neighborhood of foreign rayon price plus import duty, the

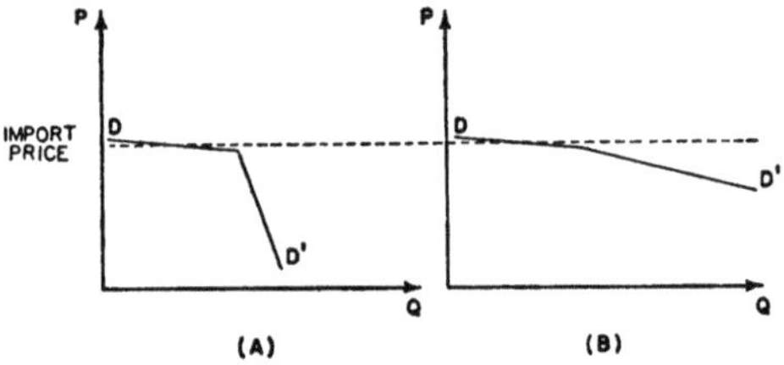

Figure 1

(A) *Approximated demand curve for rayon in 1911. (Scale of Q-axis = x.)*
(B) *Approximated demand curve for rayon in 1949. (Scale of Q-axis = 1000x.)*

demand for domestically produced rayon should have been highly elastic. A small price change upward would have decreased sales tremendously; a small downward revision of price would have given domestic producers the entire market. But price reductions below this point would probably have had little effect upon the quantity demanded since rayon was used primarily in cheap ribbons and braids, and so forth. These articles are accessories that constitute a small percentage of total cost of the finished fabricated article and, therefore, have relatively inelastic demand schedules.

The evolution of rayon from an inferior silk substitute to a high quality multi-purpose yarn, however, has brought it into closer competition with all the natural fibers. Furthermore, since 1939, new synthetic yarns which compete with rayon have been brought into commercial production. Hence, the elasticity of that portion of the demand curve falling below the point of import price (including the tariff) has probably increased significantly over the past several decades. This would seem to follow from the gradual sustained increases in the number of alternative uses of rayon and in the number of available textile fibers. This point is illustrated in Figure 1.

Moreover, rayon producers have developed markets of their own in which a higher degree of elasticity of demand should be expected. For example, a decrease in the price of rayon yarn should increase the consumption of 100 per cent rayon print dresses more than it would have increased consumption of ribbons and braids when rayon was pretty much confined to the production of these relatively insignificant accessories. Hence, since 1911, the number of factors which influence the pricing policy of rayon producers, and therefore narrow the range of arbitrary prices, has increased considerably.

3

THE RELATIONSHIP between the Size and Number of Producers in the Domestic Rayon Industry

It was suggested in the preceding chapter that economies of scale have significantly limited the number of firms in the domestic rayon industry. The financial success enjoyed by large-scale producers and the high mortality rate among small-scale enterprises indicate that the firm's long-run average total cost curve might be negatively sloped over a wide range of output. If this were so, it would be expected that a small number of large producers would constitute the industry. The purpose of this chapter is to examine the growth pattern of rayon-producing firms and the possible shape of a firm's long-run cost curve and, hence, to explain, at least in part, why the rayon industry is oligopolistic in character.

A. The Problem of Measuring Economies of Scale

An investigation into the relationship between efficiency and size in the rayon industry encounters several difficult problems, most of which would probably be encountered in any empirical cost study.[1] At the outset, nearly half of the total number of domestic rayon producers are multi-plant firms. Du Pont currently operates four rayon yarn plants in the United States; American Viscose, seven plants (not including one under construction); Industrial Rayon, three plants (not including one under construction); Celanese, four plants; American Enka, two plants; and Beaunit operates one plant and owns a controlling interest in Skenandoa, North American, and

[1] Cf. *Cost Behavior and Price Policy*, National Bureau of Economic Research Price Studies no. 4 (New York, 1943); esp. pp. 80–115.

American Bemberg.[2] Celanese also operates two plants in Mexico and Du Pont operates one plant in Argentina. There are, therefore, three entities in the rayon industry which may vary in size and efficiency: the plant, the firm, and the interest group. They are synonymous only in cases where a completely independent firm's total assets are confined to the operations of a single plant.

The most meaningful data presented in this chapter for purposes of comparing size and efficiency relate to plant size and total unit costs. These data show a strong positive relationship between size and efficiency, particularly over the range of plant sizes varying from 5 per cent to about 80 per cent of the size of the largest plants in the industry. There are possibly higher orders of economies of scale for the multi-plant firm or even the interest group. Cost curves for these entities, however, are both conceptually and empirically more difficult if not impossible to treat. For these reasons, therefore, economies of scale for the firm must be inferred from (1) the upper limit to the economical number of firms indicated by the most efficient size of plant, (2) the economies of scale which accompany the large plants operated by large firms, (3) the relative profitability of large and small firms, and (4) other less quantitative data.

Furthermore, the plant data used are based upon the experience of one of the large multi-plant firms and, although they seem to be compatible with all the evidence of a more qualitative nature furnished the author by other multi-plant firms,[3] they do not necessarily

[2] The rated annual capacities of rayon yarn plants operated by each multi-plant firm in 1949 in millions of pounds were as follows: American Viscose Corporation, 72, 45, 30, 30, two having a combined capacity of 58, and one under construction with a planned initial capacity of 25; Du Pont, 60, 48, 35, and one plant the capacity of which is not known; Industrial Rayon Corporation, 32, 17, 12, and one under construction with a planned capacity of 25; Celanese Corporation, 60, 50, one plant exceeding 60, and one plant acquired in its recent merger with Tubize Corporation with a capacity of 25; American Enka, one with a capacity of 20 and two plants on the same plant site with a capacity of 25 each (one textile yarn plant and one tire yarn plant); and Beaunit, 40, 10, 10, and 15. Most capacities exceeding 35–40 million pounds per year include capacity for producing high-tenacity yarn for automobile tires. Only a few viscose textile yarn plants have an annual capacity exceeding 40 million pounds.

[3] Every multi-plant firm in the rayon industry states that, on the basis of either its studies or past experience, large plants are much more efficient than small ones. An excerpt from the correspondence carried on with one of the largest multi-plant producers is typical: "We know that costs decrease as plant size increases since there are many items of overhead that are constant and other items which do not increase proportionately as the size of plant increases. We have made no studies to determine the most economical plant size, but such a plant would be larger than any now in existence." The most plausible reason why larger plants have not been constructed is because, at some point, the advantages of a new location more than offset the economies of scale which would result from an expansion of existing plants.

reflect the relationship between unit costs and size of plant for the industry as a whole. In many respects, however, they are superior to data which might conceivably be obtained from all plants for a given time period.

The rate of technological change has been very high in the domestic rayon industry. Hence, plants constructed several years apart possess sufficiently different physical characteristics, at a given instant of time, to make precise cost comparisons impossible. Such comparisons are further complicated by temporal differences in plant construction and equipment costs even for identical plants. Moreover, there has been a general tendency among rayon producers to build plants with considerable upward flexibility in anticipation of expansion; that is, power plants, filter plants, disposal systems, and often spinning departments are built on a scale larger than is necessary to service the initial textile department. Cost data collected from all firms in the industry, therefore, would give an upward bias to unit costs for small plants. In computing the relationship between unit costs and size of plant the industrial engineering division of the multi-plant firm adjusted its data to 1948 technology and price levels and to overhead costs consistent with its historical experience with plants of various sizes. Hence, although the sample is smaller, the data are much more homogeneous than data which might be collected from the entire industry.

Another obstacle to measuring economies of scale stems from the difficulty of distinguishing between private and social economies. Rayon firms have financed both their initial plants and subsequent expansion programs almost exclusively through the sale of equity stocks and out of retained earnings. Hence, there is no way of determining in any quantitative sense, by comparing interest rates on bonds or short-term loans, whether or not large rayon firms have held a superior position to their smaller rivals in the capital markets. However, about two-thirds of all the rayon producers have floated relatively small issues of par value cumulative preferred stock stipulating dividend rates ranging from 4.5 per cent to 5.0 per cent or no par value cumulative preferred stock stipulating annual dividends ranging from $3.50 to $4.75. There is no correlation between size of firm and either the dividend rate or the per cent of total equity represented by preferred stock issues.

One might conclude a priori that securities bearing such names as Du Pont, American Viscose, and Celanese find an easier market than those of less successful smaller producers. Even if this were demonstrably the case, however, it would indicate neither that economies associated with size were private economies nor that large rayon firms, simply because they are large, procure preferential treatment in the capital market. None of the rayon firms, even the relatively small ones, can be appropriately classified under the heading of small business; and the effects of expected earning power cannot be isolated from the effects of size.

In other factor markets, plant location appears to have had much more effect on prices than has the size of the purchasing unit. Wage rates for about three-fourths of the wage earners in the rayon industry have been determined by collective bargaining since 1937 and embodied in contracts with either the Textile Workers of America (C.I.O.) or the United Textile Workers (A.F. of L.). Historically, money wage rates in the industry have been higher in small cities and towns than average wages in the local labor market, approximately the same as the local average in the larger cities, slightly higher in the North than in the South, and higher for large firms than for small. The work force of one large rayon producer, not affiliated with either of the national unions, has consistently received higher money wage rates than the highest prevailing in the industry. Since there is no reason for suspecting large companies of paying higher wages than small ones for noneconomic reasons, it would seem reasonable to conclude that efficiency wages, if properly adjusted for regional and local labor market conditions, would show little variation between large and small rayon firms.

Rayon producers, through long-term contractual arrangements made possible by stable rates of delivery, have obtained some of their raw materials at prices lower than prevailing list prices, and several of the large rayon companies have produced some of their own chemicals and wood pulp.[4] To the extent that large rayon producers obtain either greater quantity discounts than small producers on raw material purchases, or lower interdepartmental transfer prices, than can be justified on the basis of costs, the resulting economies are of course either private or apparent rather than social or real. The available evidence, however, limited to 1940 cost data and to the outcome of correspondence and interviews with the producers themselves, would suggest that differences in size among rayon firms has resulted in no corresponding raw material price differentials. In

[4] See discussion of short-run factor price behavior, pp. 157 ff.

1940, total delivered material costs per pound of yarn produced by the viscose rayon industry amounted to $0.14, whereas material costs, excluding the cost of small quantities of magnesium sulfate, titanium dioxide, and bleaching compounds, per pound of yarn produced by one of the largest viscose rayon producers amounted to $0.13.[5] Similarly, total material costs per pound of acetate yarn produced in 1940, based on data representing 79 per cent of the industry's output, amounted to $0.143, whereas material costs, excluding the cost of small quantities of sulfuric acid, ethyl acetate, and soda ash, per pound of yarn produced by one of the largest acetate rayon producers amounted to $0.133.[6] The $0.01 difference in material costs between the industry average and the large producer in each case is probably attributable to the cost of the small quantities of chemicals included in the industry data but omitted from those for the two large firms. Furthermore, large firms who produce some of their own raw materials stated in 1949 that interdepartmental transfers are always made at prevailing market prices and nearly all rayon producers, whether large or small, indicated that whatever price advantages they have over their rivals in raw material markets derive from their location rather than their size.

B. Growth Pattern and Evidence of Economies of Scale

Limited to a single firm until 1920, the rayon industry had expanded to twenty firms by 1931. Eighteen of these producers entered the industry during the expansion period of the twenties. Between 1931 and 1947 the number of active firms declined to fourteen. Since 1947 one old firm has been revived, one new firm has commenced production, and two additional new firms have announced their plans for plant construction.

Prior to 1920, American Viscose accounted for 100 per cent of the total domestic output. Although still the world's largest rayon producer, the company's share in the market gradually decreased until by January 1949 it accounted for only 26 per cent (see Table 5). Until 1930 the two largest producers, American Viscose and the rayon division of E. I. du Pont de Nemours and Co., Inc., accounted for over 75 per cent of total domestic output and the four largest producers accounted for about 90 per cent. Since 1930 the two largest companies have produced slightly less than 50 per cent and the four

[5] *Hearings*, H. R., Project V, pp. 47–48.
[6] *Hearings*, H. R., Project V, pp. 47, 49.

TABLE 5

Historical Growth of the Rayon Industry by Firm in Terms of Output and Installed Capacity,[a] 1924–1949

(IN MILLIONS OF POUNDS)

Company	1924	1925	1926	1927	1928	1930	1931	1933	1935	1938	1942[b]	1945[b]	1949[b]
American Viscose	24.8	35.0	37.0	41.0	59.0	76.7	86.0	77.0	95	102	160	183	237.0
Du Pont	4.0	6.8	10.9	15.1	22.0	29.2	30.0	37.2	47	53	86	106	143.0
Tubize[c]	4.3	5.2	7.0	7.5	8.5	16.3	14.8	16.3	10	20	20	23	—
North American					—	9.9	14.0	17.3	20	25	30	32	40.0
Industrial	2.0	2.3	3.4	3.5	4.5	13.3	13.0	16.7	17	32	38	65	81.0
Celanese		1.5	2.5	3.5	5.0	11.0	11.0	22.0	35	37	85	112	220.0
American Bemberg					2.5	5.5	5.0	7.9	8	10	14	12	15.0
American Enka						6.6	5.0	15.0	13	30	30	37	65.0
Tennessee Eastman						—	1.0	5.5	10	21	34	35	62.0
Skenandoa					1.2	3.7	3.5	3.5	4	7			10.0
Delaware				0.5	1.5	2.2	2.0	2.0	3	3			3.5
New Bedford						1.8	2.0	3.0	4	5	22[e]	20[e]	5.0
Woonsocket						1.8	1.8	2.2	3	3			3.5
Hartford (Belamose)		0.7	0.9	1.4	1.4	1.7	2.5	2.8	4	4			6.5
National (Acme)[d]		0.3	0.4	0.5	0.7	1.1	1.0	1.2	1	1			1.5
Cuprammonium[d]					—[g]	1.0	1.0	1.0	1	1	—	—	—[g]
Amoskeag[f]						1.0	1.0	1.3	—	—	—	—	—
Carolina Mills[f]						1.0	1.0	—	—	—	—	—	—
Hampton Company[f]						1.0	1.0	1.5	2	2	—	—	—
Roseland[f]					—[g]	—[g]	—[g]	—	—	—	—	—	—
Beaunit													10.0
Total	38.3	51.8	62.1	73.0	106.3	184.8	196.6	233.4	277	356	519	625	904.0
Per Cent Controlled by:													
Largest firm	73	58	60	56	56	42	44	33	34	29	31	29	26
2 largest firms	84	81	77	77	76	57	59	49	51	44	47	47	51
3 largest firms	95	91	89	87	84	66	67	58	64	54	64	64	66
4 largest firms	100	95	94	92	89	73	74	66	71	63	71	75	75
No. of firms	4	7	7	8	13	19	20	18	17	17	15	15	16[h]

Source: *Rayon Organon; Textile World;* Willard L. Thorp, *et al., The Structure of Industry;* E. W. Axe and Company, *Rayon Common Stocks; Hearings,* H. R., Project V; Avram, *The Rayon Industry;* other trade journals, newspapers, and correspondence with rayon firms.

[a] Actual production 1924–1927, and 1945. Installed capacity other years.

[b] Staple fiber not included.

[c] Includes American Chatillon. Reported with Celanese in 1949.

[d] Closed down in several years for which capacities are shown.

[e] Estimated.

[f] Companies stopped operating shortly after last capacity shown.

[g] Very small.

[h] Does not include two new companies not yet operating plants on a commercial scale.

largest companies slightly over 70 per cent of domestic output. The decline in concentration was arrested during the war period, principally because 99 per cent of the tire yarn capacity constructed by the Reconstruction Finance Corporation for the rayon industry was placed under the custody of American Viscose and Du Pont, the two largest producers. The remaining 1 per cent went to North American, the fifth largest viscose yarn producer.[7]

The extent to which output has been concentrated in the hands of a few sellers is considerably more pronounced if each process is viewed as a separate industry. Neither capacity nor production data by process are available for all the years included in Table 5, but most recent data show that American Viscose produces between 45 and 50 per cent of total viscose rayon, Celanese from 50 to 60 per cent of total acetate rayon, and American Bemberg accounts for virtually all of the domestic cuprammonium rayon output.

Average investment data show the industry to be somewhat less highly concentrated than do output or installed capacity data. For example, in 1938 American Viscose produced 33 per cent of all rayon (including staple fiber) produced in the United States but accounted for only 28 per cent of total average investment; Du Pont accounted for 24 per cent of output but only 20.6 per cent of total average investment; Celanese for 17 per cent of output but 21 per cent of investment; and five medium-size firms accounted for 26 per cent of total rayon output and 27 per cent of total average investment.[8]

By any method of measurement, however, concentration of control in the rayon industry has been high relative to other sectors of the textile industry. The decline in concentration which has occurred since 1930 may be traced to the expansion of medium-size producers, not to an increase in the number of producers. In fact, while concentration of control in the hands of a few large firms has declined since 1931, the number of sellers in the rayon industry has also decreased.

The incidence of failure in the rayon industry has been wholly upon small-scale producers. Mortality among small firms is understated by the data presented in Table 5 since they do not reflect the attempts made to enter the industry that ended in failure before a stage of commercial production was reached. Moreover, two of the small companies for which continuous capacity data are given in Table 5 have not been in continuous operation. The Cuprammonium Corporation has hung onto life by a thread since its organization. The company has undergone four financial reorganizations and has

[7] *Hearings*, H. R., Project V, p. 61.

[8] Federal Trade Commission, *Investments, Profits, and Rates of Return for Selected Industries*, United States Government Printing Office (Washington, 1941), p. 17991. The five medium-size producers were Industrial, Tubize, American Enka, North American, and American Bemberg.

been listed as inactive in all but two or three years of its corporate existence. The National Rayon Corporation (Acme Rayon Corporation prior to 1941) has also been closed down over several prolonged intervals. When resuming operations during the last war, National was granted a higher price schedule than the rest of the industry by the Office of Price Administration because of its abnormally high production costs.[9] With the first postwar slump in the textile market, which became evident early in the spring of 1949, the company announced that it had closed down its plant for an indefinite period.[10]

Failures among very small producers stem from the same casual forces that explain why the rayon industry has been composed of relatively few firms. There is considerable evidence that unit costs fall as plant capacity is increased over a very wide range of output. Without exception, the large and medium-size producers have operated large plants, whereas small firms have operated only small plants.

Economies of Scale for the Plant. Curve A in Chart 11 shows the variation in total cost per unit of output with size of rayon yarn plant.[11] Plant size, in terms of per cent of capacity of the largest plant operated by the large multi-plant company, is measured along the horizontal axis, and the lowest point on the total unit cost curve of each plant relative to that of the largest plant is measured along the vertical axis.[12] The relevancy of the curve to the industry for analytical purposes is indicated by the frequency distribution of plants by size groups for the year 1949. However, three of the plants included in the "10 million and under" group were inactive by the middle of the year.

The shape of the curve that represents the relationship between unit costs and size of plant, which is a close approximation to the negatively sloped range of the economic theorist's envelope curve, is extremely helpful in explaining why the rayon industry has been limited to relatively few plants. Unit costs continue to decrease as plant size is increased up to the maximum size plant (approximately

[9] *Textile World*, September 1942, p. 155; *Rayon Organon*, October 1942. The price ceiling on 300-denier viscose yarn for the rest of the industry was $0.49 per pound; Acme was permitted to sell the same yarn for $0.65 per pound.

[10] *Rayon Organon*, April 1949, p. 51.

[11] See Chap. 8 for a discussion of the curves shown in Chart 11. The company currently operates plants that are normally classified as either medium- or large-size plants; hence, unit costs for small-size plants had to be estimated by adjusting data for small plants previously operated.

[12] The percentages were used so that actual cost per unit of output would not be disclosed.

40 million pounds per year) operated by the firm. Since the multi-plant firm that conducted the study has never constructed plants beyond the point of technical optimum size, it could furnish no information on variation in unit costs with size of plant beyond the size of its largest plant. The flatness that characterizes the curve between 80 per cent and 100 per cent of the capacity of the largest plant currently operated by the company, however, indicates that average total unit costs fall very slowly as plant size is increased beyond the present size of its largest plant.

The high unit costs of small-scale producers, particularly of those operating plants having less than ten million pounds annual capacity, partially account for the failure of the several smaller firms that entered the industry on too small a scale of production and failed to keep pace with the plant expansion programs of other firms. Four of the companies that collapsed or withdrew from the industry during the early thirties commenced operations with extremely small plants and never expanded capacity beyond 1.5 million pounds per year. Two additional small companies, Acme and Cuprammonium, having annual capacities under 1.5 million pounds, have experienced long periods of inactivity. The surviving small producers, Skenandoa, Delaware, New Bedford, Woonsocket, and Hartford, have increased their plant capacities at a moderate pace but their affiliations with large weaving and knitting companies and novelty yarn production have probably aided these firms considerably in maintaining their existence in the industry.[13]

Several factors contribute to the shape of the long-run plant cost curve described above. Overhead costs for a single-plant firm constitute a fairly large proportion of total costs. Historically, they have averaged one-third of total costs of production for the industry.[14] Some overhead costs remain constant over a wide range of plant sizes; some vary, but not proportionately with the size of plant.

The complexity of the chemical processes employed in the manufacture of rayon and the recognition by each producer of the necessity for continuing product improvement if he is to maintain his position in the industry have entailed large expenditures on research, experimental and physical testing laboratories, and professional per-

[13] E. W. Axe & Co., Inc., *Rayon Common Stocks* (New York, 1946). Woonsocket, the smallest of the five companies, closed down in March 1949, and offered its plant for sale. *Rayon Organon*, April 1949, p. 51.

[14] Schwarz and Mauersberger, *Rayon and Staple Fiber Handbook* (New York, 1939), p. 38.

sonnel. Many of the laboratory facilities must be maintained whether the firm operates a large or small plant or one or several plants. Moreover, a large staff of chemical and mechanical engineers is required in operations. Scientific control groups, although obviously larger for such producers as Du Pont's rayon division and American Viscose than for smaller producers, do not increase with approximate proportionality to either plant or firm capacity. This is equally true for the maintenance of various other research, production, and selling facilities.

Also, there is fairly conclusive evidence that the indivisibility of certain plant installations makes for lower fixed charges per unit of output as plant capacity is increased. According to Lockwood Greene Engineers, Inc., an engineering firm that has had a long successful history in the construction and operation of rayon and other textile plants all over the world:

Any rayon plant, no matter how small, requires the installation of certain facilities which are quite expensive and which would increase very slightly with an increased output. Among such items may be mentioned the following: boiler plant, power generating plant, water supply system, spinning bath recovery system, fume stack, repair shops, offices, toilet and locker rooms, laboratory, technical and supervisory staff, maintenance department. The experience of the plants in the U. S. A. indicates that the best quality of yarn and the best profits are produced by the larger companies. In this country six large producers with thirteen modern plants produce 88% of the total viscose yarn produced (as of April 1943). While these individual plants vary in size, the average plant capacity for the group was twenty-seven tons per day. Five small producers produced the remaining 12% of the output, with plants ranging in size from four and one-half tons per day to eleven tons per day. Of these five companies the plant with eleven tons per day production has shown better results than the others, and it is clearly shown that the overhead costs in a small plant are very high, and that this type of industry requires operation in large units to be profitable. While we believe that it is all right to start an initial plant with a capacity of two tons per day, it should be realized in the beginning that the plant investment will be unduly high in proportion to sales volume, and that it should not be expected to operate profitably until such time as it has been brought up to a larger capacity."[15]

[15] From a report which Mr. S. B. Lincoln of the New York office of Lockwood Greene Engineers, Inc. prepared for a proposed rayon plant in India. This part of the report was obtained in Boston through Mr. H. E. Cousins, Vice-President of Lockwood Greene Engineers, Inc.; the company has produced rayon and has constructed many of the rayon plants in this country, South America, and elsewhere.

The report stated further that a plant with four tons daily capacity would cost only about 50 per cent more than a plant of two tons daily capacity if the smaller plant were designed to facilitate future expansion to the larger size.

Available data on construction costs of rayon plants of various sizes are not to be interpreted too rigidly since costs will not be a unique function of the size of the initial producing unit but will vary somewhat with plans for future expansion. Correspondingly, costs of additional capacity are partially dependent upon the facilities previously installed. Moreover, available plant cost data are confined to the years 1925–1929 when initial plant units were constructed on a

TABLE 6

Cost of Various Size Plants and Plant Additions Constructed between 1925 and 1939[a]

INITIAL PLANT			PLANT ADDITIONS		
Annual Capacity (millions of pounds)	Construction Costs (millions of dollars)	Cost per Annual Pound	Annual Capacity (millions of pounds)	Construction Costs (millions of dollars)	Cost per Annual Pound
12.00	11.50	$0.96	24.40	14.60	$0.59
10.00	10.00	1.00	17.40	13.30	0.76
10.00	8.75	0.88	6.00	3.30	0.55
6.60	10.00	1.52	5.00	2.00	0.44
3.50	8.00	2.28	4.00	5.00	1.25
3.50	8.00	2.28	2.40	3.00	1.25
2.10	4.50	2.25			
0.36	1.00	2.78			

[a] As reported in *Textile World* and other sources. All plants but one were constructed between 1925 and 1929.

much smaller scale than they are today. The data presented in Table 6, however, confirm the above averred relationship between installations cost per unit of output and size of plant. The larger the initial plant or plant addition, the lower the installation cost per unit of output.

As would be expected, once a plant has been put in operation, additions to plant capacity cost considerably less per annual pound than the initial unit. Some specific examples are as follows: The initial Du Pont plant at Richmond, Virginia cost $2.28 per annual pound; the second unit of approximately the same size cost only $1.25 per annual pound. American Chatillon's initial plant at Rome, Georgia cost $1.50 per annual pound; a later addition cost only $0.40

per annual pound.[16] Industrial Rayon's large 12 million pound per year plant at Painesville, Ohio cost 11.5 million dollars, or $0.96 per annual pound; the 6 million pound per year addition cost only $0.55 per annual pound of installed capacity.

Many of the economies of large-scale production are obtained through more effective utilization of power plants, filter plants, recovery systems, laboratories, staff personnel, and other facilities and personnel that do not vary proportionately with plant size. A portion of the greater efficiency of large plants, however, is traceable to economies of scale obtained through expansion of auxiliary plant installations. During the twenties, for example, when most firms were entering the industry, hydroelectric power delivered at the power plant switchboard cost $0.026 per kilowatt-hour from a 1000 kilowatt-hour capacity power plant. Cost per kilowatt-hour decreased to $0.018 as power plant capacity was increased to 5000 kilowatt-hours.[17]

It should be mentioned, however, that some of the above economies of scale are not unique functions of size of plant. For example, centralized chemical and physical testing laboratory costs per unit of output would probably be reduced by the same amount with any given increase in output, whether from the addition of one large plant or two medium size plants having the same total capacity. Similarly, any increase in output for the firm may reduce selling, administrative, and research unit costs regardless of how such increases in output were accomplished. Reductions in unit costs such as those caused entirely by increasing output are obviously more closely associated with economies of scale for the firm than for the plant.

Economies of Scale for the Firm. For the most part, the greater technical efficiency of large plants and of multi-plant operations has reflected in correspondingly greater financial efficiency for the large firm. The relationship between size and financial efficiency obtained from an analysis of financial statements, however, is at best a rough approximation since accounting profits are neither entirely comparable among firms nor the same as profits in an economic sense.

The rate of return on average annual investment by company from 1915 to 1947 is presented in Table 7.[18] Between 1911 and 1947,

[16] Not included in table because exact capacities could not be determined.

[17] Avram, *The Rayon Industry*, p. 203.

[18] See Appendix C for methods used in calculating investment, profits, and rate of return.

TABLE 7

Annual Rate of Return on Total Investment[a] for Principal Rayon Companies, 1915–1947

Year	American Viscose Corporation	Du Pont Rayon Company	Celanese Corporation of America	Tubize Chatillon Corporation	Industrial Rayon Corporation	American Enka Corporation	North American Rayon Corporation	American Bemberg Corporation	Skenandoa Rayon Corporation	Hartford Rayon Corporation	Delaware Rayon Corporation	New Bedford Rayon Corporation
1915	26.32											
1916	109.19											
1917	95.96											
1918	100.56											
1919	268.96											
1920	156.83											
1921	87.16	2.13[b]										
1922	97.00	34.11										
1923	88.13	38.91										
1924	54.18	27.88										
1925	72.64	34.19	1.15									
1926	46.01	15.23	12.60		12.80							
1927	52.82	27.01	20.76		25.48					9.72[e]		
1928	59.36	26.63	9.09		22.03			8.34		4.81		
1929	44.55	19.04	9.88		12.42		0.96[b]	0.04[b]		3.47		
1930	10.95	0.90[b]	5.98		13.38	4.28[b]	1.30	7.25[b]	0.38[bc]	6.40[b]		
1931	4.83	4.45	3.03		6.43	1.55[b]	0.32[b]	9.72[b]	1.50[b]	7.06[db]	2.55[e]	
1932	1.32	1.21	3.47		2.10	1.29[b]	3.50[b]	10.43[b]	0.70[b]	15.70[db]	0.65[eb]	
1933	17.01	12.65	20.37	4.75	14.35	8.86	12.58	14.64	3.53	10.55[d]	n.a.	
1934	11.12	8.58	10.91	0.27[b]	9.33	1.84	5.88	9.90[b]	1.92[b]	5.94[b]	1.90[eb]	
1935	9.22	5.25	12.13	5.86	4.25	5.03	10.06	11.10[b]	1.66[b]	n.a.	3.10[e]	
1936	14.78	11.00	11.98	12.27	9.66	17.12	21.75	17.27	3.17	n.a.	11.66	
1937	15.36	13.10	10.96	16.60	1.68	21.19	24.75	29.45	12.49	14.51	7.54	
1938	4.34[b]	4.15	6.00	3.55	1.67	8.46	4.48	18.48	0.91	2.27[b]	n.a.	2.14[cb]
1939	n.a.	n.a.	13.50	13.10	7.40	17.40	26.10	29.00	7.40	5.50	8.30	4.50
1940	n.a.	n.a.	16.30	21.20	12.80	22.20	36.80	23.60	8.80	5.70	n.a.	9.40
1941	15.20	n.a.	18.20	24.80	23.50	25.60	31.70	42.10	15.40	14.00	n.a.	10.60
1942	21.40	n.a.	22.70	33.00	30.00	43.80	39.40	70.50	19.40	18.90	n.a.	14.00
1943	22.50	n.a.	18.50	33.20	25.80	50.40	36.80	41.30	15.60	12.60	n.a.	7.30
1944	20.70	n.a.	20.00	37.90	17.90	49.20	34.10	55.10	16.70	11.30	19.10	8.10
1945	18.80	n.a.	18.80	35.10	21.90	13.80	34.70	60.70	n.a.	15.30	24.80	5.70
1946	19.30	n.a.	20.70	merged with	48.30	49.50	38.90	50.80	19.60	17.90	41.10	5.10
1947	31.80	n.a.	23.80	Celanese	78.20	56.10	49.10	38.10	n.a.	4.80	44.50	8.10
Avg. 1933–1941	11.19	8.79	13.37	11.32	9.40	14.19	20.46	17.06	5.35	6.01	5.74	5.59

[a] Data for eight largest companies for the period 1915–1938 from Federal Trade Commission, *Investments, Profits, and Rates of Return For Selected Industries*, United States Government Printing Office (Washington, 1941); other data computed from financial statements of individual companies as they appear in *Moody's Manual*. In keeping with the method used by the Federal Trade Commission, investments at beginning and end of year were averaged. Total investment is sum of long-term borrowings, stock outstanding, surplus and surplus reserves. Rates of return on total investment and stockholders' investment are practically identical since there is very little long-term borrowing in the industry. Rate of return computed from net income on operations before Federal income taxes and average investment.

[b] Loss. [c] Only year end investment available. [d] Investment computed by interpolation. [e] Net profit used instead of net income from operations.

American Viscose[19] operated at a profit in all years but 1938. Until 1930, the company's rate of return on investment never fell below 26.32 per cent and in all years but one ranged between 44 per cent and 269 per cent. The rayon division of E. I. du Pont de Nemours & Company, Inc. has also operated at a high rate of return on investment and has experienced only one unprofitable year (−0.90 per cent in 1930) since 1922. Celanese and Industrial have operated at a profit in all years since 1925. The Tubize Corporation has operated at a profit in all years for which financial statements are available except one (−0.27 per cent in 1934). American Enka and North American (jointly managed with American Bemberg) have proved to be highly profitable ventures since 1933. All of these companies commenced operations with a relatively large-scale plant and expanded plant capacity rapidly, and all but one increased their number of plants. The smaller rayon producers, Skenandoa, Hartford, Delaware, and New Bedford, show more frequent losses and considerably lower rates of return.[20]

Between 1933 and 1941, the seven large producers earned an average annual return of 12.7 per cent whereas the four small producers earned an average annual return of only 5.7 per cent.[21] These data overstate the earning power of small producers since they do not include the negative earnings of small firms which have either failed or maintained little more than nominal existence. Postwar data contained in a recent study made by the Federal Trade Commission[22] show that the four largest rayon producers realized a

[19] For a brief financial history of the American Viscose Corporation, see "Mystery: the American Viscose Corporation," *Fortune*, July 1937, pp. 39–43, 106–112.

[20] The number of firms for which profit data are available is too small to compute a statistical relationship between size and earning power in the rayon industry. However, the available data suggest a pattern not greatly different from that for the manufacturing economy generally, i.e., large producers are more profitable than small ones, their earnings are more stable, but the difference in rates of return between the large and very large producers is almost negligible. See William L. Crum, *Corporate Size and Earning Power* (Cambridge, Mass.: Harvard University Press), 1939.

[21] The war years were excluded when making this comparison for several reasons: (1) Some rayon firms operated plants constructed by the Government and depreciated them more rapidly than wear and tear and obsolescence would justify. Hence, differences in accounting for profits among producers were even more accentuated during the war period. (2) The black market price for rayon by the end of the war was three times the published list price. It is not known to what extent, if at all, rayon producers sold yarn for other than list prices after 1942, but had some indulged in off-list selling more than others, their profits would have been unduly inflated.

[22] F. T. C., *Rates of Return for 528 Identical Companies in 25 Selected Manufacturing Industries, 1940, 1947 and 1948* (mimeographed release, December, 1949), pp. 9–14.

higher rate of return on stockholders' investment in 1947 and 1948 than three smaller producers among which the smallest firms in the industry were not included.

If the underlying causative forces behind the long-run plant cost curve explain its shape, they, along with what evidence there is that some economies of scale accrue to the firm, also explain in part the industry profit pattern and account for much of the economic pressure upon rayon producers to increase the size and number of their plants. They also explain to a considerable extent why there are relatively few rayon plants and, less precisely, why there are relatively few rayon producers. As plants of existing firms grew in size and number, the quantity of capital and the caliber of managerial ability required to enter the industry on a cost basis comparable to established firms increased. In the years 1920–1925, new firms entered the industry with plants ranging in capacity from one to three million pounds per year. The Textile Economics Bureau estimates, and the foregoing data seem to justify its conclusion, that the entrance fee to the industry in recent years has been sufficient capital to construct a plant having at least a capacity of from twelve to fifteen million pounds per year. On the basis of prewar construction costs this would approximate an outlay of fifteen million dollars. Additional capital would be required to tide the potential producer over the period of construction and the customary two years of operations necessary to gear the plant for production of first grade yarn in sufficient quantities to show promise of normal profitability.

Factors other than mere size, however, have been decisive obstacles to entrance since most basic patents became public property. The vigorous growth of the industry has left a dearth of rayon engineers and other highly technical personnel. It was pointed out in the previous chapter that most domestic producers acquired their technical assistance from Europe prior to 1930. The initiation of several lawsuits as a result of their transfer suggests that a high premium has been placed upon the services of trained rayon experts. For example, in August 1929 Celanese filed an injunction against American Chatillon, claiming that "Chatillon induced W. E. Crooks away from them for trade secret purposes." [23] Closely associated with the problem of obtaining top management and technical experts has been the problem of obtaining the details of the principles

[23] *Rayon Journal*, September 1, 1929, p. 36.

of production or industrial "know-how." Many production methods not protected by patents have been protected by secrecy.[24]

Moreover, factors other than economic barriers to entrance determine the number of firms in an industry. For example, the depression eliminated five producers from the rayon industry that might possibly have continued operations had the depression not occurred. Furthermore, the rate of return for rayon-producing firms, even for the more successful large firms, was probably not sufficiently high between 1930 and 1940 to attract new firms to an industry which was dependent upon tariff protection for its survival. Between 1930 and 1938 the average rate of return on operations for selected large producers was only slightly over 7 per cent and the average for the industry was substantially less (see Table 7). When adjusted for financial expenses, income taxes, and the uncertainties of future tariff policy, a 5 to 7 per cent rate of return on operations may not have been considered as particularly attractive to the prospective entrant.

Hence, since 1930, prospective rayon producers would have had to emulate the performance of large producers already in possession of the short supply of rayon engineers, "know-how," and plant facilities that would have taken millions of dollars to duplicate. The rate of return was probably too low to risk the necessary large investment. Moreover, established firms were in a position to expand more rapidly and more economically than new entrants could construct a given addition to total installed capacity. Stated briefly, since 1930 a new firm would have had to be a large firm because of cost considerations; the rate of return does not appear to have been sufficiently high to indicate that there was room in the industry for another large producer. Whatever the validity of this line of reasoning, the industry has always been composed of relatively few sellers. By most definitions, therefore, a study of price behavior in the rayon industry is a case study of an oligopoly price. And, although it is patently impossible to explain why the industry is composed of precisely the number of producers it is, the evidence presented in this chapter appears to be sufficiently strong to conclude that the rayon industry falls among the natural oligopolies.

[24] Cf. "Mystery: The American Viscose Corporation," *Fortune*, July 1937, pp. 39–43, 106–112.

4

RAYON PRICE and Product Composition and Terms of Trade

A. Price and Product Composition

Output in the domestic rayon industry may be divided into two principal classes of products: rayon yarn and rayon staple fiber. Rayon yarn is currently produced in the United States under the viscose, acetate, and cuprammonium processes and staple fiber is produced under the viscose and acetate processes. In each process, yarns are produced over a fairly wide range of deniers, lusters, and filament counts. Viscose yarns are also divided into textile yarns and high-tenacity automobile tire yarns; the former, after undergoing a special inspection room operation, are further classified into first, second, and inferior grades of yarn.

Until recent years, however, rayon was a much more homogeneous product than that of most mass-production industries in the American economy,[1] consisting mainly of 150-denier viscose yarn. Moreover, the industry's practice of designating all rayon yarn in terms of a common unit facilitates the conversion of all yarns of the same process into equivalent pounds of standard 150-denier yarn. Rayon yarn is numbered for degree of fineness on a basis of the metrical weight-length units that constitute the legal denier standard employed in measuring the size of raw silk. The rayon denier represents the weight in five-centigram units of a skein 450 meters (492.13 yards) in length. The legal denier weight of five centigrams is equiv-

[1] An account of recent developments in the rayon industry, including a discussion of recent changes in the nature of the rayon industry's output, is presented in Appendix A.

alent to 0.771618 grains; there are 7000 grains in one pound; hence:

$$\frac{7000}{0.771618} \times 492.13 = 4{,}464{,}528,$$

which is the number of yards per pound of one denier rayon or raw silk. The constant (4,464,528) divided by the denier of the rayon yarn gives the yards per pound for that denier yarn, or, conversely, the constant divided by the number of yards in a pound of yarn gives the denier of the yarn. For example, 150-denier yarn runs 29,764 yards to the pound; hence:

$$\frac{4{,}464{,}528}{29{,}764} = 150.$$

The yardage per pound varies inversely with the denier. For example, one pound of 75-denier yarn contains 59,528 yards, or exactly twice the yardage of one pound of 150-denier yarn (29,764 yards). A sample calculation will show how all rayon yarns produced under a given process may be converted to standard units of output or their 150-denier equivalent:

Denier	Quantity in Actual Pounds	Conversion Factor	Quantity in Standard (150-denier) Pounds
75	100	2.000	200
100	100	1.500	150
150	300	1.000	300
200	200	0.750	150
300	100	0.500	50
Total	800		850

Yarns are sold by the pound and all yarn prices are based upon the price of the 150-denier yarn (lowest filament count) of that process. Since the time required to produce one pound of rayon varies directly but not proportionately with the yardage, deniers finer than 150-denier, because of their greater yardage, carry a premium over the 150-denier price. Conversely, yarns heavier than 150-denier sell for slightly less.

All market barometers and trade publications use the quoted price of 150-denier viscose rayon yarn in their price series rather than a weighted average price or index number computed from prices and quantities of the various deniers sold. Several advantages obtain from employing a representative price in preference to a computed price index: Over long periods of time some deniers fade out and others take their place; the product matrix may be negligibly affected but such changes present difficulties in making the necessary allowances in the index number computation. Moreover, data are not available for the computation of index numbers that precisely locate price changes[2] with respect to time. It is essentially for the latter reason that a representative price is employed in this study in preference to a price index. A close examination of the component parts of the rayon yarn product matrix will show that this is justifiable.

Viscose yarns are produced over a range of 50-denier to 450-denier.[3] Several deniers are produced with more than one filament count and all deniers are graded, according to coloration, uniformity, and broken filaments, into first, second, and inferior qualities of yarn. The price differential between grades has gradually decreased from about $0.20 in 1926 to $0.01 in 1947. All deniers and grades are put up in skeins, cones, tubes, cops, and beams. Variations in putup have occasioned price differentials of only a few cents per pound. Most price differentials among putups had disappeared by 1940 but some producers have quoted a price differential of $0.01 between skeins and cones since February 1947. In addition, most companies produce delustered yarns in all deniers. When first introduced, delustered yarns carried a $0.05 per pound premium. By 1931, however, premiums on delustered yarns had disappeared. Acetate and cuprammonium yarns are produced in only one grade[4] but are put up in sizes and packages similar to viscose yarns.

Annual rayon yarn production by denier group and by process[5] (1928–1948) is presented in Table 8. Until 1920, only 150-denier viscose was produced in the United States. Production data by denier for viscose yarn are not available for years before 1928 and are not available for acetate yarn before 1934. There was a slight secular downward movement in the average denier of viscose yarn spun from 1928 to 1941. This trend was reversed after 1941 when

[2] Only annual data for rayon production and deliveries by denier are available.

[3] High-tenacity yarns for the tire cord and fabric trades are produced in deniers of 1100 to 2200. These yarns were quantitatively insignificant before 1939.

[4] See Chap. 2.

[5] Viscose and cuprammonium yarn production are reported together to keep from identifying the single cuprammonium producer. Since cuprammonium yarn has accounted for only 1 or 2 per cent of total yarn production since 1928, its inclusion does not materially affect viscose production data.

TABLE 8

Filament Rayon Yarn Production by Denier, 1928–1948

(MILLIONS OF POUNDS)

VISCOSE PROCESS[a]

Year	50 (62 a.u.)	75 (63–87)	100 (88–112)	125 (113–137)	150 (138–162)	200 (163–237)	300 (238–374)	375–999	1000 a.o.	Average Denier	Average Denier of Textile Yarns Only
1928	—	2.6	5.2	1.0	68.2	1.9	10.5	1.8	—	152	152
1929	—	2.5	8.6	1.9	83.6	1.9	12.7	1.8	—	151	151
1930	—	2.0	11.2	4.5	83.3	1.9	12.6	1.6	—	148	148
1931	—	2.1	16.5	2.9	95.8	1.8	13.1	2.3	—	146	146
1932	—	2.4	22.2	3.6	76.4	2.1	8.0	1.3	—	139	139
1933	0.5	2.4	36.9	5.5	106.6	3.8	14.5	2.7	—	139	139
1934	0.7	1.9	29.7	4.6	105.4	9.2	16.4	2.4	—	145	145
1935	0.6	3.3	26.7	5.3	124.1	15.8	21.7	4.5	—	149	149
1936	0.9	6.8	38.0	5.6	128.4	10.3	19.5	5.4	—	142	142
1937	1.2	7.1	41.1	4.5	145.0	9.1	22.9	7.3	—	143	143
1938	1.3	8.8	39.8	3.8	97.2	6.5	17.8	6.3	—	137	137
1939	4.1	16.2	45.3	3.2	122.1	6.6	26.1	7.2	0.5	134	134
1940	4.1	20.7	50.2	3.7	141.3	3.8	21.5	7.5	4.3	132	129
1941	4.2	20.1	51.7	3.0	155.4	3.6	26.6	9.9	13.0	139	132
1942	5.8	23.0	60.9	5.0	148.1	2.7	28.6	6.5	29.9	140	126
1943	6.6	26.9	54.1	4.1	126.3	2.5	43.5	7.5	67.0	158	133
1944	5.3	29.5	50.4	12.8	102.4	1.6	45.7	10.6	125.2	184	132
1945	5.1	29.9	51.3	12.7	95.2	1.5	41.0	13.7	198.4	215	129
1946	5.0	30.7	56.1	15.4	104.7	1.5	39.2	14.2	224.4	220	129
1947	5.0	32.1	60.8	10.7	120.1	1.5	40.5	14.7	239.8	222	130
1948	4.3	34.0	71.3	4.2	130.3	1.7	35.6	17.8	263.1	225	129
ACETATE PROCESS											
1934	0.4	3.9	19.3	8.2[b]	5.8	0.4[c]				105	
1935	0.6	5.3	17.5	13.4	17.1	1.6				114	
1936	0.5	7.9	13.5	11.9	25.2	3.7				118	
1937	1.5	13.6	17.8	10.0	33.4	6.0				115	
1938	3.3	14.5	15.2	5.8	32.0	5.3				111	
1939	6.8	20.9	14.1	4.2	42.9	8.4				108	
1940	9.8	35.5	12.8	5.3	56.1	13.5				106	
1941	11.0	40.9	17.4	9.8	66.3	18.3				107	
1942	13.9	51.6	21.7	20.5	56.5	4.6				98	
1943	12.5	48.7	20.8	28.7	45.4	6.5				98	
1944	13.5	52.7	26.1	28.4	44.5	6.5				97	
1945	13.9	53.5	25.3	34.8	37.4	10.6				97	
1946	16.4	59.1	24.5	29.4	51.2	5.7				96	
1947	17.0	70.1	30.3	23.5	65.1	15.5				99	
1948	22.7	82.8	35.1	25.0	97.9	30.3				104	

Source: *Rayon Organon*, Annual Supplements.

[a] Viscose includes cuprammonium.

[b] 120-denier for acetate.

[c] Includes all deniers over 163.

production of heavy denier tire yarn was greatly increased. For the period before 1941, however, 150-denier yarn possesses the usual qualifications of representativeness: It is the modal denier class, accounting for from 53 to 75 per cent of all viscose yarn produced; the average denier spun, except for three years, falls within the range included under 150-denier yarn (138-denier to 162-denier); it is also the approximate median denier spun; and the distribution about the 150-denier class is moderately symmetrical.[6]

The selection of a representative acetate yarn for purposes of price analysis is more difficult. Rayon producers state that they use 150-denier acetate yarn as a basis for pricing other deniers but the average denier spun has been closer to 100. Since it is desirable for price comparison purposes, however, to select an acetate yarn comparable to the representative viscose yarn, and since the 150 class more nearly represents the typical pound of acetate yarn, 150-denier acetate yarn prices will be used in the chapters that follow.

The primary purpose behind the careful selection of a representative denier for the two yarn processes is to give the correct *level* to the price series. Actually, the price of almost any denier class would adequately reflect the price *movement*. The fairly constant relationship maintained among the prices of all denier classes in both yarn processes can be demonstrated by comparing price series based upon the representative prices selected above with an average price series based upon all deniers. In a recent study,[7] Professor Daniel Vandermuelen employed the weighted aggregative method with fixed (1928) quantity weights for computing an average yearly price series for rayon yarn. This price series (Chart 2) and one based upon the prices of only 150-denier viscose yarn and 100-denier acetate yarn, the average deniers spun for each process over this time interval, weighted by total viscose and total acetate production respectively (weighted Average A in Chart 2), are almost identical from 1931 to 1939, the terminal year of Professor Vandermuelen's price series. A weighted average using 150-denier acetate yarn prices and quantities (weighted Average B) instead of those for 100-denier

[6] The degree of "normality" of the frequency distribution depends somewhat upon the number of classes used. The classification used in Table 8 shows decided dips immediately adjacent to the modal class due to the small output of 125- and 200-denier yarns. These two deniers lie between fine and medium, and medium and coarse yarns respectively. They have never been used as extensively as the more popular fine, medium, and coarse denier yarns.

[7] Daniel Vandermuelen, "Intertextile Competition" (MS.), Claremont College, Claremont, California.

acetate yarn gives an average price approximately 5 per cent less than the other two series for all years. Presumably, therefore, the representative denier prices should satisfactorily reflect the price behavior of rayon produced under the two major processes — a fortunate condition since a study based upon the precise timing of price changes necessitates their use.

Chart 2

Comparison of Three Rayon Annual Price Series, 1930–1939

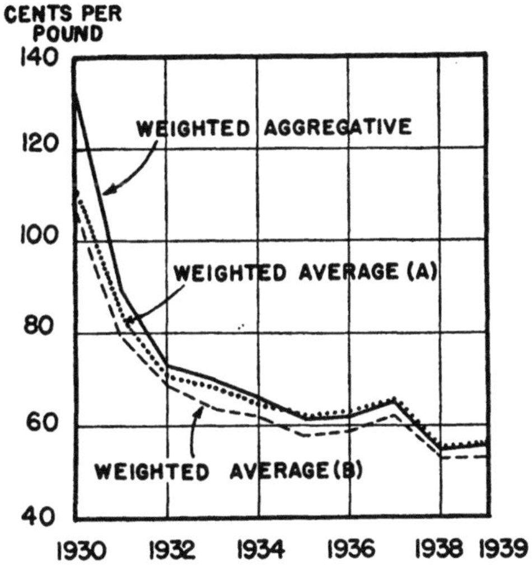

Source: See text.

Wherever data permit, acetate and viscose rayon yarn should probably be treated separately but as quite similar commodities. The price differential between the two types of yarn, however, has gradually decreased since 1925.[8] Since the middle thirties, the average annual price differential between the two types of yarn has been only a few cents per pound on all but heavy deniers, most of which is accounted for by slight differences in timing of price changes. For certain purposes of analysis, it is necessary to treat acetate and viscose rayon yarn as the output of a single industry. The high degree of substitutability between the two types of yarn in

[8] See Chap. 5 and Chart 8. In a number of market areas, acetate and viscose yarns are almost perfectly substitutable, but acetate yarn cannot be used in tire fabric construction because it breaks down when subjected to heat. Hence, since the tire fabric industry has become the most important single market outlet for viscose yarn, the two types of yarn have recently become less substitutable for each other.

many market areas and the virtual identity of their representative prices since 1935 indicate that such a treatment, within limits, is justified.

B. Terms of Trade in the Rayon Industry

Unlike natural fibers, the prices of which are determined on the open commodity exchange market, rayon has no organized market. Sales are made direct from producers through their sales offices to consuming mills.[9] Sellers periodically publish price lists setting forth the terms of sale. Generally, the published price lists hold over fairly long periods of time. The quoted price is for point of shipment with minimum freight paid by the producer to the railroad siding nearest the mill on shipments east of the Mississippi River. Yarn-consuming mills in the West are allowed minimum freight to the Mississippi but bear the remainder of the total freight charge.[10] Until June 16, 1941, a term discount of 2 per cent was allowed on all shipments paid for in 30 days. On that date all producers changed their terms from 2 per cent 30 days, net 31, to net 30 days.

Until the passage of the Robinson-Patman Act, the price of rayon was subject to a fairly complicated system of quantity discounts. Since individual producers have from time to time revised their quantity rebate schedules in order to circumvent the price rigidity imposed by price lists, discounts have not been consistently uniform among sellers. When first employed, quantity rebates were on a sliding scale, increasing 0.5 per cent for each 100 thousand dollars of purchases made by a single firm during a calendar year up to a maximum of 5.0 per cent on purchases of 1 million dollars or more.

The decline in consumption during the depression, following on the heels of the rapid expansion in productive capacity which took place during the twenties, led to frequent rebate revisions in 1930.[11] Early in 1930, several producers revised their schedules so that a 5 per cent discount was allowed after a firm's purchases had reached 500 thousand dollars and commenced carrying accounts for rebate purposes on a yearly basis commencing with the day the account was opened. These two changes increased the total rebate and permitted

[9] An insignificant percentage of rayon sales is handled through yarn brokers.

[10] Because of the recent basing-point decisions, a few rayon companies have discontinued the practice of granting freight allowances altogether but, at the time of this writing, most prodûcers still bear the freight to all destinations in the United States east of the Mississippi River.

[11] See *Rayon Organon,* November 1930, pp. 11–15, for a full discussion of the competitive aspects of the rebate system and some suggested remedies.

new customers to enjoy rebate privileges earlier. Some producers also permitted the grouping together of accounts of companies having financial connections. As the depression deepened, this requirement was dropped in favor of simple group purchasing. By the end of the year most sellers were allowing a straight 5 per cent discount on all rayon purchased regardless of quantity.

Constant pressure for reform through trade publications (presumably exerted by the producers) brought a fairly uniform quantity rebate system into effect in 1931.[12] Under the new schedules quantity discounts increased at a rate of 0.5 per cent for each 100 thousand dollars' worth of rayon purchased per customer up to a maximum of 3.0 per cent on purchases of 600 thousand dollars.[13] In May 1932, the scale was changed to allow 0.5 per cent on the first 50 thousand dollars of annual rayon purchases and increased to 5.0 per cent on 500 thousand dollars. These terms were generally effective in the industry until July 1936. A few differences existed among producers with respect to quantity rebates throughout the latter half of 1936 because of the various interpretations of the meaning of the Robinson-Patman Act. Since January 1, 1937, no quantity rebates have been granted in the rayon industry.

Two other practices of the industry which bear upon price behavior are the booking period and the price guarantee. Rayon is sold on both a spot and booked order basis. Until September 1932, rayon producers booked business for indefinite forward periods. In late September, a generally adopted plan provided that spot business would be accepted at any time and that producers would open their books on the first of the month to take orders for a maximum of 90 days ahead. The booking period has alternated between 60 and 90 days since 1932, the current booking period being 60 days.

Advance bookings of orders are regarded as options rather than contracts but the booking period system introduces a signficant modification to list-price behavior. In a tight rayon market most producers are usually booked 60 to 90 days ahead to deliver yarn at the price effective when the orders were placed. Heavily booked production is usually a necessary prelude to a price increase; conversely, slim bookings usually precede a price decrease.[14] Hence, price increases probably do not become fully effective in the market

[12] United States Tariff Commission, *The Rayon Industry*, p. 256.
[13] United States Tariff Commission, *The Rayon Industry*, p. 256.
[14] See Chap. 5.

until about 60 to 90 days after the announced price increase, whereas price decreases become effective a few days after the announced price decrease.

Similarly, price guarantees alter the effective dates of announced list-price changes. Rayon producers introduced the price guarantee in order to give textile yarn purchasers some of the protection against price fluctuations made possible through hedging in the cotton and silk markets. Rayon consumers had often taken severe inventory losses during periods of falling rayon yarn prices. To prevent hand-to-mouth buying when a rayon price cut was rumored, producers offered protective guarantees against price fluctuations for a period of 90 days. If, while price guarantees were in effect, the price fell within 90 days after the date of invoice, the customer was credited with the difference between the amount of the actual invoice and the amount of the invoice computed on the new low price. If the price rose, the old price obtained.

Price guarantees were offered unofficially and selectively in mid-1930. In November 1930, guarantees against price change were uniformly offered by all producers for 60 days retroactive. The period was lengthened to 90 days on January 9, 1931.[15] On October 1, 1931, all guarantees except those on acetate and nitrocellulose yarn prices were withdrawn but were restored on April 7, 1932.[16] On June 20, 1932, all price guarantees were withdrawn.[17] They were restored on December 20, 1937, but were offered only against price declines. Price guarantees were withdrawn on viscose yarns on January 14, 1938, and on acetate yarns one week later; they have not been employed in the rayon industry since that date.

A significant feature of the price guarantee is that it makes a price decrease effective from 60 to 90 days before the price decrease is announced. Hence, it has been a strong deterrent against price reductions in a sluggish rayon market. Producers contemplating a price cut must consider not only additions to total revenue expected to result from the price cut and increased sales, but also the cost of the necessary refunds on all sales that have been made over the past 60 or 90 days.

Such terms of trade as those set forth above subject rayon prices to several significant conditioning factors not usually allowed for in

[15] United States Tariff Commission, *The Rayon Industry*, p. 255.
[16] United States Tariff Commission, *The Rayon Industry*, p. 255.
[17] See Chap. 5.

the simpler price models of economic theory. Price guarantees and booking period arrangements might quite possibly effect such discontinuities in a firm's marginal revenue curve that, purely upon theoretical grounds, we should not expect a shift in demand, *ceteris paribus,* to result in an instantaneous price change, irrespective of possible "administered price" phenomena. There must have been occasions, for example, where sellers have delayed an otherwise profitable price reduction only because the price guarantee in effect made such a reduction retroactive for 90 days. On the other hand, rayon producers have probably hastened to announce price increases since booking period arrangements delay the applicability of the price increase by the length of the booking period. Hence, conclusions reached through an analysis of published prices are at all times subject to the modifications introduced by the foregoing extraordinary terms of trade.

5

PRICE BEHAVIOR among Firms

Much of the analysis presented in this study is in terms of an industry price for rayon. Business barometers ordinarily employ the price of 150-denier viscose yarn, as quoted by the largest producer, to reflect the price prevailing in the rayon market at any given instant of time.[1] Implicit in the analysis presented in this study and in the price series published by various statistical agencies is the assumption that the price of the largest producer is also the price applicable to all other rayon producers. That is, the price quoted by the largest producer is the prevailing price for all rayon yarn. This chapter proposes to test the validity of such an assumption by examining the price relationship among producers.

The output of all rayon firms that employ the same process is fairly homogeneous. Practically all of the medium- and large-size firms have at all times produced yarns having identical denier and filament count designations over the range of 50- to 450-denier for viscose yarn and 45- to 300-denier for acetate yarn. The smaller firms do not produce such a wide range of deniers but those they produce are comparable to the similarly designated output of large producers.

Several factors make for a moderately high degree of homogeneity of output among rayon-producing firms. Rayon is knit or woven into fabric by standardized machinery. This places severe limits upon the denier and filament count variations that may be

[1] The Textile Economics Bureau, Inc. publishes the prevailing list price on all deniers of viscose rayon for the American Viscose Corporation. These are the prices used in price series published in such standard sources of statistics as the *Monthly Labor Review*, the *Survey of Current Business*, the *Federal Reserve Bulletin*, etc.

initiated by yarn producers without consulting fabricators. Also, rayon is a chemically controlled product. Laboratory analysis permits any producer to imitate a new denier that has met with success in the market.[2] Imitation is rapidly effected since denier change-over in production is accomplished by simply changing spinnerette nozzles on the spinning machines. Hence, there is not the degree of product differentiation that such highly advertised brand names as "Crown Yarns," "Du Pont Rayon," "Celanese," "Nardura," and so forth, would ostensibly indicate.[3] The rayon industry is, therefore, oligopolistic with a very small degree of product differentiation. This seems to be substantiated by the persistence of identical quoted prices by all producers on yarns having the same denier and filament count designation. However, since the largest three or four rayon producers have accounted for about 75 per cent of total production, the two largest producers for 50 per cent, and the largest producer for 33 per cent, one might reason a priori that the industry's price and output policy has been dominated by a few large firms.

It is generally conceded that individual firms in an industry clearly characterized as oligopolistic do not chase each other down the industry's demand schedule in a fit of ruinous price-cutting;[4] nor do they live in a haze of complete uncertainty as to what the reaction of the rest of the industry will be to an initiated line of action when mutual dependence is recognized. Both ruinous price-cutting and much uncertainty are often circumvented through the development of a code of behavior that falls under the broad classification of "business practices." Scattered references appearing in trade and government publications agree that the *modus operandi* in the rayon industry is one of price leadership.[5] That is, they all state,

[2] For example, in late 1937 Du Pont introduced a heavy denier viscose yarn to be used in the manufacture of tire fabric. Almost all of the large- and medium-size firms were producing yarn with the same denier designation several years before the war.

[3] The Rayon Institute was formed in 1929 for the purpose of conducting joint advertising by all producers. There is much evidence in the trade literature that most advertising has been designed to make consumers "rayon conscious"—to shift the industry's demand schedule to the right rather than a single producer's demand schedule at the expense of the rest of the industry.

[4] For a synthesis of the arguments raised by Bertrand, Marshall, Pareto, Cournot, Edgeworth, and others in connection with the duopoly solution, see Edward H. Chamberlin, *Monopolistic Competition* (5th ed.; Cambridge, Mass.: Harvard University Press, 1946), pp. 34 ff.

[5] "Price changes are usually announced by one of the larger producers; within a few days or weeks virtually all the other manufacturers bring their prices more or less in line with the newly named quotations of the initiating company, minor differences occurring, however, in some instances. Under the present procedure of

or at least infer, that list prices are generally static until a change is announced by one of the large producers. However, the pattern of price leadership in the industry has never, to the author's knowledge, been determined. The following pages will be devoted to an examination of the evidence that price leadership does in fact exist, and to the presentation of evidence that should indicate the particular pattern of price leadership which prevails in the industry.

With respect to inter-firm price behavior, the lines between overt price collusion, price leadership, and perfectly competitive pricing are often thinly drawn. In any case, prices quoted by all firms in the industry would move in consonance. Hence, it is necessary at the outset to decide upon some method of differentiating among the three types of pricing mechanisms.

Presumably, overt collusion would entail the simultaneous issuance of new price lists by all parties to the collusive agreement. It is true, of course, that producers might agree to change their prices upon a signal from any one of them, but it seems unlikely that they would concede to any single producer the privilege of always being the first to change price unless the designated price leader already possessed some of the attributes of either a "dominant" or a "barometric" firm.[6] Hence, it is highly probable that the more tacit form of price leadership would have prevailed had no collusive agreement been reached. Should such an agreement be reached, therefore, the industry would contain a price leader, but price leadership would be of a more stereotyped form than is usually conceived.[7]

---

pricing no advance notice is made by producers of anticipated action in price changing; the changes go into effect immediately upoon announcement." United States Tariff Commission, *The Rayon Industry* (Washington: April 1944), p. 252.

"Rayon prices are quoted by the producers on a list price basis. The larger producers ordinarily originate a new price list on any given date and these prices hold until the next list price change is announced. The smaller producers invariably revise their list prices to conform to those of the larger producers. *Rayon prices usually hold for relatively long periods of time.* In this sense the rayon pricing policy is similar to that used by steel companies in setting their price for rails, or by copper producers who collectively set an export price for copper." E. W. K. Schwarz and H. R. Mauersberger, *Rayon and Synthetic Yarn Handbook* (New York: 1934), pp. 71–72.

See also, E. W. K. Schwarz and H. R. Mauersberger, *Rayon and Staple Fiber Handbook* (New York: 1939), pp. 43–44; and Clair Wilcox, *Competition and Monopoly in American Industry,* p. 202. The latter identifies American Viscose and Du Pont as price leaders in seven of the eight price changes announced in the industry between 1930 and 1937.

[6] See Chap. 6 for a discussion of these two types of price leadership.

[7] As a practical matter of public policy, the two types might receive different interpretations in the courts. Overt agreements to follow a leader would probably be construed as "price fixing," whereas the more tacit form of price leadership would not.

On the other hand, all producers would be expected to change prices simultaneously in a perfectly competitive market, but in response to a common market stimulus. Imperfections in the market might result in some producers' prices lagging behind others, but price leadership in this case should be random.[8] Hence, an industry possesses a price leader when one particular firm is usually the first to announce changes in price, and the announced prices are customarily followed by nearly all the producers comprising the industry.

Aside from any conclusions which may be drawn from the following statistical examination of company price lists, there is ample evidence presented in rayon and textile trade literature that price leadership is an important tenet of rayon price behavior. Editorial comment to the effect that a price change was led by one of the large producers and followed by others has been made after practically all important rayon price revisions. Typical examples are as follows: "A rayon yarn price cut was initiated by Viscose Corporation May 3 [1930] and followed by Du Pont and American Enka May 4, and Tubize May 5, . . . the rest of the industry is expected to follow."[9] Nor is price leadership confined simply to price quotations. In reporting one withdrawal of price guarantees, the *Organon* stated, "On October 1, 1931, all viscose price guarantees were withdrawn by one producer, all other viscose producers followed as usual."[10]

Moreover, comments made by spokesmen for individual firms strongly indicate that producers do not usually exercise independent control over their pricing policy but wait for the price pattern to be set by recognized leadership. On June 26, 1926, Samuel A. Salvage, President of American Viscose, announced to the industry that his firm had drastically cut viscose prices to meet foreign competition; the price reduction would be effective July 1.[11] Commenting upon the announced price cut, Bertrand Clark, President of Industrial Rayon Corporation, stated, "The move on the part of Viscose Corporation was a matter of gratification to everyone in the industry."[12] Industrial, Tubize, and Du Pont followed immediately

[8] Unless, of course, persistent price leading by one or several producers could be explained in terms of locational factors. When the market is distinctly national and not composed of several concentrated points around which producers are unevenly distributed geographically, no single producer should always be the first to feel the impact of changing market forces.

[9] *Textile World*, May 10, 1930, p. 109.

[10] *Rayon Organon*, November 1931, p. 12.

[11] *Rayon Journal*, June 30, 1926, p. 4.

[12] *Rayon Journal*, June 30, 1926, p. 4.

with revised price lists. Again, when American Viscose cut prices May 26, 1932, the rest of the industry leveled caustic criticism against the action taken by Viscose but, in spite of ostensible reluctance, they all followed within a few days.[13] When summoned before the Federal Trade Commission to testify on pricing practices in the viscose rayon industry, the spokesmen for all the small- and medium-size producers stated that they set their list prices to correspond with those of the larger producers, particularly the list prices of American Viscose.[14] The editor of *Textile World* indicated the traditionally passive role played by most rayon producers in determining the price of their commodity when he stated: "Tubize, forsaking its traditional role as a price follower, initiated its first price cut June 20 [1932]." [15] Viscose followed on June 21, but undercut Tubize by $0.05 on each denier. Viscose Corporation's new price schedule was in turn followed by Tubize as well as the rest of the industry a few days later.

The recurrence of statements similar to those above after nearly all important changes in rayon *quoted* prices is virtual proof of the presence of price leadership in the rayon industry. Moreover, the identity of the firms which usually initiate the list price changes is not difficult to establish. Editorial references can be found in the trade literature to the company[16] first to announce the new price in twenty-five of the forty-two major price changes which have occurred in the rayon industry since 1925.[17]

It is important, however, to draw a distinction between the behavior of *list* price and actual *net realized* price. These two prices are seldom identical in any industry because of freight allowances granted buyers by the sellers, term and quantity discounts allowed, and other terms of trade discussed in the preceding chapter.

With the exception of quantity discounts most of the usual terms of trade have been uniform among the domestic producers of rayon.

[13] *Textile World*, June 1932, p. 110.

[14] F. T. C., Docket No. 2161, *Record*, see especially the testimony of Mr. Fuller, pp. 746–750; Mr. Kerman, p. 848; Mr. Carr, p. 947; Mr. Ryan, p. 1213; and Mr. Bassill, p. 1476.

[15] *Textile World*, July 1932, p. 82.

[16] The *Rayon Organon* usually does not refer to the name of the company, but uses such descriptive terms as "the largest viscose producer," "the second largest producer," "the largest acetate producer," etc. These terms readily identify the company. The *Rayon Journal*, *Textile World*, and *Silk and Rayon Journal* often mention company names.

[17] See Appendix C for an explanation of how price change dates for individual companies are determined.

Until the recent basing-point decisions were handed down, all producers paid the freight on all shipments east of the Mississippi River; and until 1941, all producers allowed a 2 per cent discount on bills paid within 30 days of the date of invoice. A more important point of inquiry, however, is the extent to which producers sell rayon at prices other than those which appear on their published price lists. Off-list selling not only widens the gap between published and net realized prices, but also results in price differentials among sellers — differentials that would remain undiscovered in an analysis confined only to published price lists.

Generally, list price less the usual freight and discount allowances fairly accurately reflects the net realized price on rayon yarn except for periods characterized by a severe and protracted slump in rayon sales. The rayon yarn industry has been a rapidly expanding one (from 0.4 million pounds in 1911 to 1.3 billion pounds in 1950). Throughout most of its forty-year history, demand at published list prices has either equaled the industry's installed capacity or, at worst, fallen little short of it. When either one of these conditions has prevailed in the industry, all producers adhere rather closely to list prices published by the larger firms.

During acute business recessions such as the 1930–1932 recession, however, abnormally high inventory accumulations produce what the trade terms "a highly competitive situation." In a period of high inventory accumulation most producers frankly admit that there is no meaningful price. Mr. Scott, President of the Tubize Company, testified before the Federal Trade Commission that, "customers always took advantage of surplus inventory conditions by spreading rumors that other companies were undercutting and misbranding." [18] He stated that his company sold under list price during 1931 and 1932 and that, in spite of his admiration and affection for his competitors, he believed that they did also; it was an accepted industry practice. Purchasers of rayon testified before the Commission that smaller producers usually offered them yarn at lower prices than larger producers when yarn inventories were high.[19]

Some indication of the extent to which even the larger rayon producers ignored their published price lists during the depression may be obtained from the data presented in Table 9, where

[18] F. T. C., Docket No. 2161, *Record*, pp. 441–442.

[19] Cf. F. T. C., Docket No. 2161, *Record*, p. 5315 ff. Buyers and sellers of rayon frequently refer to all the producers except Du Pont and American Viscose collectively as "small" producers.

TABLE 9

Monthly Summaries of Yarn Sales of Rayon Yarn Producers, Showing Ultimate Net per Pound Prices for 150-Denier 1st Quality Cones for the Period from November 1, 1931 to December 31, 1933

(CENTS PER POUND)

	American Viscose		Du Pont Company		Industrial Rayon		North American		American Enka		Tubize Chatillon		List	All Companies	
	High	Low	High	Low	High	Low	High	Low	High	Low	High	Low		High	Low
1931															
Nov.	74.7(½)	71.3(3)	72.9	72.8	73.9	61.9	71.4	61.4	—	—	—	—	75	74.7 V	61.4 NA
Dec.	74.6(½)	71.3(3)	72.9	72.5	71.4	61.9	75.0	66.6	—	—	—	—	75	75.0 NA	61.9 I
1932															
Jan.	73.9(1½)	69.9(5)	71.4	71.4	75.0	65.0	73.5	63.7	—	—	68.0(3)	68.0(3)	75	75.0 I	63.7 NA
Feb.	73.9(1½)	69.9(5)	71.8	71.4	73.7	65.0	73.5	73.5	—	—	68.0(3)	68.0(3)	75	73.9 V	65.0 I
Mar.	73.9(1½)	69.9(5)	71.5	71.4	75.0	61.6	73.5	71.3	75.0(0)	75.0(0)	75.0(0)	63.2(3)	75	75.0 I, E	61.6 I
Apr.	69.9(5)	51.2(5)	61.9	52.3	75.0	53.4	73.6	63.5	73.5(0)	73.5(0)	65.0(0)	64.6(3)	75	75.0 I	51.2 V
May	54.2(1½)	51.2(5)	52.3	52.3	57.1	52.4	47.8	47.8	—	—	48.6(3)	48.6(3)	65–75	57.1 I	47.8 NA
June	54.2(1½)	53.2(1½)	61.9	52.3	61.9	45.2	49.0	49.0	45.5(5)	45.2(5)	48.6(3)	48.6(3)	50–68	61.9 I, D	45.2 I, E
July	51.2(5)	51.2(5)	52.3	52.3	47.6	42.8	45.0	44.1	50.0(0)	45.5(5)	50.0(0)	50.0(0)	50–55	52.3 D	42.8 I
Aug.	54.2(1½)	53.2(1½)	52.4	52.3	47.6	47.6	50.0	44.1	50.0(0)	46.7(5)	50.0(0)	40.5(5)	50–60	54.2 V	40.5 I
Sept.	59.1(1½)	53.2(1½)	57.1	52.4	52.4	47.6	60.0	44.1	50.0(0)	46.7(5)	—	—	60	60.0 NA	44.1 NA
Oct.	59.1(1½)	54.2(1½)	57.1	52.4	59.4	44.4	60.0	44.1	51.3(5)	46.7(5)	—	—	60	60.0 NA	44.1 NA
Nov.	58.0(1½)	51.3(5)	57.1	52.4	57.1	44.4	60.0	52.5	52.5(5)	52.5(5)	52.4(5)	52.4(5)	60	60.0 NA	44.4 I
Dec.	59.1(1½)	51.3(5)	57.1	57.1	57.1	57.1	60.0	52.5	52.5(5)	51.5(0)	52.4(5)	52.4(5)	60	60.0 NA	51.3 V
1933															
Jan.	59.1(2½)	58.0(2½)	57.1	57.1	57.1	57.1	56.0	53.9	60.0(0)	47.6(5)	52.4(5)	52.4(5)	60	60.0 E	47.6 E
Feb.	60.0(5)	57.4(2½)	—	—	57.1	57.1	58.9	45.0	56.0(5)	46.7(5)	52.4(5)	52.4(5)	60	60.0 V	45.0 NA
Mar.	60.0(5)	56.0(5)	57.1	57.1	47.6	47.6	58.8	42.0	56.0(5)	46.7(5)	52.4(5)	52.4(5)	60	60.0 V	42.0 NA
Apr.	48.8(2½)	47.6(5)	47.6	47.6	47.6	45.7	47.8	42.0	46.7(5)	46.7(5)	42.9(5)	42.9(5)	50–55	48.8 V	42.0 NA
May	52.4(5)	47.6(5)	47.6	47.6	50.5	45.7	52.4	45.8	46.7(5)	46.7(5)	47.6(5)	47.6(5)	50–55	52.4 V, NA	45.7 I
June	52.4(5)	46.6(5)	52.3	47.6	61.9	45.7	52.4	52.3	51.3(5)	46.7(5)	—	—	55–60	61.9 I	45.7 I
July	53.7(2½)	51.3(5)	52.3	52.3	52.4	47.6	65.0	52.4	51.3(5)	46.7(5)	—	—	60–65	65.0 NA	46.7 E
Aug.	57.1(5)	51.3(5)	57.2	52.3	52.4	47.6	65.0	52.4	51.3(5)	51.3(5)	—	—	65	65.0 NA	47.6 I
Sept.	58.6(2½)	55.9(5)	61.9	57.1	57.1	52.4	61.9	52.4	60.6(5)	56.1(5)	—	—	65	61.9 NA, D	52.4 I, NA
Oct.	63.4(2½)	58.6(2½)	61.9	61.8	61.9	57.1	65.0	61.9	60.6(5)	60.6(5)	—	—	65	65.0 NA	57.1 I
Nov.	63.4(2½)	60.6(5)	61.9	61.8	61.9	61.9	65.0	61.9	60.6(5)	60.6(5)	—	—	65	65.0 NA	60.6 V, E
Dec.	63.4(2½)	60.6(5)	61.9	61.8	61.9	61.9	65.0	65.0	60.6(5)	60.6(5)	—	—	65	65.0 NA	60.6 V, E

Source: *Hearings*, F. T. C., Docket 2161, Exhibits No. 925 ff. Prices were compiled from the following invoices: American Viscose to Beaunit and Globe; Du Pont to Algro; Tubize to Argus Knitting Mills, Elkind Knitting Mills, Koenegsberg Bros., and Raynit Mills; Industrial to 11 commercial mills, Enka to 9 commercial mills, and North American to approximately 24 commercial mills. The customer lists of the last three companies overlapped each other and those of American Viscose, Du Pont, and Tubize. When given on the invoices, quantity discounts in effect are shown in parentheses. In some instances the lowest price shown is not the lowest offer price because in some months large buyers entitled to larger quantity discounts than those shown made no purchases. Where no prices are shown, no sales were made to the above mills during that month. For a similar comparison of list and net realized prices (1937–1940) for the American Viscose Company only, see note 12, Chap. 9

published list prices are compared with the high and low ultimate net per pound prices charged selected customers by six[20] leading rayon producers for 150-denier viscose knitting yarn from November 1931 to December 1933. By and large, the differences between list prices and the highest net realized prices received by each producer are negligible; that is to say, most producers sold at least a part of their output at list price even during the 1930–1932 depression. Nearly all rayon producers, however, lowered their actual prices during the depression a few weeks before they revised their published price lists and sold some yarn at less than list price. For example, the list price of 150-denier viscose rayon was not lowered from $0.75 per pound to $0.65 until May 26, 1932; but all producers for whom actual prices are available, except one, had commenced selling some 150-denier yarn for from $0.65 to $0.52 per pound as early as April. Similarly, the medium-size producers, Enka, North American, and Industrial, lowered their actual prices from one to two months before list prices were revised downward in April 1933.

It is almost certain that the small rayon producers, several of whom have seldom published price lists, adhere even less rigidly to list prices when market slumps occur than the larger producers who usually issue them. President Bassill of Tubize testified before the Federal Trade Commission that

> it generally happens in this business that there are certain times . . . when the demand is greatly in excess of current supply. On those occasions most of the producers can get the full [list] price for yarn; at other times, when the demand is not so great and there are large stocks on hand, some of the smaller producers, ourselves included, must of necessity be a little under the price of Viscose and Du Pont in order to move our product in certain fields.[21]

Moreover, virtually all rayon producers sold fairly large quantities of "obsolete" yarn during the depression and most small producers further reduced actual prices below list prices by offering larger quantity discounts than were customarily offered in the trade. The introduction of new types of yarn, particularly dull and semi-dull yarns, during 1929 and 1930 had in fact rendered obsolete some

[20] Ultimate net per pound prices are also available for the Delaware Rayon Corporation for the months of April and September 1932, and February and April 1933. In each month they fell between the high and low prices shown in the right-hand column of Table 9.

[21] F. T. C., Docket No. 2161, *Record,* p. 1476. See also pp. 750–752, 848, 947, 1206, 1337, and 5315 for similar testimony by other rayon producers.

yarns held by producers in their inventories throughout the early thirties. In order to move these yarns, the value of which was rapidly declining, producers offered them for sale at prices from 10 per cent to 20 per cent below published prices on active yarns with similar denier and filament counts.

The obsolete yarn price, however, also served as a convenient and more subtle means of cutting prices on active yarns without departing from published prices or issuing new price lists. Most producers, particularly the small- and medium-size producers, admitted before the Commission that they sold considerable quantities of their active yarns at "obsolete" prices between October 1931 and May 1932. Mr. Yerkes, President of the Du Pont Rayon Company, testified before the Federal Trade Commission that much yarn "was sold as 'obsolete' long after the supply had been exhausted . . . [a practice which] ruined the name of rayon and the market for high quality yarn." [22] Some indication of the extent to which major rayon producers engaged in the practice of "misbranding" may be obtained from the following data: During the first quarter of 1932, during which time the Federal Trade Commission subsequently found the ten principal producers of viscose yarn to have been in collusion on price and production policy, North American sold 152.4 thousand pounds of viscose yarn at "obsolete" yarn prices; Industrial sold 216.4 thousand pounds, and American Enka sold 11.9 thousand.[23]

It is not likely that off-list selling, "misbranding," and abnormally high quantity discount allowances have ever been resorted to on such a wholesale scale in the history of the rayon industry as in the 1930–1932 depression. Rayon company officials characterize the two years between June 1930 and June 1932 as a period of distress selling, chiseling, off-list selling, and large-scale indulgence in the "inferior and obsolete racket." [24] The list price reductions initiated by large rayon producers on January 9, 1931, and May 26 and June 21, 1932, were admittedly only clarifications of the price situation since they simply took public cognizance of prices which already existed.[25]

The rayon yarn market had reached such a state of disorder by

[22] F. T. C., Docket No. 2161, *Record*, p. 599.

[23] *Hearings*, F. T. C., Docket No. 2161, company exhibits.

[24] In appraising the previous month's activities in the rayon industry, the June 1931 *Organon* quipped: "and the chisellers chiselled and business fizzled in the merry month of May!"

[25] *Rayon Organon*, February 1931, pp. 13–14; June 1932, p. 12; July 1932, p. 12.

1931 that even a collusive agreement among viscose yarn producers was not a sufficiently strong weapon alone to overcome the above trade practices. Greatly concerned over the lack of price discipline during the early stages of the depression, the large rayon producers tried to obtain the coöperation of the rest of the industry on a price and production policy.[26] Although ten viscose rayon firms consented to have the firm of Price, Waterhouse and Company make a survey of their capacities and to make a monthly audit of their stocks, sales, and prices charged, below list selling and "misbranding" continued over the period from October 21, 1931 to May 23, 1932, while the agreement was in effect.

Whatever the long-run effects of the agreement may have been, the immediate aim to stabilize prices seems to have met with little success. Although no changes were made in the list price of rayon between October 21, 1931 and May 23, 1932, "misbranding" and off-list selling continued and by April, one month before the association was dissolved, even such large producers as Viscose, Du Pont, and Industrial were selling rayon at 30 per cent below list price (see Table 9). Vice-President Scott of the Tubize Corporation, when he testified before the Federal Trade Commission, stated that one of the probable reasons why the agreement was ineffective was that

> no rayon association could ever survive a protracted period of slack demand. It is almost impossible to get together men to consider seriously the statistics of our industry without injecting into the discussions transactions by one and the other which bring on accusations of unfair business dealings. A man always thinks it is unfair for his competitor to sell goods below him. And the time of these meetings is usually taken up by that sort of thing. Nothing constructive ever came out of any of them, and I think I know as much about them as anyone.[27]

[26] Cf. Viscose Company *et al.*, Docket No. 2161, *Federal Trade Commission Decisions, Findings, Orders, and Stipulations*, XXV, 421–433. The ten viscose yarn producers were heard before the Federal Trade Commission from 1934 to 1937 on charges of entering into and carrying out "an agreement, combination, understanding and conspiracy among themselves to fix and maintain, and by which during said period [October 21, 1931 to May 23, 1932], they fixed and maintained uniform prices to be exacted by them from their purchasers of viscose rayon yarn, and thus to fix the price of viscose rayon yarn entering into interstate commerce." *Ibid.* at p. 431. The Commission found the rayon producers guilty of the practices and ordered them to cease and desist on July 3, 1937. Because no specific practices of which rayon producers had been guilty were mentioned in the cease and desist order, and because it was stated in the complaint that the conspiracy had been terminated voluntarily by May 23, 1932, the cease and desist order was presumably a mere formality.

[27] F. T. C., Docket No. 2161, *Record*, p. 473.

A more significant and perhaps a more certain cause of the association's failure, however, can probably be found in the behavior of prices of closely competing products. Even if the rayon association could have resolved all internal conflicts, it would have had no control over the highly competitive prices of cotton, silk, and wool, upon which the price of rayon is largely dependent.

The revival of the rayon market in August 1932 and the subsequent more complete acceptance of the leadership of large producers by the rest of the industry were important factors in restoring price discipline soon after the trough of the 1930–1932 depression had passed.[28] Although there is some evidence that producers resorted to the "insidious" pricing practices of the early thirties in subsequent market slumps, since 1932 they seem to have been both sporadic and short-lived.[29] There are several possible explanations as to why deviations from list prices were much less noticeable after 1932: (1) Except for the 1937–38 recession, the industry has been able to sell near-capacity output at prevailing list prices. (2) Many small rayon producers failed between 1929 and 1933; it was this sector of the industry that initiated much of the price-shading in the depression. (3) Nearly all of the viscose yarn producers who survived the depression were parties to the collusive agreement; although the agreement formally lasted only seven months, it is highly probable that the objectives of the association, once they had been fully and freely discussed, were borne in mind by most rayon producers after the association was dissolved. (4) The industry's interpretation of the application of the Robinson-Patman Act effectively eliminated the employment of various scales of quantity discounts as a means of price competition. And (5) natural fiber prices since 1932, due in part to price supports, have remained at a much higher level relative to rayon prices.

With but few highly publicized exceptions, all producers appear to have followed a uniform policy on term discounts, shipping terms, booking periods, and price guarantees.[30] Term discounts and shipping terms are usually given on the published price lists and, less often, quantity discount provisions and the length of booking period

[28] *Rayon Organon*, March 1933, p. 9. See editorial entitled "Production Control in Rayon Industry Proves Price Safe-Guard" — "the rayon industry showed benefits of good leadership, large producers shut down plants entirely to prevent overproduction. Shows that leadership in any industry is an asset."

[29] *Infra.*

[30] See *Rayon Organon*, special annual supplement, February 1944, pp. 34–36, for a brief history of prices and terms of trade from 1925 to February 4, 1944.

and price guarantee are included. No differences among producers are discernible on term discounts, shipping terms, or booking periods, but in several instances producers have had different policies toward price guarantees. Prior to 1930, various guarantees were offered unofficially and selectively. From November 1930 to October 1, 1931, price guarantees were uniformly offered by all producers. They were removed from viscose yarns on October 1, but remained on acetate and nitrocellulose yarns. When price guarantees were restored on viscose yarn on April 7, 1932 by the Tubize Chatillon Corporation, American Viscose Corporation alone did not follow.[31] The price guarantee was short-lived. All producers removed it from knitting yarns by June 1 and from weaving yarns by June 20.[32]

For a period of several years during the depression some differences existed among rayon producers on published quantity discount schedules (see Table 10). Published discount schedules, however, were applied rather loosely during the depression. Also, as a result of the enactment of the Robinson-Patman Act on June 19, 1936, one large producer of viscose and acetate yarns announced on July 31 that "all quantity discount schedules in effect as of June 19 are to be discontinued. From June 19 to September 30, 1936, a flat five per cent rebate is allowed to all customers on yarn actually shipped. No discount after September 30 is to be allowed, except the usual cash discount." [33] All except one producer had followed by September 8, but had substituted "until further notice" for "September 30." One large company still used a sliding scale, waiting further clarification of the Act. This difference disappeared when all producers in the industry simultaneously discontinued giving quantity discounts on December 31, 1936.

Extremely tight yarn markets occasionally have given rise to the practice of charging small price premiums. Generally, this practice seems to have been limited to a few producers and to very short

[31] American Viscose traditionally has been against the price guarantee. On this occasion President Salvage of American Viscose stated, "customers can rely on our twenty-year record instead of a price guarantee . . . ," *Rayon Journal,* April 1932, pp. 9–10.

[32] The price guarantee was costly to all who followed Tubize in adopting it. The following month, on May 26, American Viscose announced one of the largest price cuts in the history of the rayon industry. All producers reluctantly followed. As a consequence, all producers except American Viscose had to make refunds to customers on all sales between April 7 and May 26. Advance rumors concerning the price cut by American Viscose on June 21 led to complete abandonment of the price guarantee by all producers by June 20.

[33] *Rayon Organon,* July 1936.

TABLE 10

Progressive Range of Quantity Discounts in Effect for Six Leading Rayon Producers, 1931 and 1932

Volume in Excess of:	1931 Du Pont %	1931 American Glanzstoff %	1931 Tubize %	1931 American Enka %	1931 American Viscose %	1931 Industrial %	1932 Du Pont %	1932 American Glanzstoff %	1932 Tubize %	1932 American Enka %	1932 American Viscose %	1932 Industrial %
50,000					.25		.5				.25	
75,000												
100,000	.5	.5	.5	.5	.5	1	1	1	1	1	.5	1
125,000										1.25		
150,000				.75	.75	1.5	1.5	1.5	1.5	1.5	.75	1.5
175,000										1.75		
200,000	1	1	1	1	1	2	2	2	2	2	1	2.0
225,000										2.25		
250,000				1.25	1.25	2.5	2.5	2.5	2.5	2.5	1.25	2.5
275,000										2.75		
300,000	1.5	1.5	1.5	1.5	1.5	3	3	3	3	3	1.5	3
325,000										3.25		
350,000				1.75	1.75	3.5	3.5	3.5	3.5	3.5	1.75	3.5
375,000										3.75		
400,000	2	2	2	2	2	4	4	4	4	4	2.0	4
425,000										4.25		
450,000				2.25	2.25	4.5	4.5	4.5	4.5	4.5	2.25	4.5
475,000										4.75		
500,000	2.5	2.5	2.5	2.5	2.5	5	5	5	5	5	2.5	5
525,000												
550,000				2.75	2.75						2.75	
575,000												
600,000	3	3		3	3						3	
650,000											3.25	
700,000											3.5	
750,000											3.75	
800,000											4	
850,000											4.25	
900,000											4.5	
950,000											4.75	
1,000,000											5	

Source: *Hearings*, F. T. C., Docket No. 2161, Exhibit No. 921.

intervals. Also, postwar demands upon the yarn industry led to small published price differentials on identical deniers among producers.[34] Although these differentials did not exceed $0.02 per pound, they were the first to appear on 150-denier yarns in the history of the industry. Demand for rayon at list price immediately after the war considerably exceeded supply and the supply curve of rayon in the short-run is, for all practical purposes, perfectly inelastic. While such conditions prevailed, it was possible for published price differentials to exist.

Hence, acute yarn shortages or severely depressed yarn markets introduce imperfections into any analysis based upon list prices, but the only wholesale abandonment of the customarily accepted price leadership of the largest (and second largest) producer occurred in the depression of the early thirties. In 1931, price shading by small- and medium-size producers threw the rayon market into such disorder that large producers attempted to stabilize the industry through a collective agreement reinforced by accounting check-ups. For the most part, however, the evidence indicates that the rayon industry has generally accepted the price policy of the largest and oldest producers and, under fairly normal market conditions, has transacted most sales at the price leader's price.

A. Price Leadership among Viscose Yarn Producers

From 1926 to 1949, about 85 per cent of the total domestic rayon yarn output was produced under the viscose process. Until 1928, nearly all domestic rayon output was viscose yarn. Steady increases in acetate capacity after 1925 had reduced the viscose producers' share of the market to about 70 per cent by January 1940 and, in spite of wartime and postwar demand for heavy denier viscose tire yarn, to 64 per cent by the last quarter of 1948.

Except for the three or four small companies that produce chiefly for a parent knitting or weaving company, sporadic price quotations can be found for all viscose yarn producers. With occasional gaps, continuous price quotations are available for all the large- and medium-size producers, and a complete price history is available for American Viscose, the largest and oldest viscose producer. Therefore, price change dates for American Viscose can be conveniently used as reference points for measuring price lags and leads for other

[34] *Rayon Organon,* March 1947, p. 42, and January 1948, p. 7.

TABLE 11

United States Viscose Rayon Yarn Producers' Price Changes, 1926–1949
(Lags and Leads Expressed Relative to Price Changes of the American Viscose Corporation)

American Viscose	Du Pont	Tubize	Industrial	North American	American Enka	Delaware	Commercial Fiber	Belamose	Acme	Skenandoa	Celanese
1926: July 1	lagged	lagged	lagged					lagged			
Sept. 1	(a)	(a)	(a)					(a)			
Nov. 1	same	lagged	lagged					lagged	lagged		
1927: Mar. 16[b]	lagged	lagged	lagged				lagged	lagged	lagged		
April 1	lagged	lagged[c]	lagged				lagged	lagged			
1928: No price changes											
1929: Feb. 25	*led*	lagged	lagged	—			—	lagged			
June 18	*led*	lagged	lagged	lagged			lagged[d]	lagged		lagged	
1930: May 1	lagged	lagged	lagged	lagged	lagged	lagged		lagged[e]		lagged	
July 22	lagged	lagged	lagged	lagged	lagged	lagged				lagged	
1931: Jan. 9	lagged	lagged	lagged	lagged	lagged	(f)				lagged	
Oct. 23	lagged	lagged	lagged	lagged	lagged	lagged				(f)	
1932: May 26	lagged	lagged	lagged	lagged	lagged	lagged					
June 21	lagged	*led*	lagged	lagged	lagged	lagged					
Aug. 22	lagged	lagged	lagged	lagged	lagged	lagged					
Aug. 29[g]						(f)					
1933: April 3	lagged	lagged	lagged	lagged	lagged						
April 26	lagged	lagged	lagged	lagged	lagged						
June 20	lagged	*led*	lagged	*led*	lagged						
July 27	*led*[h]	lagged	lagged	lagged[h]	lagged						
1934: May 24	lagged	lagged	*led*	lagged	lagged						
Dec. 13	lagged	lagged	lagged	lagged	lagged						
Dec. 31	lagged	lagged	lagged	lagged	lagged						
1935: April 17	*led*	lagged	lagged	lagged	lagged						
Aug. 8	lagged	lagged	lagged	lagged	lagged						
Dec. 30[i]	*led*	lagged	lagged	*led*	led						
1936: June 15	lagged	lagged	lagged	lagged	lagged						
1937: April 12	*led*	lagged	lagged	led	*led*						
Dec. 20	lagged	lagged	lagged	lagged	lagged						
1938: Jan. 14	same[j]	lagged	lagged	lagged	lagged						

TABLE 11 (Continued)

American Viscose	Du Pont	Tubize	Industrial	North American	American Enka	Delaware	Commercial Fiber	Belamose	Acme	Skenandoa	Celanese
Jan. 21	same	lagged	lagged[k]	lagged	lagged						
May 20[g]	0	0	—	0	—						
July 29	lagged	lagged	lagged	lagged	lagged						
1939: Sept. 20	lagged	lagged[l]	lagged	lagged	lagged						
Dec. 4[g]	—	—	—	—	lagged						
1940: Jan. 2[g]	lagged		lagged	lagged	(m)						
1941: July 1	lagged		lagged	lagged	lagged						
Sept. 15	lagged		lagged	lagged	lagged						
1946: Nov. 19	*led*		lagged	led	lagged						led
1947: Jan. 28	lagged		lagged	lagged	lagged						same
Dec. 15	*led*		lagged	lagged	lagged						lagged
1948: Aug. 9	lagged		lagged	(n)	lagged						—
1949: May 19	lagged		lagged	lagged	lagged						lagged

Source: *Rayon Organon*, *Rayon Journal*, and *Textile World*.

[a] Price change affected only 75- and 100-denier yarn. Du Pont and Tubize, the only competitors quoting prices on these two deniers, did not follow this list price change but made adjustments on these deniers with the November 1 price change.

[b] The *Rayon Organon* lists March 16 as the official date of price change. Price changes on some deniers, however, had been announced by American Viscose in time to be included in the March 15 issue of the *Rayon Journal*. Hence, it was assumed that American Viscose led the price change.

[c] The April 1 price change affected only one denier having a filament count comparable to yarn produced by American Viscose. Tubize did not publish a new price list until November 15.

[d] Commercial Fiber Company did not publish a revised price list to reflect this price change until October 15; at that time it undercut the rest of the industry on all deniers except 150-denier. The October 15 price list remained in effect until March 5, 1930, at which time the company ceased publishing price lists. Commercial Fiber, an agency of Snia Viscosa in the United States, sold but did not produce rayon yarn.

[e] Belamose Rayon Corp. followed the price change June 1, but undercut the rest of the industry on 150- and 300-denier yarn, the only two deniers the company was then producing. Belamose published no price list after 1930.

[f] Companies advertised "Prices on Application Only" instead of their usual price lists.

[g] Price leader cannot be determined.

[h] Both Du Pont and North American issued new price lists in July before American Viscose announced its price change on July 27; however, both companies brought their lists into full agreement with American Viscose prices on July 27 by introducing a few minor changes.

[i] Price change announced to the industry simultaneously by North American and Du Pont. American Enka followed the next day, American Viscose eleven days later.

[j] Du Pont did not publish the effective date of its first January price change; however, the *Rayon Organon* stated that the two January price changes were led by the two largest producers, i.e., American Viscose and Du Pont. *Textile World* credited American Viscose with initiating both price changes; *Textile World*, February 14, 1938, p. 82.

[k] Industrial Rayon Corporation issued only one price revision in January; this was effective January 18.

[l] From September 20, 1939, until its merger with Celanese, Tubize published prices on only 75-denier rayon yarn.

[m] The January 2 price change affected only 75-denier yarn. American Enka had included this price adjustment in its December 30, 1939 price change when it revised prices to agree with those announced by American Viscose December 4, 1939. Industrial waited three months before formally making this slight adjustment in its price list.

[n] North American Rayon Corporation and American Bemberg Corporation were controlled by the War Assets Administration when O.P.A. price controls were removed. The War Assets Administration waited six months before following the December 15, 1947 price increase and did not follow the August 9, 1948 price increase.

producers.[35] Lags and leads by company for all major list price changes in the viscose rayon industry are shown in Table 11.[36]

A summary of price changes initiated by each company independently[37] and jointly with one other company is presented in Table 12. Since, for the most part, price lists are available for only seven producers and the highest number available at one time is ten,[38] price leadership shared by more than two producers is not shown. When three or more producers simultaneously announce price changes in an industry, the price leader is obscured. Hence, such cases are included under "no price leader identified." [39] For the purpose of further analysis, price changes have been broken down by company into increases and decreases.

Size and Price Leadership. The data presented in Table 12 indicate a close relationship between size and the willingness to announce new list prices. Of the 32 price changes announced in the industry by a single producer (see column 2, Table 12), American Viscose, the largest producer of viscose yarn, accounted for 23, or 72 per cent of them. Du Pont, the second largest producer, accounted for all except two of the remaining price changes led by a single producer, or 22 per cent of the total. The two remaining price changes were led by Industrial Rayon Corporation and Tubize, both moderately large viscose yarn producers. Of those price changes announced independently or jointly with one other producer, American Viscose led in 27 of the 38 major price changes for which price leaders can be designated. The Company announced 23 of these price revisions independently, three simultaneously with Du Pont, the second largest

[35] For price quotations on representative deniers, see Appendix C.

[36] The table begins with 1926 since the July 1, 1926 price change was the first to occur after the publication of individual company price lists in the *Rayon Journal.* Throughout 1925, the first year the *Journal* was published, rayon prices were quoted for the industry as a whole; a notation was made to the effect that such prices held for American Viscose Corporation, Tubize Artificial Silk Corporation, Industrial Rayon Corporation, and the Du Pont Corporation. See Appendix C for a more detailed explanation of how price-change dates for individual companies were determined.

[37] Independence in this context connotes absence of obvious collusion rather than independence in any real sense. A price leader may act on the historical evidence that all other producers will surely follow. This would not be absolute independence.

[38] See early 1930. New Bedford is not shown in the table since no price changes occurred while the company was publishing price lists.

[39] The three possible interpretations of this kind of price behavior have already been mentioned, namely, (1) price collusion; (2) all producers reacting independently to a common market stimulus; or (3) price leadership by a single producer with the rest of the industry following so quickly that no time lag appears on published price lists.

viscose yarn producer, and one with Celanese, the third largest producer.[40]

Hence, in the viscose sector of the domestic rayon industry, there is an unmistakably high degree of correlation between size and price

TABLE 12

Price Leadership among Viscose Rayon Yarn Producing Companies, 1926–1949

Producer	Price Changes Initiated Alone		Price Changes Initiated Simultaneously with One Other Producer		Total		Grand Total	No. Times[b] Followed
	Increase	Decrease	Increase	Decrease	Increase	Decrease		
Viscose	13	10	1	3	14	13	27	11
Du Pont	4	3	1	3	5	6	11	26
Tubize	0	1	1	0	1	1	2	29
North American	0	0	2	0	2	0	2	29
Industrial	0	1	0	0	0	1	1	38
Celanese[a]	0	0	1	0	1	0	1	3
No Leader Identified	—	—	—	—	3	1	4	—
American Enka	0	0	0	0	0	0	0	32
Delaware	0	0	0	0	0	0	0	5[c]
Commercial Fiber	0	0	0	0	0	0	0	3
Belamose	0	0	0	0	0	0	0	8[c]
Acme	0	0	0	0	0	0	0	2[c]
Skenandoa	0	0	0	0	0	0	0	4[c]
Total	17	15	6					

[a] Merged with Tubize Rayon Corporation February 6, 1946. Prior to merger, Celanese produced acetate yarn only.

[b] Includes only the number of times followed which can be documented by available published price lists or by a published statement in rayon trade journals.

[c] All of the smaller companies stated before the Federal Trade Commission that they usually followed the prices set by the larger producers; since they did not publish their prices it cannot be determined conclusively whether they followed a large number of price changes or not. Hence, the number of times each of the four small companies followed the price leader is probably greatly underestimated.

leadership with the largest company accounting for all except a few list-price changes.

No significant difference can be observed between upward and downward list-price movements. Of 32 list-price changes announced

[40] When price lists of two companies have the same effective date, there is no necessary implication that they jointly led the price change. One company may change price because it has anticipated the other company's price change; or, one of the price lists may be antedated. Moreover, rayon producers frequently make their new prices, particularly in the case of price decreases, effective on the date the price leader changed his price regardless of the published effective date. See testimony of L. A. Yerkes, President of Du Pont Rayon Company, F. T. C., Docket No. 2161, *Record*, p. 566.

independently, American Viscose accounted for 76 per cent of the increases and 64 per cent of the decreases. The difference, in and of itself, is probably not sufficiently large to lead to any significant conclusions. As previously mentioned, however, several of the downward list-price revisions initiated by American Viscose and Du Pont came after it was discovered that a substantial volume of rayon sales was being transacted at less than published list price. Hence there is some evidence that the industry relies more upon large producers to raise than to lower price.

Magnitude of Lag Behind Price Leader. Although price lists published before 1934, since few carried the date they became effective, cannot be used in computing an average time lag, they throw some light on the question of how quickly an announced price change pervades the market. Taking the issue of the *Rayon Journal* in which the price leader announced its new price as the point of reference, between 1925 and 1934 seventy-two individual company price lists were received in time to be published in the same issue; twenty-five were published in the following issue; five, two issues later; and four were published more than two issues later. Of the last four, three were only "technical" price changes.[41]

This information, while denying precise calculation, permits the determination of limits to price lags. Twenty-seven revised price lists must have lagged from zero to thirty days; three from sixteen to thirty days; twelve from one to fifteen days; thirteen from one to thirty days; two from thirty-one to sixty days; and one from ninety-one to one hundred and twenty days.[42] A weighted arithmetic average of the mid-points of the limits is 13.8 days. The computation assumes that the dates of price lists in each lag group were dispersed symmetrically about the mid-point of the limits — an assumption difficult to justify since the limits are completely determined by the date of publication of the *Journal.* Nevertheless, the fourteen-day average time lag gives some clue to the extent producers lagged in response to the price leader's revised price schedules over the time interval for which data for the small producers are available. The computations that follow, although more precise, are based principally upon the published price lists of the seven large producers. A

[41] Trade journals refer to minor adjustments of prices on specific deniers occurring after a list-price change as "technical" price changes.

[42] The three "technical" price changes are not included. See Appendix C for method used to determine the limits to price lags.

negligible few of the small companies advertised their price lists in the *Journal* after August 1932.[43]

Price lags in days by company, as computed from the effective dates of price lists published in the *Journal*, are shown in Table 13. The results are based on somewhat incomplete data since effective dates were occasionally omitted. Also, there are lengthy intervals

TABLE 13

Number of Days' Lag behind Price Leader, 1935–1949[a]

Date of Price Change	American Viscose	Du Pont	Tubize	Industrial	North American	American Enka	Celanese	Average
Apr. 12, 1935	5	led	—[b]	—[b]	—[b]	—[b]		5
Dec. 19, 1935	11	led	—[b]	—[b]	led	1		6
June 15, 1936	led	0	—[b]	—[b]	0	3		1
Mar. 31, 1937	12	led	—[b]	—[b]	1	5		6
Dec. 20, 1937	led	24[c]	—[b]	3	0	7		11
Jan. 14, 1938	led	led	—[b]	4	—[b]	—[b]		4
Jan. 21, 1938	led	led	—[b]	—[d]	10	10		10
July 29, 1938	led	0	3	—	3	—[b]		2
Sept. 20, 1939	led	33	—[b]	41	—	41		38
Sept. 15, 1941	led	16		0	1	1		4
Nov. 2, 1946	7	led		9	3	13	3	7
Jan. 28, 1947	led	7		15	13	7	led	10
Dec. 8, 1947	7	led		22	—[e]	15	10	14
Aug. 9, 1948	led	32		7	—[e]	2	—[f]	14
May 19, 1949	led	1		4	1	13	0	4
Average	9	14	3	12	4	10	4	9

[a] Based on effective dates of price lists published in *Rayon Journal*.
[b] Followed, but no effective date shown on price list.
[c] Absorbed in price change announced jointly with American Viscose on Jan. 14, 1938.
[d] See fn. k, Table 11.
[e] See fn. n, Table 11.
[f] Did not follow.

for which no quotations are available for the Tubize Corporation.[44] The results, however, approximate the rough conclusions drawn from the 1926–1934 data. The average time lag for bringing prices in line with those of the price leader is nine days. Forty-one of the forty-seven lags were sixteen days or less. The single price advance

[43] Small companies' price lists were published sporadically between 1932 and 1949, but not on the dates price changes occurred. When published, they agreed with price lists of the larger companies.

[44] On February 6, 1946, Tubize merged with Celanese to become the Tubize Division of The Celanese Corporation of America. This explains the appearance of viscose yarn prices under the Celanese name in 1946. The pending merger may be a possible explanation for the intermission in price advertisements under the Tubize name.

announced by American Viscose on September 20, 1939 accounts for three of the six company lags that exceed sixteen days. The data do not permit generalization on the relationship between size and magnitude of lag. The higher average lags for Du Pont, Industrial, and American Enka are almost wholly accounted for by the fact that these three companies (and American Viscose) were the only producers who published price lists with effective dates for the September 20, 1939 price increase.

On the average, rayon producers are slightly more hesitant in following a price increase than a price decrease; the average time lag behind announced price increases is ten days while the lag behind decreases is seven days. However, since most firms meet their competitors' lower prices immediately, regardless of the effective dates they show on their published price lists,[45] the actual difference is probably about ten days between the time price increases and price decreases are followed. The statistical evidence that price decreases pervade the market more rapidly than price increases, moreover, is supported by the testimony of price followers before the Federal Trade Commission. Several producers testified that they followed price decreases as quickly as possible, but that they frequently delayed in following an announced price increase long enough to see whether or not the new price would stick.[46]

B. Price Leadership among Acetate Yarn Producers

The relative importance of the acetate process increased steadily from 1925 to 1942. In 1925, the year commercial production of acetate yarn commenced, this process accounted for only 2.9 per cent of total domestic rayon output. By 1942, it accounted for 35 per cent. It has failed to increase its relative position substantially since that date because of the sharp increase in demand for heavy-denier viscose yarns for automobile tire production.[47]

There are a number of reasons why the acetate process merits special treatment in an analysis of rayon price behavior: There are differences in (1) the physical properties of acetate and viscose yarn,[48] and (2) the number of producers supplying each type of

[45] *Supra*, fn. 40.

[46] F. T. C., Docket No. 2161, *Record*, p. 1481.

[47] Acetate yarns disintegrate when subjected to fairly intense heat; hence, they cannot be used in tire cord and fabric construction.

[48] The technical difference may be stated briefly: Viscose yarn starts as cellulose, is then reduced to a xanthogenic ester in solution, and in the spinning process is coagulated back into a cellulose fiber. Viscose yarn is therefore a regenerated cellulose.

yarn. At present, there are four producers of acetate yarn. Over most of the period covered in this study (until the Tubize-Celanese merger) there were five. Two acetate yarn producers, American Viscose and Du Pont, are also the two largest producers of viscose yarn. Relative to both their total yarn capacity and to total domestic acetate yarn output, they are small acetate producers. Tennessee Eastman Corporation produces only acetate yarn, and Celanese, until its merger with Tubize, produced rayon only by the acetate process. Celanese, the oldest producer of rayon by this process in the United States, has accounted for considerably over 50 per cent of the total domestic acetate rayon production.

Price behavior among acetate producers, therefore, is far more elusive and more difficult to interpret than is the price behavior among the viscose producers. The reasons are obvious. There is no large independent acetate yarn market per se. Rather, it constitutes a small segment of a total rayon market in which the two types of rayon are at once substitutable, complementary, and independent of each other. Many fabrics may be woven or knitted from either acetate or viscose yarn. In this area price may be the sole determining factor. On the other hand, particular style creations call for the interweaving of the two types of yarn. For example, variety in color patterns may be obtained by subjecting fabric woven from both types of yarn to dye to which the two yarns react differently. In a small fraction of the yarn market, where specific coloring or resistance to water or heat is essential, viscose and acetate yarns may be viewed as dissimilar commodities. Hence, within this market setting, price leadership among acetate producers becomes somewhat ambiguous. One could reason a priori that the price policy of acetate yarn producers is greatly conditioned by the price of viscose yarn. Consequently, there are two relationships to be examined: the relationship between viscose and acetate yarn prices on the one hand and the relationship between each acetate yarn producer and his rivals on the other.

Viscose and Acetate Yarn Prices. Acetate yarn prices have moved

---

On the other hand, the chemical treatment of the cellulose in the acetate process causes alterations in molecular arrangement and composition so that it remains an ester when coagulated; it is not a regenerated cellulose. The principal commercial difference is that the two types of yarn react to the same dyeing process differently and react differently to heat and water. See Celanese Corporation, *Notes on the Chemical Fiber Industry*, No. 2 in a series of informative bulletins to stockholders, January 1948.

more closely with viscose yarn prices as the relative significance of acetate yarn has increased. This is clearly shown in the comparison of viscose and acetate yarn price change dates in Table 14. From 1925 to 1930, the period over which acetate yarn accounted for less than 6 per cent of total rayon output, price policies of the two types of yarn producers appear to have been formulated independently. All price changes on both yarns, except for the price increases on viscose yarn in the early spring of 1927, were downward, but in no case were price changes on the two types of yarn timed closely together.

From May 1930 to the end of 1936, acetate yarn output advanced from 8 per cent to about 23 per cent of total rayon output. Over this period a relationship between prices of the two types of yarn began to appear. Of the nine acetate price changes which occurred within this period, six were closely timed with major price changes on viscose yarn. There was a fairly strong tendency for acetate prices to lag slightly behind viscose prices (from zero to fifteen days), but the computation of a precise average lag based on all the data for this period is made difficult by the occasional steplike price movements. For example, the spring, 1932 price decrease on viscose yarn was taken in two steps, one on May 26, and one on June 21; both were approximately 15 per cent decreases. The acetate price reduction on June 24 was about 25 per cent and presumably absorbed both viscose yarn price reductions. Again, in the spring and summer of 1933, viscose yarn prices were advanced three times in fairly rapid succession: on April 26, June 20, and July 27. The acetate price increases were made in two steps, one occurring on June 7 between the first and second viscose price increase and the other on July 20 between the second and third viscose increase. For the six acetate price changes that can be directly paired with viscose price changes, however, the lag is from zero to fifteen days.

The acetate process has accounted for slightly less than 30 per cent of total rayon production since 1937. A comparison of viscose and acetate price changes over this period is more meaningful. Prior to April 1937, acetate prices were higher than viscose prices on identical deniers and filament counts. In April, price differentials between the two yarns were all but eliminated: Prices on 150-denier yarn for both processes were made the same; on finer deniers, acetate was quoted a few cents cheaper per pound than viscose, and on heavier deniers, just the opposite was true. These almost identical

TABLE 14

Date of Price Change Comparisons for Viscose, Acetate, and Cuprammonium Yarn, 1925–1949

Viscose (Price Leader Dates)	Acetate	Lag in Days Behind Viscose	Cuprammonium (Bemberg)	Lag in Days Behind Viscose
1925: Feb. 1	: May 1			
1926: July 1	: No Change			
: Sept. 1				
: Nov. 1				
1927: Mar. 16	: Feb. 1		: Sept. 30	
: Apr. 1	: Nov. 14			
1928: No Change	: Aug. 10		: No Change	
1929: Feb. 25	: No Change		: Sept. 15	
: June 18				
1930: May 1	: Jan. 15			
: July 22	: May 16	15	: Aug. 15	
1931: Jan. 9	: Sept. 9		: Jan.	
: Oct. 23			: Nov.	
1932: May 26	: June 6[a]	11	: June	
: June 21	: June 24	3	([d])	
: Aug. 22	: Sept. 6[a]		([d])	
: Aug. 29	: Oct. 11[a]			
1933: Apr. 3			([d])	
: Apr. 26			([d])	
: June 20	: June 7		([d])	
: July 27	: July 20		: Aug.	
1934:	: Feb. 19		: June	
: May 24	: May 24	0		
: Dec. 13				
: Dec. 31				
1935: Apr. 12	: Apr. 17	5	: Apr. 17	5
: Aug. 8			: Aug. 9	1
: Dec. 19				
1936: June 15 (Increase)	: Oct. 7 (Decrease)		: Jan. 2[e]	14
			: June 17	2
			: Dec. 7	
1937: Mar. 31	: Apr. 1	1	: Apr. 13	13
: Dec. 20				
1938: Jan. 14			: Jan.	
: Jan. 21	: Jan. 22	8	: Jan. 21	0
: May 20	: May 20	0	: May 30	10
: July 29	: July 29	0	: July 29	0
1939: Sept. 20	: Sept. 20	0	: June 19	
	: Dec. 1		: Nov. 2	
1940: No Change	: No Change		: No Change	
1941: Sept. 15	: Sept. 15[b]		: Sept. 15	0
	: Oct. 6[b]	21		
	: Oct. 28			
	: Nov. 1			
1946: Nov. 12	: Nov. 15	3	: Nov. 25	13
1947: Jan. 28	: Jan. 28	0	: Feb. 7	10
: Dec. 8	: Dec. 8	0		
1948: Aug. 9	: No Change		: July 6	
1949: May 19	: May 2	17[c]	: May 20	1

Source: *Rayon Journal* and *Rayon Organon*.
[a] Only Celanese changed prices on these dates, see Table 15. [b] See Table 15. [c] Led.
[d] No published price lists available. [e] 1936.

prices greatly facilitate the comparison of price lists. Moreover, since 1937, prices of the two types of rayon have moved in concert so that the impact of viscose producers' price policies upon acetate yarn prices is unmistakable. Every acetate price change except one can be readily paired with a comparable viscose price change. Of ten acetate price changes between April 1, 1937 and May 1949, five were announced as having the same effective date as viscose price changes; one lagged a viscose price change by one day, one by three days, one by eight days, and one by twenty-one days. The May 2, 1949 acetate yarn price decrease preceded the price change on viscose yarn by seventeen days.

It may be fairly concluded that acetate producers have geared their prices more closely to viscose yarn prices as acetate yarn has increased in importance. This trend is unquestionably accounted for in part by the entrance of the two largest viscose rayon producers into the acetate field in 1929, and the merger of Celanese and Tubize in 1946, making a total of three firms that produce both types of rayon.

Price Behavior among Acetate Yarn Producers. The dates of price changes for domestic acetate rayon producers are presented in Table 15. Since a continuous price history for no single company is available, all lags and leads are measured with reference to the official price change dates as recorded in the *Rayon Organon.* Of the fourteen price changes for which a leader can be designated, Celanese, the largest acetate producer, initiated eight of them. As already pointed out, however, nearly all announcements of new acetate yarn prices have followed a viscose yarn price change. Du Pont and American Viscose, both small acetate producers, independently initiated two price changes each and Tubize initiated one; the three producers jointly announced one price change on the same date. Tennessee Eastman Corporation, over the period for which its price lists are available, did not initiate a single price change. American Viscose and Du Pont, the two largest viscose yarn producers, although extremely active in setting viscose prices, have initiated only a few acetate rayon price changes.

Hence, the chainlike pattern of price transmission in the two main sectors of the rayon yarn industry seems to be as follows: The large viscose yarn producers initiate a list-price change on viscose yarn which other viscose producers and the largest acetate producer usually follow within a few days. Acetate producers, including the

TABLE 15

Price Change Dates for Acetate Yarn Producers, 1931–1949

Official Date of Price Change (*Rayon Organon*)	American Viscose	Du Pont	Tennessee Eastman	Tubize	Celanese
Sept. 9, 1931	—	—	—	—	—
June 24, 1932	—	—	—	—	—[a]
June 7, 1933	—	—	—	—	—
July 20, 1933	—	—	—	—	—
Feb. 19, 1934	lagged	lagged	lagged	lagged	led
May 24, 1934[b]	lagged	lagged	lagged	lagged	led
Apr. 17, 1935	—	—	—	—	—
Oct. 7, 1936	lagged	lagged	lagged	lagged	led
Apr. 1, 1937	led	led	lagged	led	lagged
(Apr. 29, 1937)	lagged	led	—[c]	—[c]	—[c]
Jan. 22, 1938	lagged	lagged	—	led	lagged
May 20, 1938	lagged	lagged	lagged	lagged	led
July 29, 1938	lagged	lagged	lagged	lagged	led
Sept. 20, 1939	—	—	—	—	—
Oct. 17, 1939	lagged	lagged	—	—	lagged
Dec. 1, 1939	—	—	—	—	—
Sept. 15, 1941	led[d]	lagged	lagged	—	lagged
Nov. 1, 1941	lagged	lagged[e]	lagged	—	led
Nov. 15, 1946	lagged	lagged	lagged	—	led
Jan. 28, 1947	lagged	lagged	lagged	—	led
Dec. 8, 1947	lagged	led	lagged	—	lagged
May 2, 1949	led	lagged	lagged	—	lagged
Average lag (days)	5	4	8	3	7

[a] Celanese list prices were uniformly $0.05 higher than those of other producers in 1932. The company initiated price changes on September 6 and October 11, 1932 that were not generally followed. On November 3, 1932, Celanese revised its price list to conform with prices then prevailing in the market.

[b] American Viscose increased prices on 120-denier yarns by $0.02 and on 150-denier yarns by $0.05 on December 13, 1934, but only one other acetate yarn producer followed. No official price lists were published during this period, but it is believed that all acetate yarn producers' list prices were back in agreement after April 17, 1935. See *Rayon Organon*, January 1935, p. 13, and May 1935, p. 65.

[c] Price change initiated by Du Pont and followed by American Viscose but is not included in official price change table since it is believed that other producers did not follow. Tubize did not follow; no price lists are available for Celanese and Tennessee Eastman.

[d] American Viscose announced a price increase on both acetate and viscose yarns on September 15, 1941, but subsequently revised its prices on acetate yarns to agree with those announced by Celanese on October 28.

[e] Du Pont's price list on November 1 did not exactly agree with those of other producers; it was brought into agreement on December 1.

viscose producers who also produce relatively small quantities of acetate, follow with revised acetate yarn price lists after the largest acetate producer has revised his. There are exceptions to this pattern: Ocasionally, new price lists for almost all viscose and acetate producers are published with the same effective date.[49] Also, small

[49] See May 24, 1934; May 20, July 29, and September 20, 1938; September 15, 1941; January 28, 1947; and December 8, 1948 (Table 14).

acetate producers occasionally have been apathetic to price changes initiated by Celanese. When such was the case, Celanese usually readjusted its prices to agree with the rest of the industry.[50] On one occasion (September 15, 1941) American Viscose independently announced new prices on both types of rayon yarn in the same price list. Celanese made a temporary price adjustment on October 6 but published a revised acetate yarn price list on October 28 that was followed by the entire acetate industry, including American Viscose.

Largely, however, the pattern of price behavior is as outlined above. Price leadership is strongly associated with size. This holds within each of the two processes and between the two processes. A price change by a large producer usually sweeps through the entire industry in several days and the lag rarely exceeds two weeks. In a few instances, where nearly all large firms in the industry issue identical price lists on the same date, no price leader can be identified.

C. Cuprammonium Prices[51]

The American Bemberg Corporation has accounted for virtually all rayon yarn produced under the cuprammonium process in this country. All price comparisons between cuprammonium and other rayon yarns have been based upon the published price lists of this single company.[52] Unlike acetate yarn prices, cuprammonium prices have always been higher than viscose prices on identical deniers and filament counts. The differential has decreased since 1926, but has not disappeared.

A comparison of cuprammonium and viscose price change dates is presented in Table 14. Data prior to 1935 are shown merely to indicate the general proximity of cuprammonium price change dates to those of viscose before effective dates appeared on published price lists. Cuprammonium price changes have been timed closely with viscose price changes since August 1930. Since 1935, all except four cuprammonium price changes appear to stem directly from price changes initiated in the viscose segment of the industry. For the

[50] See fn. to Table 15.

[51] Quantitatively, the cuprammonium process is relatively insignificant; currently, it accounts for less than 2 per cent of total domestic rayon yarn output.

[52] Price lists were published for the Furness Corporation, the only other cuprammonium yarn producer, from September 1932 to January 1, 1933. Since no price changes occurred in the industry over this period, Furness price quotations cannot be used. In 1933, the company was one-eighth the size of Bemberg.

cuprammonium price increase on December 7, 1936, there is no comparable viscose price change; the June 19 and November 2, 1939 cuprammonium price increases straddled a viscose yarn price increase initiated on September 20; and the July 6, 1948 cuprammonium price increase preceded a comparable price increase on viscose yarns by one month.

On the average, cuprammonium prices have lagged behind viscose prices about six days and in no case has the lag exceeded two weeks. On three occasions cuprammonium price changes were announced on the same day as viscose yarn price changes. Such price behavior further substantiates the thesis that size and price leadership are closely associated in the rayon industry — the list price of cuprammonium yarn varies systematically with list-price revisions initiated by large viscose rayon producers.

D. Implications and Qualifications of the Evidence of Price Leadership

The conclusions reached in this chapter play a significant role in shaping the method of approach to much of the investigation that follows. First, the identification of certain large price leaders is of tremendous help in the selection of segments of inquiry into the rayon industry. To investigate severally all the data relevant to the pricing policy of each of the ten to twenty corporations that have comprised the domestic rayon industry over the past 30 years would present a nearly impossible task. If it can be satisfactorily demonstrated, however, that, for the most part, the smaller producers play a passive role; that is, they change their prices *because* the price leader changes his, an explanation of the leader's price behavior largely explains the behavior of price for the industry.

With infrequent exceptions, most list-price changes are initiated by the very large producers. By far the greater part of them are accounted for by the largest producer alone. The impact of the pricing policy of the few large firms can be traced throughout all segments of the rayon industry. Hence, not only is the scope of the study narrowed to a more manageable number of points of attack, but it is narrowed to the activities of the large corporations that trade journals and newspapers are prone to publicize — they have these corporations in mind when they refer to the industry.

Secondly, it has been demonstrated that a newly announced price by a large producer quickly pervades the industry and that, for the most part, all producers quote identical prices on the same deniers and filament counts. Such behavior obviates much price ambiguity that would exist should the various producers quote noticeably different prices or should the time lag extend over several months. Moreover, identical prices among the various producers strongly imply a homogeneous commodity.

The establishment of price leadership, identification of price leaders, and computation of price lags have rested largely upon an analysis of published price lists. It is demonstrably true, however, that large quantities of rayon yarn sold at prices considerably below published list prices in the depression of the early thirties. Largely, these departures from published list prices were initiated by the small producers and quickly led to subsequent price-list revisions by large producers such as American Viscose and Du Pont.

Although the records of actual prices charged by individual firms are not nearly as complete for subsequent years as they are for the period included in the Federal Trade Commission's investigation, such evidence as there is available strongly suggests that list prices, except for a few months in 1938, are a much more reliable indicator of actual price behavior after 1933 than during the depression.

"Spirited competitive price cutting" led to downward revisions in list prices by American Viscose on January 14 and January 21, 1938.[53] There is little evidence, however, that off-list selling was either engaged in by many of the producers or accounted for a significant volume of total rayon sales. Authoritative spokesmen for the industry stated that the list-price cut initiated by Du Pont in May 1938 officially put an end to off-list selling in the 1937–38 recession; the price cut reduced list prices below any previous level in the industry's history and substantially below any unofficial prices known to have been in existence at the time.[54]

Since wartime and postwar demand for rayon has generally exceeded supply at quoted prices, there is no reason to suspect any off-list pricing of rayon over the past ten years. Hence, except for the 1929–1932 depression and a few months in 1938, published list prices and actual prices can probably be viewed as substantially the same for purposes of price analysis.[55]

[53] *Textile World,* February 14, 1938, p. 82.

[54] *Textile World,* June 1938, p. 92.

[55] Fairly reliable evidence that this is reasonably true may be found in the published reaction of rayon sellers to an editorial which appeared in the January 23, 1950 issue of the *Daily News Record,* summarizing this author's views concerning

E. Institutional Factors Conducive to Price Leadership

While the domestic rayon industry is structurally the type of industry in which, according to the theories of oligopolistic behavior, a tacit observance of some sort of price discipline is likely to arise, institutional and historical factors have undoubtedly influenced the relationship among rayon-producing firms.

Many of the firms that operate in the United States have been loosely associated with each other through the European cartel.[56] Until 1943, Courtaulds, Ltd. held 95 per cent of the capital stock of the American Viscose Corporation. In 1926, the leading German producer, Vereinigte Glanzstoff Fabriken, A. G., founded with Courtaulds the Glanzstoff-Courtaulds firm. The German company held stock in the American Bemberg Corporation and the North American Rayon Corporation in this country. The 1929 merger of Glanzstoff and a Netherlands company resulted in the establishment of the Dutch firm Algemeene Kunstzijde Unie, N. V., in which Courtaulds also held shares. This merger virtually brought the three American firms, North American, American Enka, and American Bemberg, under joint control. Also, the firm of Glanzstoff-Courtaulds had an exchange of shares with Snia Viscosa of Italy, which held some of the shares of Industrial Rayon Corporation, and Courtaulds had a working agreement with the French rayon combine. Until 1929, a French company held 40 per cent of the stock of Du Pont Rayon Company and continued to maintain patent agreements with Du Pont until recent years. French interests had also participated in the establishment of the Hartford Rayon Corporation, Skenandoa Rayon Corporation, and the Delaware Rayon Corporation. Thus, most of the productive capacity in the United States was loosely associated through the tangled mass of interlacing European interests.

Moreover, many of the same firms that operate in the United States had worked in harmony with each other in Europe several years before American subsidiaries were established. The price lead-

---

the administered features of rayon prices. They did not object to an analysis which, with the above qualifications, associated actual prices with list prices. They did point out, however, that many rayon producers frequently revised prices on extremely fine denier yarns without waiting for American Viscose or Du Pont to do so. See *Daily News Record,* January 23, 1950, pp. 2, 16; January 24, 1950, p. 33; and February 6, 1950, p. 2.

[56] Clair Wilcox, *Competition and Monopoly in American Industry,* pp. 202–205.

ership of Courtaulds, for example, was the accepted price relationship among firms in Great Britain until 1938. In that year, price leadership gave way to price agreements and market sharing after it had been demonstrated "that price leadership could be maintained without consulting other firms when the desire was to stabilize prices or lower them, but there was no guarantee that the other firms would raise prices if the dominant firm chose to do so; hence, the agreement on prices." [57] Therefore, most American rayon producers had previously accepted the leadership of Courtaulds in Great Britain. Such a precedent probably paved the way toward accepting the leadership of the Courtaulds-owned American Viscose Corporation in the United States.

Furthermore, American producers have had several points of contact through their jointly operated advertising, statistical, and trade associations.[58] Also, the two largest producers occupy adjacent home office buildings in Wilmington, Delaware, and their central sales offices and the home or principal sales offices of nearly all the other producers in the United States are located close to each other in New York City. Whether by accident, by design, or for business purposes, such proximity could be instrumental in keeping each producer informed of the activities of his rivals.

The foregoing historical and institutional factors, particularly the formal arrangements among the parent rayon firms in Europe, have hardly encouraged completely independent action in the domestic market. Since the overt price and market sharing agreements that took place in Great Britain in 1938 would have been illegal in the United States, tacit acceptance of the leadership of the American Viscose Corporation (or any other large producer) may have been the best alternative, albeit not sufficiently strong to maintain price discipline when the rayon market was severely depressed.

[57] Edgar Jones, "Price Leadership in the Rayon Industry," *Manchester School of Economics and Social Studies*, XII (October 1941), 86.

[58] See Appendix B.

6

OLIGOPOLY THEORY
and the Domestic Rayon Industry

The possibility of a number of relationships between firms and their rivals is the distinguishing feature of oligopolistic markets — a possibility excluded from the areas of perfect competition and monopoly. Because the number of possibilities is great, theoretical constructions yield market solutions that range, according to the assumptions made concerning each firm's behavior, all the way from the purely competitive to the pure monopoly price.

Since the purely competitive price solution follows from the rather unrealistic assumption that each firm assumes its rivals' prices to be independent of any of its own actions, such a theoretical construction is of little use as an explanatory hypothesis for markets where sellers are few. Hence, there is pertinence in the observation made by Professor Chamberlin: "When a move by one seller evidently forces the other to make a counter move, he is very stupidly refusing to look further than his nose if he proceeds on the assumption that it will not." [1]

On the other hand, the assumptions which underlie the monopoly price solution, when viewed against the dynamic aspects of industrial growth and change, are equally as unrealistic. The monopoly price solution presupposes, for example, that cost functions are identical among firms and that they would remain unchanged if the several firms which comprise the oligopoly were to unite and behave as a pure monopolist under a single entrepreneur. Moreover, the monopoly price solution for oligopolistic markets is a static concept.

[1] Edward H. Chamberlin, *Monopolistic Competition* (5th ed.; Harvard University Press: Cambridge, 1946), p. 46.

In a dynamic economy where all factors are subject to unpredictable change, where entrepreneurs hold different expectations of the future, and where ambition and the desire to grow, even at the expense of rivals, is not yet dead, the monopoly price solution in markets where sellers are few has, at best, very limited applicability as an explanatory hypothesis. It is probably for these reasons that Professor Chamberlin offers it as only one of many conceptually possible solutions.

Nevertheless, the fundamental principle of oligopolistic rationalization, that is, that each seller will consider both the direct and indirect effects of his actions, holds a degree of relevancy for rayon price behavior. For example, when asked before the Federal Trade Commission why his company did not publish prices lower than those of American Viscose and Du Pont, President Fuller of the North American Rayon Corporation replied that, "It would be bad business since other firms would surely meet the lower prices." [2] Mr. Fuller added, however, that he frequently sold rayon at less than list price and sometimes quoted lower prices on deniers other than 150-denier. Officials of virtually all viscose yarn companies gave the same reason for not quoting lower prices than American Viscose and Du Pont — the indirect effects of such a move would be a lower price for all.

Although such rationalization on the part of each producer probably does not result in the monopoly price, it does frequently lead to the tacit adoption of a *modus operandi* which eliminates much of the uncertainty over what rivals' reactions to a given move might be. As previously indicated, among the most important of such conceptual arrangements that might possibly explain the relationship among rival firms in the rayon industry would be those which embrace some form of price leadership.

At least three theoretical market models which make price leadership of some sort virtually inevitable have gained currency in the writings of economists:[3] (1) the partial monopolist or dominant firm

[2] F. T. C., Docket No. 2161, *Record*, p. 750.

[3] The dominant firm and barometric firm types of price leadership are discussed by Professor G. J. Stigler in "The Kinky Oligopoly Demand Curve and Rigid Prices," *Journal of Political Economy*, October 1947, pp. 432–449. See also Professor Stigler's "Notes on the Theory of Duopoly," *Journal of Political Economy*, August 1940, pp. 522–523; and A. J. Nichol, *Partial Monopoly and Price Leadership* (Philadelphia: Smith Edwards Co., 1930). For a discussion of price leadership by low-cost high-output firms and in industries containing firms having identical cost curves but different shares of the market, see Kenneth E. Boulding, *Economic Analysis* (rev. ed.; New York: Harper & Brothers, 1948), pp. 582, 586.

industry; (2) an industry containing one low-cost high-output firm and one or more high-cost low-output firms; and (3) an industry containing firms having identical cost curves, different shares of the market, and constant proportional shares over the entire range of possible prices. A fourth type of price leadership, which can more appropriately be viewed as an institutional or historical phenomenon than as a product of theory, is centered upon the barometric firm.

It has already been suggested in Chapter 3, and it will be more fully demonstrated later, that a model which presupposes identical cost curves for all firms does not fit the rayon industry at all well. Plants and firms vary in size, and size is an important determinant of costs. Furthermore, in view of the computed relationship between size and efficiency in the rayon industry, the largest firm would probably be the low-cost high-output firm. The largest rayon firm, however, has also occupied the position of a dominant firm over a significant period of the industry's history. Hence, the logic behind the dominant firm and barometric firm types of price leadership, at least at first blush, promises to shed the most light on price-making in the rayon industry.

The rationale behind the partial monopolist type of price leadership is as follows: In an industry composed of one large producer and a number of small ones, the large producer sets a price on the basis of the visualized demand schedule for the commodity, after allowing for the quantities that will be supplied at all possible prices by the small producers. The required conditions are that the dominant firm sell a sufficiently large proportion of the commodity, that the small firms individually ignore any effect they may have on price, and that the dominant firm must behave passively — it sets a price and sells the remainder after the small producers have sold all they wish at the prevailing price. It is assumed that the large producer has some means of estimating the demand curve for the product, that he can predict fairly accurately the sum of the marginal cost curves of all the other producers, and that each small producer behaves rationally, that is, attempts to maximize his profit by producing up to the point where his marginal cost is equal to price. It is further assumed that the small producers act independently. In other words, they do not join forces to restrict the price-setting power of the partial monopolist. Under these conditions small producers accept the price set by the partial monopolist just as a firm accepts a perfectly competitive price. No small producer would raise his price since this would result in the loss of his entire sales. There would be no incentive for him to lower his price since he sells all he wishes at the price set by the largest producer. Hence, each small producer views the demand schedule for his product as horizontal.

The actual equilibrium price set by the partial monopolist depends upon his profit-making motives. If he behaves passively, i.e., merely equates his marginal cost with his marginal revenue as computed from his own derived demand schedule, the solution is, conceptually, perfectly determinate with an equilibrium price automatically set. If, however, the partial monopolist is motivated by forces other than short-run profit maximization, there is a range of possible prices. The price he actually sets will depend upon the share of total output the partial monopolist wishes to maintain, his desire to suppress profits so that new firms will not be attracted to the industry, his long-run market expectations, and so forth. Professor Stigler holds that the largest firm should produce a minimum of 40 per cent of the output of an industry in order to be classified as a dominant firm and that his percentage should be considerably greater if the second largest firm is fairly large.[4] Since the determinateness of the solution of the partial monopoly problem does not depend so much upon the complete inability of any firm other than the largest producer to influence price, but rather upon whether any one of these firms can influence price sufficiently to warrant the serious consideration of a price other than that set by the partial monopolist, this limitation would appear to be reasonable although perhaps somewhat arbitrary.[5]

Conditions in the domestic rayon industry up to 1931, however, would fulfill essentially all of Professor Stigler's criteria. Between 1920 and 1931, the American Viscose Corporation accounted for from 99 per cent to 44 per cent of total rayon output in the United States. Over the twelve-year period, American Viscose ranged from three to ten times as large as Du Pont, the second largest producer. As late as 1931, fourteen of the twenty rayon producers were less than one-seventeenth the size of American Viscose and the combined output of the remaining five firms was less than that of American Viscose.

Moreover, it was possible for the dominant firm to estimate fairly

[4] Stigler, "The Kinky Oligopoly Demand Curve and Rigid Prices," p. 444.

[5] By applying these criteria, Professor Stigler did not include the rayon industry among those having a dominant firm price leader between June 1929 and May 1937; *ibid.*, p. 443.

accurately the combined output of the other producers. The computed marginal and average cost curves for a representative rayon plant[6] shows that all producers except American Viscose, because their marginal costs decline nearly up to the rated capacity of their plants, should have produced in the neighborhood of full capacity over a very wide range of possible prices. At any price between the price P_2 and say P_1 (Figure 2), the quantity supplied by the rest of the industry would probably have varied within very narrow limits. Throughout the twenties, a period characterized by rapid expansion, fairly large profits, and infrequent excess inventories, the burden of adjusting its output to equate demand and supply in the rayon market was probably a small price for the partial monopolist to pay for the privilege of setting the price. There is no evidence that American

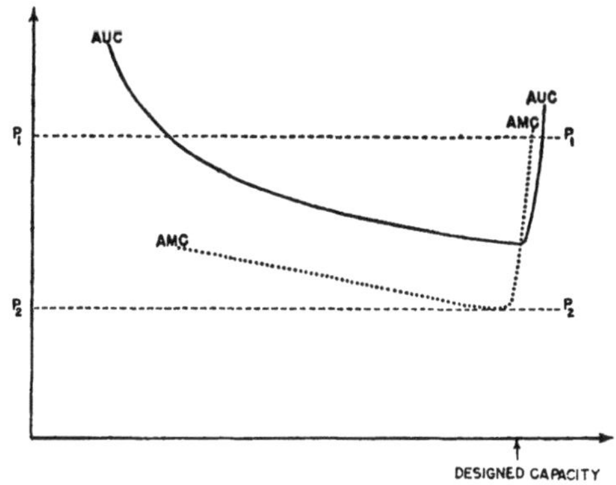

Figure 2

Viscose or any other firm found it necessary to curtail output prior to 1930 for any appreciable length of time. In spite of the obvious shortcomings of the above static analysis when applied to the dynamic features that characterized the domestic rayon industry during this period of its development, the reasoning behind the partial monopolist concept might explain the price leadership of American Viscose extant in the comparative price lists analysis.

Several changes which occurred in the rayon industry make it difficult to explain the continued price leadership by the American Viscose Corporation after 1931 in terms of the foregoing partial monopolist analysis. As production facilities expanded to satiate demand for rayon, it became less feasible for one firm to bear the impact of

[6] See Chart 11. Average and marginal costs beyond installed capacity (Fig. 2) are estimated.

cyclical variations in demand. Moreover, by 1931 several producers had reached a size sufficiently large so that any one of them could have affected price by altering its rate of output. The fact that American Viscose and several other large producers tried to secure, and in some instances succeeded in securing, the coöperation of the rest of the industry on output curtailment after 1930 is sufficient evidence that the company was not behaving as the theoretical partial monopolist; the collusive agreement in effect from October 1931 to May 1932 is further evidence.[7]

Nevertheless, from 1931 until the present time, the American Viscose Corporation has continued to be the largest producer and, hence, has been in a position to exert more influence on the price of rayon (by altering its rate of production) than any other single firm. In this respect the American Viscose Corporation has continued to be the dominant firm in the rayon industry over the past twenty years, although it has not fulfilled the criteria for a partial monopolist as set forth by Professor Stigler.

Another type of price leadership that could conceivably explain the price relationship among firms in the rayon industry after 1931 is centered upon the barometric firm. No extensive treatment of the rationale behind this type of price leadership has been set forth in the economic literature, but it has been briefly stated as follows: In a market characterized by a limited number of producers, one of the selling firms may take the initiative to set a price agreeable to the rest of the industry. According to Professor Stigler, the barometric firm "commands adherence of rivals to his price only because and to the extent that his price reflects market conditions with tolerable promptness." [8] The precise industrial structure likely to produce this particular type of price leadership as envisaged by those who have touched upon it is not quite clear. But since the adherence of rivals to the price set by the barometric firm is contingent upon that firm's past performance, the answer to why a particular firm is the baro-

[7] A partial monopolist, by definition, has the power to dictate the price; hence, he does not have to seek the coöperation of the rest of the industry.

[8] Stigler, "The Kinky Oligopoly Demand Curve and Rigid Prices," p. 444. As employed in this study, the term "barometric price leader" refers to the firm that conventionally first announces price changes. The illustrative case used by Professor Stigler, however, conflicts with such a definition since one of the market forces that the barometric firm's price was supposed to reflect was "secret price cutting by dealers in some particular area . . ." (cf. p. 445). In such a case it seems that the barometric firm no longer plays the role of a "price leader" but, in truth, becomes a "price follower."

metric firm would more likely be found in the historical and institutional features of an industry than through the speculative construction of theoretical schema.

There are several good reasons, in addition to those mentioned previously in connection with the existence of price leadership, why American Viscose should have fallen heir to the job of price-setting in the rayon industry after its partial monopoly status had been weakened, if not extinguished. It was the oldest and still the largest producer of rayon in the United States. From 1911 to 1920, the company had enjoyed a complete monopoly of rayon production and, until the early thirties, had fulfilled the criteria for a partial monopolist. Hence, it was the only firm that had acquired experience at adjusting the price of rayon to the dynamic features of the industry's expansion and technological change, and to such exogenous forces as the price movements of silk, cotton, wool, and foreign-produced rayon.

Also, until recently, American Viscose produced only rayon, whereas a number of its larger rivals such as Du Pont and Eastman Kodak were producers of many commodities in addition to synthetic yarns. The multi-product firms might well have reasoned that it was an unnecessary expenditure of funds and effort to attempt to compute for themselves the equilibrium price for rayon when a more experienced and larger producer was already making the market analysis for them. Since only these larger firms stood as potential contenders for the role of price leader, their passivity would have automatically delegated to American Viscose the task of setting the price.

Moreover, it is unlikely that other firms, in view of the industry's profit history, would have been quick to challenge the advisability of a price set by American Viscose. It is even more unlikely that the producer who had been the unchallenged price leader for twenty years should voluntarily relinquish its role only because its relative share in the market had gradually decreased from 45 per cent of total output in the twenties to about 30 per cent by the end of World War II.

Whether or not the industrial structure of the domestic rayon industry since 1931 has been compatible with the conditions likely to give rise to price leadership of the barometric type, American Viscose has set list prices for the remaining producers since that year without benefit of the power of a partial monopolist. In view of their almost uninterrupted willingness to adopt the price schedules issued by American Viscose, the exact year in which the price leader ceased to be a dominant firm and became a barometric one may be of no particular significance. From the standpoint of public policy, however, it is important that the two types of price leadership be clearly distinguished.

When a firm occupies the position of a partial monopolist, the remaining firms in the industry have no choice but to accept its price, whether the partial monopolist attempts to maximize its short-run profits or pursues some other line of action. No price other than the price set by the partial monopolist is contemplated by the competitive sector of the industry. Dominant firm price leadership, then, is patently a form of monopoly pricing.

When firms are somewhat more evenly matched in size, however, and a leader emerges because its past performance has commanded the respect of the rest of the industry for its sound price and output policy, its ability to quickly appraise the forces at work in the market, etc., the term "price leader" is particularly descriptive of the role it plays.[9] Under these circumstances, each firm in the industry may contemplate prices other than those published by the adopted price leader and in some instances may elect to use them, either because it temporarily rejects the price leader's price as an accurate barometer or for other reasons. Here, however, each of the moderately large firms has a choice — it may follow the leader or issue a price independently. When all the conditions of a partial monopolist are fulfilled, no such choice on the part of producers is admissible.

Hence, between the terms "price control" and "price leadership," at least a subtle difference should be recognized. The former results from a fairly high order of monopoly inherent in the structure of the industry, the latter may yield a price pattern consistent with moderately strong competition. It is the latter term that more nearly describes the relationship that has existed among rayon-producing firms since 1931, at which time a number of American Viscose Corporation's rivals became significant in size and commenced to initiate price changes occasionally on their own.

[9] This is particularly true if price leadership of the barometric type can be viewed as an instrument rationally employed in an industry to reduce the uncertainties of the relationship among firms. Under the partial monopolist type of price leadership no uncertainties with respect to the price relationship exist; an equilibrium market price presupposes a known price relationship among firms, i.e., the power of the partial monopolist to set a price that other firms have no choice but to accept.

The foregoing demonstration of the extent to which the theory of monopolistic competition, particularly the principle of oligopolistic rationalization, is helpful in explaining price behavior in the rayon industry is limited, of course, to list-price behavior. Although sellers of rayon may rely upon the price leader to change the official price, they have demonstrated a willingness to sell much of their output at less than list price when the market is severely depressed. Hence, the applicability of the theory of monopolistic competition and of the theory of price leadership as a *modus operandi* in markets where sellers are few may vary considerably with the various phases of the business cycle. In the depression of 1930–1932 and, to a lesser extent, the recession of 1938, each seller, although unwilling to risk the indirect effects of a downward revision of his list price, competed with his rivals for available business by cutting actual prices. Actual price competition was engaged in so vigorously, in fact, in the first half of 1932 that even the price leader sold a substantial portion of his output at less than list price. Although such pricing practices substantiate the thesis that oligopolistic rationality prevails in markets where sellers are few (there would be no such manifest reluctance to make price revisions known to rivals if this were not so), they also vitiate the argument that oligopolistic rationalization necessarily leads to anything that closely resembles a monopoly price.

7

SHORT-RUN MOVEMENTS
Cycles, and Trends in Rayon Price and Output

A. Short-Run Movements in Rayon Price

If we define an administered price simply as one that does not reflect conditions of short-run demand and supply, rayon price will qualify as a candidate for the administered price group. Price lists issued by producers usually hold over relatively long time intervals. Since 1911, there have been forty-nine list-price changes for 150-denier viscose yarn, or an average of about one and one-quarter price changes per year. Rayon price has remained unchanged over some prolonged intervals. From early 1911 to January 1914, 150-denier rayon sold at $1.85 per pound; from January 1914 to November 1915, at $2.00 per pound; from October 1921 to February 1924, at $2.80 per pound; from March 1927 to February 1929, at $1.50 per pound. Except for two rather insignificant 4 per cent price increases initiated from fourteen months to two years apart, the price of rayon remained unchanged from July 1939 until September 1946. It must be borne in mind, however, that price ceilings were imposed upon the industry for four of these seven years.[1]

Acetate yarn and staple fiber prices have remained unchanged for longer intervals: 150-denier acetate yarn sold for $2.90 per pound from January 1925 to August 1928, a period of over three and one-half years. There were, however, two price revisions on finer denier yarns over this period. There have been several instances in which acetate yarn price remained unchanged for at least two years. The

[1] Price ceilings were not placed upon rayon until June 22, 1942.

price of viscose staple fiber has changed only nine times since 1928. In this segment of the rayon industry a price usually holds for two or three years. Except for a $0.01 per pound price cut in May 1943 that was quickly restored, the price of staple fiber remained at $0.25 per pound from September 1937 to November 1946, a period of nine years.

There is fairly conclusive evidence, apart from infrequent list-price changes, that stable rayon prices are a result of rayon producers' positive policy. The industry has highly advertised the price stability of its product to textile fabricators, emphasizing the unusual merits of a stable rayon price in a world of fluctuating natural fiber prices. In addition to sporadic offers of 90-day guarantees against price changes, corporation officials have frequently given advance notice to consumers that no price change would be initiated for the next several months in the face of unknown future market conditions. For example, the *Journal* stated in September 1927 that "steady prices on rayon yarns create wider markets, . . . the Viscose Company announces that there will be no price change for the November 1 to January 31 quarter. Other producers [are] taking similar action." [2] In this instance consumers were notified of the price that would prevail in the market five months later. Again, in September 1928, after the price of rayon had remained unchanged for over one and one-half years, the American Viscose Company gave similar assurances to rayon consumers that its prices would not change over the ensuing quarter.[3] Large rayon producers have frequently made such price guarantees to the rayon trades.

Infrequent price changes and guarantees against future price change usually are sufficient evidence that the price is administered and not an automatous result of short-run market forces. Short-run price stability can be effected by permitting inventories to fluctuate and/or by adjusting production schedules to meet conditions of shifting demand at the prevailing price. Consequently, in unregulated markets an administered price is usually associated with in-

[2] *Rayon Journal*, September 1927, p. 5.

[3] *Rayon Journal*, September 1928, p. 7. For further evidence, see the following articles in the *Journal*: "Rayon Price Stability Declared Leading Factor in Textile Recovery," March 15, 1928, p. 5; "What Stability Implies," June 15, 1929, p. 30; "Rayon Prices Regulated," March 1, 1930, p. 36; "Rayon Prices to Remain Stable," April 1, 1930, p. 7; "Price Stability of Rayon," October 1939, p. 29. See also: "No General Price Change in Rayon in 1940," *Rayon Organon*, April 1940, p. 13; Clair Wilcox, *Competition and Monopoly in American Industry*, TNEC Monograph no. 21, p. 203; Mauersberger and Schwarz, *Rayon and Staple Fiber Handbook*, pp. 43–44.

dustries in which sellers are few and the commodity is storable. The rayon industry, as described in previous chapters, falls into such an industrial classification; hence, there are a priori reasons for suspecting rayon prices to be "sticky," in the short-run, even after allowance is made for known deviations from list prices. There are, however, various orders of price rigidity. Hence, the following analysis is addressed to the problem of determining *how* insensitive rayon price is to the various orders of economic fluctuations.

Rayon Price and Seasonal Demand Patterns. Similar to practically all fibers used in the textile fabricating industry, rayon is subject to fairly broad seasonal swings in demand. The evolution of rayon from a novelty yarn to one of more general use, however, has produced such year-to-year changes in the seasonal demand pattern that summary seasonal indexes are difficult to calculate. From 1923 to 1937, the seasonal variation was somewhat progressive. The seasonal slump, which in previous years had commenced in April and lasted through September, by 1937 occurred in May, June, July, November, December, and January.[4] The over-all effect of the seasonal shifts has been to spread demand somewhat more uniformly throughout the year by producing early summer and midwinter seasonal slumps and late summer, fall, late winter, and spring seasonal bulges. In 1923, for example, the year was divided approximately into six months of relatively high activity (October through March) and six months of relatively low activity (April through September). Three specific seasonal patterns of demand for rayon for the year 1940 are shown in Chart 3.

Up to this point the evidence of an administered rayon price has been limited to the admitted price policy objectives of corporation officials and the relative infrequency of price changes. This evidence alone does not conclusively prove that rayon prices are administered. Producers' pricing policy objectives, once formulated, might be defeated when carried to the market; or short-run price stability might be perfectly compatible with prevailing conditions of supply and demand. For this reason it is necessary to subject the price data to some sort of test that should reveal the extent to which prices are insensitive to seasonal fluctuations in demand.

[4] Monthly seasonal indexes (1923–1937) appear in various issues of the *Rayon Organon* where these movements may be traced. Publication of seasonal indexes in the *Rayon Organon* was discontinued in 1938. The introduction of industrial yarns (such as tire fabric yarns) has undoubtedly altered the seasonal demand pattern significantly since 1940.

A simple statistical test would be to correlate price changes and monthly indexes for rayon deliveries.[5] If rayon prices have been sensitive to seasonal shifts in demand, there should have been a general tendency for prices to increase during months having a seasonal index greater than 100 and for prices to decrease during

Chart 3

Monthly Rayon Yarn Shipments in 1940 to (A) Three Types of Consumers Combined, (B) Print Cloth Weavers, (C) Underwear Weavers, and (D) Underwear Knitters

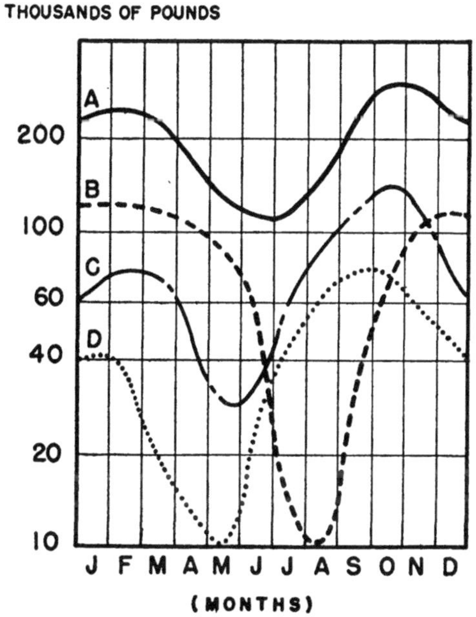

Note: Logarithmic Vertical Scale.
Source: *Rayon Organon*, February 1941.

months having a seasonal index less than 100. There is no evidence of such a relationship between seasonal demand and price movements. Between 1923 and 1941 viscose yarn list price increased fourteen times and decreased eighteen times. Eight price increases and eight price decreases occurred in months having indexes greater than 100,

[5] Ordinarily, price sensitivity to seasonal demand fluctuations could be detected by computing monthly seasonal price indexes. This procedure is obviously unwarranted when price often remains unchanged for several years. Hence, it is fairly certain at the outset that rayon price does not equate short-run demand and supply, but the above test may detect how often seasonal variations in deliveries affect price.

whereas six price increases and ten price decreases occurred in months having indexes less than 100. Over the same period, two acetate yarn price increases and five price decreases occurred in months having indexes exceeding 100, whereas four price increases and eight price decreases occurred in months having indexes less than 100. For both viscose and acetate rayon yarn, price increases and decreases seem to occur at random over the seasonal cycles. Hence, it can be fairly concluded that rayon producers have been successful in their efforts to maintain a short-run stable price although confronted with fairly wide shifts in seasonal demand.[6]

Rayon Price and the "Textile Cycle." The "textile cycle" is rarely included among the cyclical phenomena that dominate our economic data in the more general cycle analyses; hence, a brief description of the cycle is necessary. Since the end of the first World War, consumption of all textiles has been relatively high in odd-numbered years and relatively low in even-numbered years. The phenomenal regularity with which this cycle occurs in textile consumption data has never been adequately explained.

Stanley B. Hunt, director of the Textile Economics Bureau, Inc., has observed these cycles in textile consumption series since 1930 and has concluded that they are a result of a general textile inventory cycle that derives from expectations based upon consumers' replacement demands.[7] According to his data, the normal supply of stocks held on hand in the textile industry at all stages of production and distribution, from the yarn manufacturer to the finished textiles retailer, will last approximately six months. That is to say, if yarn production should be stopped completely, pipeline stocks would ordinarily insure a supply of fabricated textiles for about six months. But, if in a period of low production, stocks are permitted to dwindle to a four-month supply and, subsequently, under the impetus of higher prices (or expected higher prices), stocks are again built up, production snowballs all along the line until an eight-month supply is reached. At this point buying and production will fall off until inventories again decrease to a four-month supply, and the cumulative process is repeated. The time required to complete one of these inventory cycles is two years. Mr. Hunt does not categorically set the limits to inventory fluctuations at four and eight months' supply

[6] Since 1933, July rayon sales consistently have been only 54.7 per cent of September sales.

[7] *Rayon Journal,* December 1937, pp. 171–173.

but offers these points as possible limits suggested by the available data.

The entire cumulative process appears to stem from expected consumer replacement at the retail end. Simply stated, this merely means that retailers, presumably from experience, expect alternative years of high and low finished textile sales. The repetitious pulsations of the effects of retailers' expectations backward through all stages of the textile productive process have given rise to similar expectations all along the line.

It is not within the scope of this study either to test the above theory or to develop an explanatory hypothesis for this cyclical phenomenon peculiar to textile consumption series. The two-year requirement to proceed from one inventory level to the other and return is a convincing argument for associating the cycle with inventory fluctuations. The consumer replacement stimulus to retailers' expectations offers a fertile field for investigation.

Regardless of the plausibility of the theory, however, the phenomenon is beyond dispute. Annual consumption of cotton, rayon, silk, wool, and total fibers for the years 1912–1948 is shown in Chart 1. The two-year cycle has appeared with remarkable regularity in all textile fiber consumption data since 1920. With the single exception of 1936, all odd-numbered years are peaks and all even-numbered years are troughs. The cycle that began in 1935 lasted only nineteen months instead of the usual two years. As a consequence, the textile market experienced an upward swing in midsummer, 1936, instead of the first of 1937, which tended to increase fiber consumption in 1936 relative to 1935, and to decrease consumption in 1937 relative to 1936. The usual pattern of the cycle is therefore interrupted in the neighborhood of 1936. In spite of the sharp persistent upward trend in the rayon consumption data, the two-year textile cycle is clearly marked except for the period around 1936.

Frequencies of price change by odd-numbered and even-numbered years from 1920 to 1947, for viscose and acetate yarn, are presented below:

Years 1920–1947	Viscose Yarn Price Increases	Viscose Yarn Price Decreases	Acetate Yarn Price Increases	Acetate Yarn Price Decreases
Even-numbered	6	12	2	9
Odd-numbered	12	6	7	3

If rayon prices have been sensitive to the textile cycle, more price increases than decreases should have occurred in the odd-numbered years of relatively high demand and more price decreases than increases in the even-numbered years of relatively low demand. Obviously, the trend and cyclical movements of the price series influence the above tabulation[8] but, on balance, should not completely vitiate the results.

Of the eighteen upward price revisions on viscose yarn over this period, twelve occurred in odd-numbered years and six occurred in even-numbered years. For the eighteen downward price revisions, the frequencies were exactly reversed, twelve occurring in even-

Chart 4

Trend in 150-Denier Viscose Yarn Average Annual Price, 1919–1947

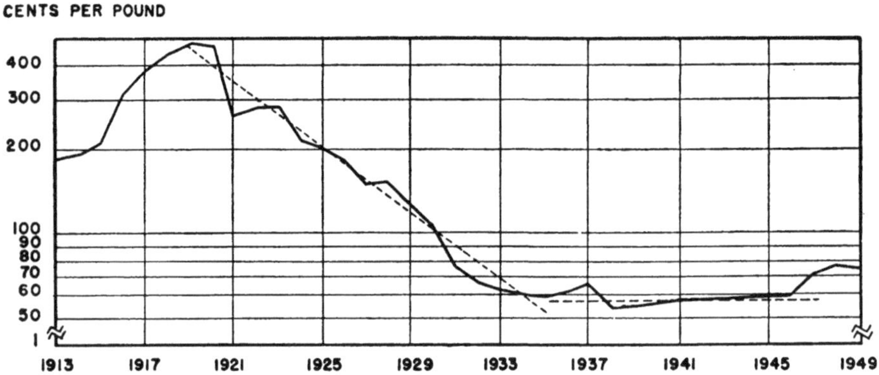

Note: Logarithmic Vertical Scale.

numbered years and six occurring in odd-numbered years.[9] The effect of the two-year cycle upon price movements is somewhat more pronounced in the case of acetate yarn. Of the nine price increases, seven occurred in odd-numbered years and two occurred in even-numbered years; of the twelve price decreases, nine occurred in even-numbered years and three in odd-numbered years.

The tendency for upward price revisions to take place in years of active demand for rayon and for downward price revisions to occur in the less active years is evidence of at least some degree of price sensitivity to the textile cycle. There are no ready statistical

[8] The trend in the price series seems to be effected through the *intensity* rather than the *frequency* of price changes; hence, it does not greatly influence an analysis confined to annual price change frequencies.

[9] The relationship between the two-year cycle and viscose yarn price movements is somewhat strengthened if the price increase in August 1936 is omitted on the grounds that 1936 did not conform to the usual two-year cycle pattern.

means for measuring the degree of sensitivity since the amplitude of the two-year price swings (if, in fact, they exist) would be considerably influenced by other cyclical movements.[10] A visual comparison of the rayon price series (Chart 4) and the rayon consumption series (Chart 1), however, will show that the textile cycle is much more apparent in the latter than in the former.

B. Trends and Cycles in Rayon Price

In making an analysis of the historical data for rayon over moderately long time intervals, it is important to keep the evolutionary aspects of the commodity in mind. It was pointed out in Chapter 2 that, between the two World Wars, rayon progressed from an inferior silk substitute to a high quality yarn having many uses. Hence, any trend line fitted to price data would have a strong upward bias. Similarly, trend lines fitted to production data are strongly biased downward.

Casual inspection of the average annual price series for rayon (Chart 4) reveals three clearly defined trend movements; each is coincident with a particular stage of growth of the industry. From 1911 to 1920 the American Viscose Corporation completely monopolized the domestic rayon industry by virtue of its ownership of the Cross and Bevan, and Topham patents. Over this period the price movement was steadily upward, having risen from $1.85 per pound in 1913 to $6.00 per pound by February 1920, an increase of 224 per cent. Although sometimes attributed to the monopoly position held by American Viscose,[11] much of this price spiral was undoubtedly due to general wartime inflation.

Between 1920 and 1931 the productive capacity of the domestic rayon industry was greatly increased. A number of new firms entered the industry in the early twenties after the expiration of the American Viscose Company's patent rights (1918). Over this period, and up to April 1933, the trend in domestic rayon yarn prices was sharply downward. The average annual price in 1919 was $4.77 per pound; by April 1933, rayon was selling for $0.50 per pound, or only slightly

[10] Other cyclical movements have also influenced the frequencies. For example, 1932 and 1938 were business cycle troughs and 1923, 1929, and 1937 were business cycle peaks. Hence, the textile cycle does not uniquely determine the above results. See *infra.*

[11] United States Federal Trade Commission, *Investments, Profits, and Rates of Return for Selected Industries,* p. 17984; a study submitted to the Temporary National Economic Committee Congressional Committee by the Federal Trade Commission pursuant to public resolution number 113, 75th Congress, Third Session.

over 10 per cent of the 1919 price. This striking downward trend has sometimes been attributed to the price competition brought about by the entry of new firms.[12]

A gradual cessation of the sharp downward trend in rayon prices occurred between 1933 and 1935. From 1935 until the removal of price controls in late 1946, the general movement has followed a straight horizontal line. This movement has coincided with the developmental phase of the industry marked by a complete absence of new entrants, the death of several small and financially weak firms, and a mild but perceptible tendency toward vertical integration.[13]

If trend lines were useful only in that they defined the general directional movement of a series over a given time period, there actually would be little need for mathematically fitting such lines to the rayon price series. The trend is so pronounced in each of the three time periods described above it could be stated that the series itself is sufficiently descriptive of the trend. Chiefly because the trend has been so pronounced as to somewhat obscure the cyclical price movements, however, it must be eliminated. For example, most price series for manufactured and semimanufactured goods show fairly well-defined peaks in the years 1920, 1923, 1929, and 1937, and troughs in the years 1921, 1924, 1927, 1932, and 1938. The downward trend in rayon prices between 1919 and 1935 was so pronounced that similar peaks and troughs are difficult to locate. This is particularly true in the neighborhood of 1933 where the trend seems to break but is still sufficiently strong to push the visible upturn in rayon prices ahead to 1936.

The periods for which trend lines could logically be fitted to the rayon price series, from both an economic and a statistical point of view, have already been described. The behavior of the series and the history of the industry have delineated three distinct time periods. Almost any trend line fitted to the 1913–1919 data, however, would give an obvious trough in 1914 and a peak around 1917 or 1918. Similarly, data for the 1935–1947 period, where the trend is virtually horizontal, shows a peak in 1937 and a trough in 1938. For this period the trend safely can be assumed as horizontal and the average price for the period taken as a point from which deviations can be measured. Horizontal linearity was imposed upon the data for much of this period, of course, by price controls. A compound

[12] *Ibid.*, p. 17984.
[13] See Appendix A.

interest rate curve (negatively sloped) was selected as the trend that best represents the general price movement for the 1919–1935 period.[14]

The resulting cyclical pattern is reproduced in Chart 7, where the trend ratios computed from the fitted trend line for the period 1919–1935, and from the average price for the period 1935–1942,[15] are plotted. Although not apparent in the original data, rayon price is fairly sensitive to general economic fluctuations. The amplitudes of cyclical swings in rayon prices are indicated by trend ratio values that fall between 118 and 77.0. The trend ratios are not particularly informative in themselves, but will be more indicative of the flexibility of rayon prices when they are later compared with cyclical swings in the price series of competing fibers and with those in the rayon production series. Some estimate can be made of the sensitivity of rayon priccs to general economic fluctuations, however, by comparing the timing of rayon price movements with some acceptable bench mark of economic activity. If, for example, the peak and trough dates of Professor Mitchell's reference cycles[16] for this time period be superimposed upon the rayon price cyclical pattern, an extremely high degree of conformity may be noted. The few instances in which peaks and troughs of rayon price cycles do not precisely coincide with those of the reference cycle are almost completely eliminated when peaks and troughs obtained by fitting the same trend lines to average monthly instead of average annual prices are used. This high degree of covariation with respect to timing between the cyclical price pattern for rayon and Professor Mitchell's reference cycles also helps justify the type of trend line employed; for not only does the compound interest rate curve apparently fit the data best, but it also yields a cyclical pattern that coincides closely with general economic fluctuations.

. . . . . .

Relative to the three clearly indicated directional movements in the rayon price series described above, a few comments should be

[14] See Appendix C. The trend line probably should terminate in 1934; 1935 was included so that both the initial and terminal phases of the cycles would lie above the indicated trend line.

[15] The fitted curve obviously overstates the 1935 trend ratio. For this year, therefore, the ratio to average price is probably more descriptive of the cyclical behavior.

[16] Arthur F. Burns and Wesley C. Mitchell, *Measuring Business Cycles* (New York, National Bureau of Economic Research, 1946), Table 16, p. 78.

made upon the relationship between the number of firms in the rayon industry and prices. The contrasting behavior of rayon price before and after 1920 occasionally has been used to demonstrate the differences between competitive and monopoly price behavior. The trend from 1911 to 1920 was sharply upward, rising from $1.85 per pound to $6.00 per pound. Over this period the Cross and Bevan, and Topham patent rights gave American Viscose a complete monopoly over domestic production. From 1920 to 1933 the trend in rayon price was steadily downward, falling from $6.00 per pound to $0.50 per pound. Fifteen new rayon producers entered the industry between 1920 and 1931, after the expiration of the American Viscose Corporation's patent rights. Since 1931, no new firms have entered the industry and price has remained fairly stable with no perceptible upward or downward trend.

In a special report before the Temporary National Economic Committee Congressional Committee, the Federal Trade Commission stated, "It is of interest to correlate the rayon production and consumption shown heretofore with the price of rayon as these price trends definitely reflect the influence of the early monopolistic position of American Viscose Corporation and the later competitive conditions of the industry." [17] It is important to point out, however, that much of this contrast in price behavior can be explained in terms of differences in the general economic conditions of the two time periods that are unrelated to the monopoly question.

Between 1914 and 1920 the price of virtually all manufactured goods more than doubled. The price index of semimanufactured goods increased from 70 to 198, or by 185 per cent. The wholesale price index increased by approximately the same per cent. The behavior of silk prices over this period, however, is even more relevant than the behavior of aggregative price indexes. The average price per pound for silk in 1914 was $3.69; by January 1920, the price of silk had risen to $17.46, an increase of over 378 per cent. Over the same period the price of rayon increased 206 per cent.

Hence, to explain the contrasting trend movements in rayon prices for these two time periods solely in terms of the extent of monopoly power ignores the consequences of other important economic

[17] F. T. C., *Investments, Profits, and Rates of Return,* part 31, p. 17984. See also, Clair Wilcox, *Competition and Monopoly in American Industry,* pp. 202–205; and *Fortune,* July 1937, pp. 40, 106.

phenomena that existed apart from the number of firms in the industry. From 1915 to 1920 the Viscose Corporation was realizing frictional gains and enjoying the fruits of the Schumpeterian innovator[18] in a more real sense than it was reaping the extraordinary profits of an established patent-protected monopoly. The rayon industry had, after several unsuccessful attempts, been permanently established in the United States only four years by 1915, just in time to ride the crest of wartime inflation. In spite of the fact that American Viscose more than quadrupled its output between 1914 and 1920, demand far outstripped supply at prevailing prices due to interruptions in foreign trade.

Moreover, since the time lag between a decision to enter the rayon yarn producing industry and a finished plant in full operation is from three to four years, the productive capacity over this period would not have been greatly increased had the Viscose Corporation's patent rights expired several years before they did. It is important to point out also that the decline in silk prices after January 1920 and the resumption of foreign trade forced the price of rayon from $6.00 per pound down to $2.55 per pound while the American Viscose Corporation was still the sole producer of rayon in the United States. Fundamentally, therefore, a comparison of price behavior over these two time periods is not one of monopolistic as against competitive pricing, but a comparison of two periods characterized by different economic forces.

This brief digression to meet the argument advanced in the Federal Trade Commission's report and elsewhere has been made at this point because much of what follows (and, in fact, much of what has already been stated) will bear out the thesis that the price of rayon is a function of many factors other than the number of firms in the industry. Hence, there are objections to the imputation of an upward secular trend in rayon prices prior to 1920 to monopoly on the one hand and the downward secular movement since 1920 to competition on the other.

C. Short-Run Aspects of Rayon Production

No published rayon monthly production series extends back beyond 1940; however, data are available from which a monthly

[18] Joseph A. Schumpeter, *Capitalism, Socialism and Democracy* (New York, Harper and Bros., 1942), chaps. vii and viii; see esp. fn. 5, pp. 90–91.

production series on an *actual* poundage basis can be computed from 1930 to date.[19] It is emphasized that the series to be used is on an actual rather than a standard poundage basis because a small error is introduced; namely, no allowance is made for changes in the average denier of the yarn spun over the period. All rayon yarn, as previously explained, may be converted to homogeneous units by expressing all pounds in terms of 150-denier yarn. The method employed in the industry is to divide actual pounds for a given time period by the average denier spun for that time period, and to multiply the resultant by 150, as follows:

$$\text{Standard Pounds}_t = \frac{\text{Output in Actual Pounds}_t}{\text{Average Denier Spun}_t} \times 150$$

This conversion supposedly takes due cognizance of yardage differences per pound among the various deniers, whereas actual poundage data do not. Hence, when the average denier spun is less than 150, actual poundage data give the production series a downward bias, and when the average denier is greater than 150, a corresponding upward bias is introduced.

Monthly production data cannot be converted to a standard poundage basis since only annual denier spun data are available. There would be several objections to the conversion, however, even if it could be performed. From the standpoint of materials, the quantity required in the production of all pounds of rayon is about the same; the diameter of the thread is made larger or smaller than that of 150-denier yarn simply by altering the size of the spinnerette orifices through which the viscose is forced. Moreover, a portion of the direct labor used in producing a pound of rayon is the same regardless of denier spun and, in many operations where labor varies inversely with the denier of the yarn, adjustment of machine speeds, within narrow limits, somewhat reduces the error introduced in the actual poundage data.

A theoretically homogeneous rayon output series, therefore, would fall somewhere between the actual poundage series and the

[19] The *Rayon Organon* contains a monthly domestic deliveries series, producers' month-end stocks on hand (since 1930 only), and domestic producers' monthly exports. The three series are given for acetate yarn separately and for viscose and cuprammonium yarn combined. Since cuprammonium makes up only 1 or 2 per cent of the total, the second series may be treated as all viscose. A monthly production series may be quite easily obtained from the following equation:

Monthly production (actual pounds) = domestic deliveries + producers' exports ± monthly inventory change.

standard poundage series.[20] Since the average denier spun between 1930 and 1944 was a little less than 150-denier, the actual poundage series will understate monthly output over this period. For the most part, however, the understatement will seldom exceed 5 per cent and in no case will the short-run movements of the series, which are of chief interest, be significantly disturbed.

Monthly production, producers' month-end inventories, and monthly deliveries (sales) for viscose and acetate rayon combined appear in Chart 5. The relative stability of the production series

Chart 5

Monthly Rayon Yarn Production, Sales, and Inventories, 1930–1941

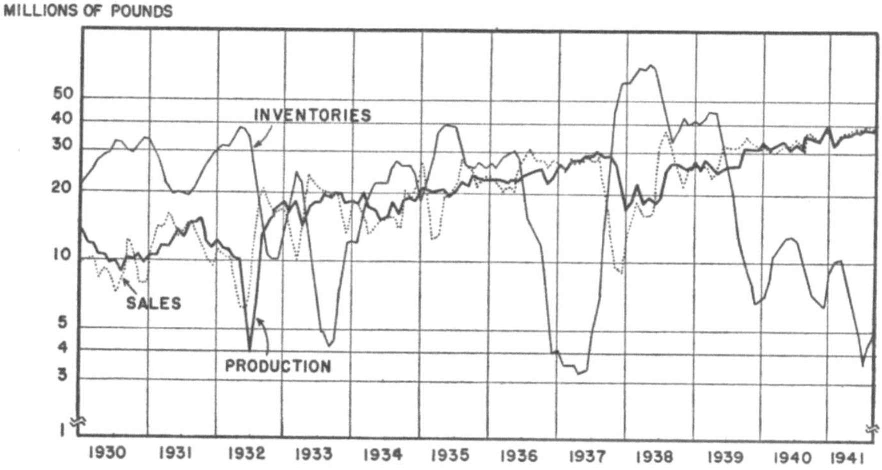

Note: Logarithmic Vertical Scale.
Source: *Rayon Organon.*

when compared with the sales series, and the highly oscillatory inventory series, indicate the sluggishness with which production schedules react to short-run demand conditions. The production series, except for fairly well-defined business cycles, is dampened to the extent that it suggests the trend about which the sales series fluctuates. The small oscillations can easily be accounted for by denier change-overs, labor difficulties, the variation in operating hours per month,[21] minor power failures, and so forth.

[20] The Textile Economics Bureau, Inc. uses the converted series for computing output per man-hour in the rayon industry; the Bureau of Labor Statistics uses the unconverted data. A discussion of the merits of each may be found in the September 1946 *Rayon Organon*, pp. 140–148.

[21] Rayon plants operate on a continuous 24-hour-day basis. Thus, rayon plants operate 672 hours in February but 744 hours in a 31-day month.

There is no apparent purposive production curtailment to meet decreases in demand until such decreases persist over a period of several months. Hence, inventories are permitted to fluctuate to cushion short-run variations in deliveries. The insensitivity of production schedules to short-run demand conditions is attested by the fact that the rayon industry operated at virtually 100 per cent capacity from June 1933 to March 1934, from December 1934 to November 1937, and except for two months in 1940, from October 1939 to March 1949.[22] In the midsummer of 1940 the industry operated at from 3 per cent to 13 per cent under capacity chiefly because of a mild pulp shortage and peak summer vacations. Yet, over these periods, demand shows considerable month-to-month variation.

Such relative stability of output over short time intervals is to be more or less expected in an industry where capacity output has not often greatly exceeded demand for more than five or six months at a time, where the supply curve for the industry is highly inelastic in the short-run beyond the point of "technical" installed capacity, and where total unit costs rise rapidly with decreased output under given wage and material costs.[23] There is considerable evidence, however, in addition to the statistical features of the production series, that producers hesitate to curtail output when initially faced with decreases in demand. For example, between January and February 1935, deliveries decreased by 30 per cent, and between February and March, by approximately another 30 per cent. In a market review of the first quarter of 1935, the *Organon* commented, "A continued lull may bring on curtailment, but there is no feeling [among producers] that immediate curtailment is necessary." [24] This attitude prevailed in spite of the fact that the weaving industry, the rayon industry's largest customer, had curtailed operations about 40 per cent. Two months later, after the volume of sales had sub-

[22] A computation of seasonal indexes for the production series reveals little or no variation in output to meet seasonal demand variations. Indexes for May, June, and July are slightly less than those for other months, but this is probably a result of heavy summer vacation schedules. Capacity figures were assembled from operation reports made in the *Rayon Organon*, *Silk and Rayon Journal*, the rayon section of *Textile World*, and other sources such as individual companies' annual reports, newspapers, etc. The duplicative nature of per cent capacity operations reported by independent sources and their agreement with reported *installed* capacity data for the industry indicate that they are substantially correct. For further per cent of capacity operating data, see "Cyclical Price-Production Patterns," this chapter.

[23] See Chap. 8.

[24] *Rayon Organon*, April, p. 136.

stantially increased, the *Organon* announced that "producers have definitely shelved their ideas of embarking upon a curtailment plan, output still exceeds sales, but by such a small margin it is of little concern."[25] Similar statements appearing elsewhere in the trade literature indicate a decided reluctance on the part of rayon producers to adjust price or production schedules to short-run market oscillations.

D. Price and Production in the Textile Cycle

The annual rayon production series (1919–1941) in Chart 6 shows a trough in all even-numbered years after 1919 except 1922, 1926, and 1940. For the most part, however, the troughs are practically imperceptible except for the years 1924, 1932, and 1938, in which the downward movement of the textile cycle coincided with a general business recession. Nevertheless, they occur with such regularity that they hardly can be dismissed as random fluctuations. It must be assumed, therefore, that they represent purposive alterations, however slight, in rayon production schedules. Of the eleven even-numbered years between 1919 and 1941, eight coincide with troughs in the production series; of the eleven odd-numbered years (1919 excluded), eight coincide with production peaks. The peaks and troughs in the production series are so subdued relative to those in the deliveries series that they hardly can be used to emphasize the sensitivity of production schedules to shifts in market demand but, on balance, they appear with more regularity than those in the price series.

[25] *Rayon Organon,* June, p. 116. The behavior of price and output in the spring of 1935 does not conform to the cyclical price-output pattern developed in this chapter. Unlike the pattern, output over this period was maintained and a price reduction was used to equilibrate production and sales. The hesitancy on the part of producers to curtail output in this particular instance may have been influenced by a ten-week strike shutdown at Industrial Rayon's Cleveland plant that decreased output for the industry by 0.5 million pounds in May and by approximately 1.0 million pounds by June. This involuntary decrease in production might have supplanted in part the plans to curtail output that producers had supposedly held under consideration since early spring. It is significant to note that this slump in the rayon market is the only instance marked by a price cut not accompanied by noticeable production curtailment initiated by the major producers. There are scattered fragments of evidence that some of the smaller producers were faced with such large inventories that they curtailed output from 5 per cent to 15 per cent. The larger producers, led by American Viscose, initiated a 10 per cent price cut on April 17, 1935, after it was suspected that small producers had been shading prices for about two weeks in order to increase sales. The large producers, however, maintained their output schedules.

Chart 6

Trend in Annual Rayon Yarn Production, 1919–1941

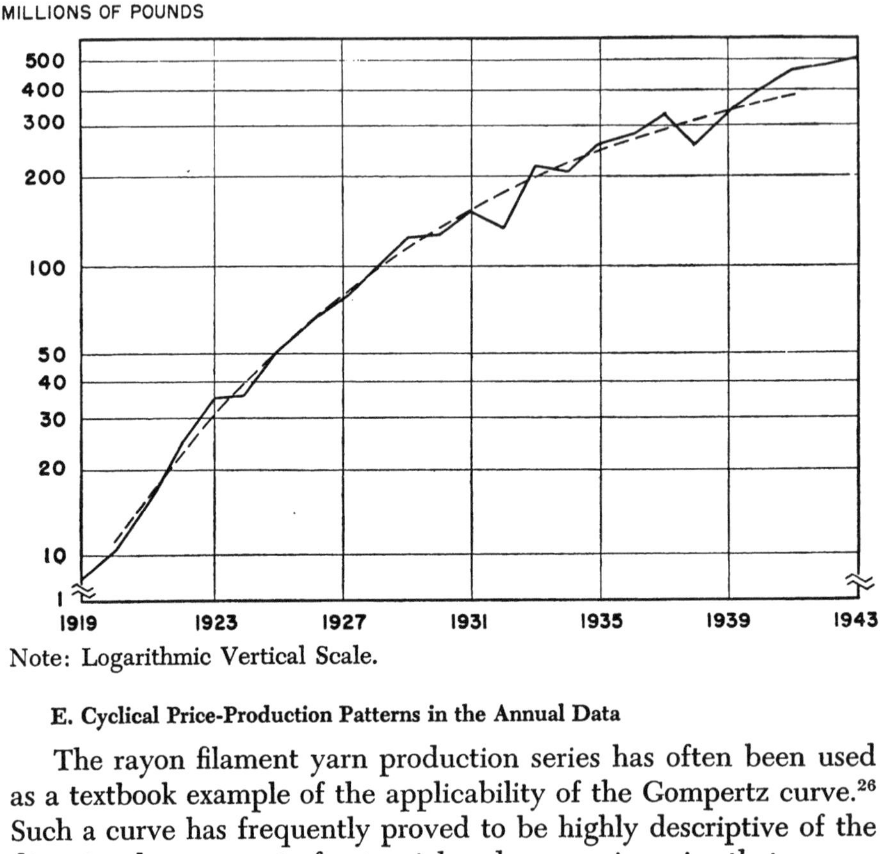

Note: Logarithmic Vertical Scale.

E. Cyclical Price-Production Patterns in the Annual Data

The rayon filament yarn production series has often been used as a textbook example of the applicability of the Gompertz curve.[26] Such a curve has frequently proved to be highly descriptive of the directional movement of actuarial and economic series that are related in some way to growth. Whether or not there are economic justifications for assuming that the rayon industry has followed a "law of growth," the appropriateness of the Gompertz curve as a statistical measure of trend in the rayon production series is hardly subject to controversy.[27]

[26] F. C. Mills, *Statistical Methods Applied to Economics and Business* (rev. ed.; New York: Henry Holt, 1938), Appendix D, p. 675.

[27] The rayon yarn production series demonstrates the dependency of the type of trend line upon the time period used. For example, a modified exponential curve fits the data from 1919 to 1929 rather well; on the other hand, a projection of the Gompertz curve beyond 1940 does not fit the data for the war and postwar years. As Professor Mills has stated, however, "within the limits of the observations . . . the Gompertz curve serves as a satisfactory measure of trend." Mills, *Statistical Methods,* Appendix D, p. 675.

So that the cyclical aspects of the rayon production series may be more closely examined, a Gompertz curve is fitted to the series in Chart 6 [28] and the resultant production trend ratios are compared with those of the rayon price series in Chart 7. Output and price, for the most part, appear to follow a similar cyclical pattern with respect to timing and amplitude. With but one exception (1926) in the trend adjusted production series, both series show peaks and troughs located approximately at the turning points of the "reference cycle."

There is a persistent tendency, however, for output trend ratios to fall above price trend ratios in odd-numbered years and below price trend ratios in even-numbered years. This relationship holds

Chart 7

Peaks and Troughs in Trend-Adjusted Rayon Production and Price Series and in Mitchell's Reference Cycles, 1919–1941

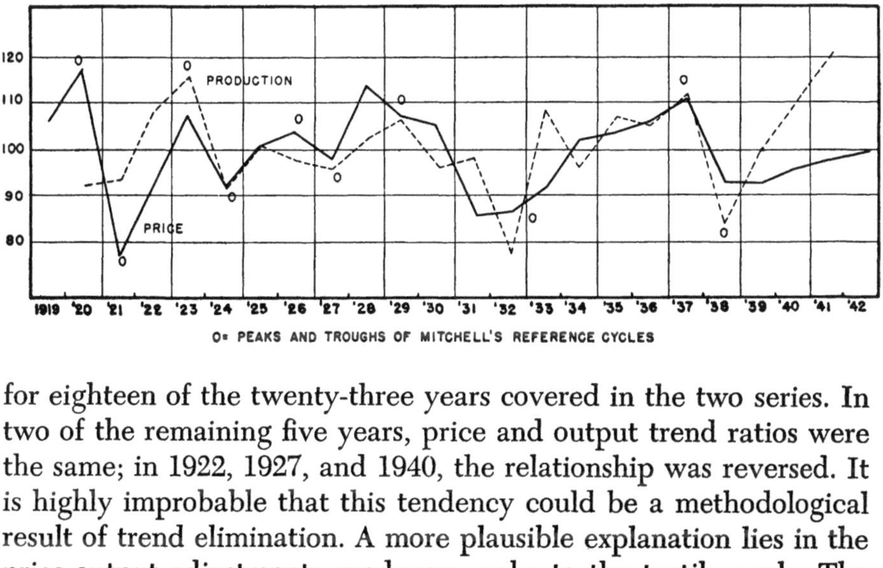

for eighteen of the twenty-three years covered in the two series. In two of the remaining five years, price and output trend ratios were the same; in 1922, 1927, and 1940, the relationship was reversed. It is highly improbable that this tendency could be a methodological result of trend elimination. A more plausible explanation lies in the price-output adjustments producers make to the textile cycle. The textile cycle is more apparent in the trend-eliminated production

[28] The trend values computed by Professor Mills up to 1938 were used. Trend values for the three remaining prewar years were obtained from his equation:

$$\text{Log } y = 5.822848 - 1.777493\ (.911351)^x$$

where y is the production trend value and x is the deviation in years from an origin at 1920. If it were desirable to take the trend through the war years, it is obvious from inspection that it would be necessary to calculate a new set of constants for the equation. Since this part of the study is concerned with price-output behavior indicative of the policy of producers, it is unnecessary to deal with the period in which policy was determined by governmental authority.

series than in the trend-eliminated price series,[29] thus producing peaks within the cyclical pattern in all odd-numbered years except 1921 and 1927, and troughs in all even-numbered years except 1922 and 1928. Another manifestation of the effect of the textile cycle upon the production series is the appearance of an additional cycle with a peak in 1933 and a trough in 1934. This secondary cyclical behavior superimposed upon the broader cycles in the production series distorts but does not obliterate the covariation between rayon prices and rayon output.[30]

Although conclusions concerning price and production policy to be drawn from the timing and amplitude of price and production cycles must await an examination of available monthly data, there is no evidence in the annual data that rayon prices are maintained at the expense of wide fluctuations in output over the course of the business cycle. The lack of such evidence in an industry which has had a concentration ratio greater than 75 per cent throughout most of its history, and in which price leadership of the largest producer is usually accepted, has some significance. In the trend-eliminated data, however, there is some evidence that output is more responsive than price to the textile cycle.

The price and production policy of rayon producers, to the extent that it is admissible to refer to them collectively, to be inferred from the foregoing analysis is as follows: There is no tendency to alter either price or output to meet short-run demand fluctuations that occur within a year. Statistical and other evidence would suggest that irregular and seasonal demand shifts are recognized as transient market elements that can be absorbed by inventory fluctuations and call for no revamping of price or production schedules. Demand fluctuations evidenced by the two-year cycle in the rayon deliveries series call for greater revision of output than price schedules. Over the course of broader cyclical movements, output and price seem to move together. No differences between the two series with respect to timing and amplitude are perceptible in the annual data.

[29] If even and odd-year "indexes" are computed from the average price and production trend ratios, the following results are obtained:

	Odd Year	*Even Year*
Production	100	91
Price	100	95

[30] A scatter diagram of price and output trend ratios indicates a fairly high degree of correlation between the two but there are several extreme items.

The fact that output is more sensitive than price to the textile cycle, however, strongly suggests that a closer examination of the data should reveal a timing difference; namely, that price adjustment lags production adjustment under the impact of shifting demand over the business cycle. For, unless some reason can be found for according rayon company executives the ability to differentiate always between textile and business cycle effects (and this is unlikely), producers' behavior, to be consistent with the results of the foregoing statistical analysis, would be as follows: A decrease in orders not usually encountered in the seasonal or irregular fluctuations within the year would be met by curtailing production. This would seem to follow since output is more sensitive than price to the textile cycle. Should the decrease in orders be, in fact, a result of a two-year cyclical downturn, business will shortly recover and price will have been left largely undisturbed. But should the decrease in orders prove to be a result of a business recession, price will be reduced also, but in the meantime output will have already been curtailed. Hence, unless rayon producers are unusually adept at judging the particular type of cycle responsible for fluctuations in orders, it would be expected that output adjustment would precede price adjustment (except, of course, in cases where orders increase and the industry is already operating at maximum capacity). The greater part of the remainder of this chapter will be devoted to an examination of this hypothesis through the available monthly data.

F. Cyclical Price-Production Patterns in the Monthly Data

Several comments must be made by way of qualification of the monthly data that are to be used. Most of the available price data are list-price quotations. It was pointed out in Chapter 5 that list prices, although sufficiently reliable in most instances, are not altogether to be trusted in periods of extreme prosperity or depression, particularly the latter.

Small producers have resorted to off-list pricing when faced with the alternatives of maintaining sales volume by selling below list price but inviting price retaliation from the large producers on the one hand, or risking serious loss of sales by adhering to list prices on the other. Price-shading was obvious in the declining rayon market of 1930–1932, and less noticeable in 1934 and 1938. Moreover, premiums over list price were demanded by some producers in the

1937 prosperity and in the postwar shortage of 1947 there were small discrepancies among producers in quoted prices.

Since 1932, however, there is little indication that deviations from list price have been quantitatively significant. Yet, such deviations as have occurred necessitate a cautious approach to questions to be answered on the basis of list-price behavior since they conceal the true timing of price changes. The extent to which off-list selling has obscured the timing of major cyclical price movements since 1932 is believed to be slight for several reasons: (1) Price-shading is usually resorted to only after the market situation has become fairly intensified; (2) there is considerable evidence that large producers quickly detect the price-shading of smaller producers through keeping close check upon fabricators' mill margins,[31] the loss of orders from repeat customers, and rumors of price-shading spread by fabricators; and (3) the quantity of yarn sold at prices other than list price should have been quite small after 1932 since such large producers as American Viscose, Du Pont, Celanese, North American, American Enka, Tubize, and Industrial Rayon appear to have held rather closely to published price lists. These producers have accounted for over 90 per cent of total sales.

In spite of the apparent insignificance of off-list selling since the depression, it is quite obvious that all price-shading cannot be detected. The mere use of off-list prices behooves the seller to employ extreme secrecy, otherwise the anticipated gains are wiped out. Moreover, some detected price-shading probably goes unpublicized because the large producers have no desire to admit to the consuming fabricators that the market is softening. To do so sets up expectations of a price reduction and, therefore, leads to declining sales for all producers. In such instances the large firms might refrain from retaliating with lower list prices and hope that the "price chiseler" will voluntarily mend his ways or that the market will soon revive and eliminate the downward pressure on list price.

The precise extent and nature of price-shading in the rayon industry, therefore, would be extremely difficult if not impossible to determine. All of the available evidence indicates that list prices are trustworthy in moderately normal times but are virtually meaning-

[31] For example, it was observed that fabricated rayon sold for $0.75 per pound in May 1932, while the list price of filament yarn was also $0.75 per pound. The Textile Economics Bureau, Inc. pointed out that this was almost conclusive proof that some small yarn producers were selling below list price. *Rayon Organon,* June 1932.

less for the years 1930–1932. The sporadic price-shading which occurred in 1934 and 1938 was quickly detected and brought about downward revisions in list price. Qualitatively, it is doubtful that a more thorough investigation of off-list pricing would reveal much more than this.

A monthly production series for both viscose and acetate yarn after January 1930 can be computed on an actual poundage basis from monthly domestic deliveries, stock changes, and domestic producers' exports. It was pointed out earlier in this chapter that the use of actual instead of standard poundage data does not seriously impair the analysis. This is particularly true for the viscose yarn series since the average denier spun between 1930 and 1942 did not deviate substantially from 150. If this series could have been converted to a standard denier basis, the upward trend between 1932 and 1943 would have been somewhat more pronounced but the difference would have been small. In any case, the cyclical movement in the two series would be approximately the same. It is this aspect of the series that is of paramount interest.

The nature of the production series makes it fairly easy to locate periods in which output was curtailed. It will be observed (see Chart 8) that the series is not subject to frequent broad fluctuations but

Chart 8

Month End Inventories, Monthly Production and Prices, Viscose and Acetate Rayon Yarn, 1930–1949

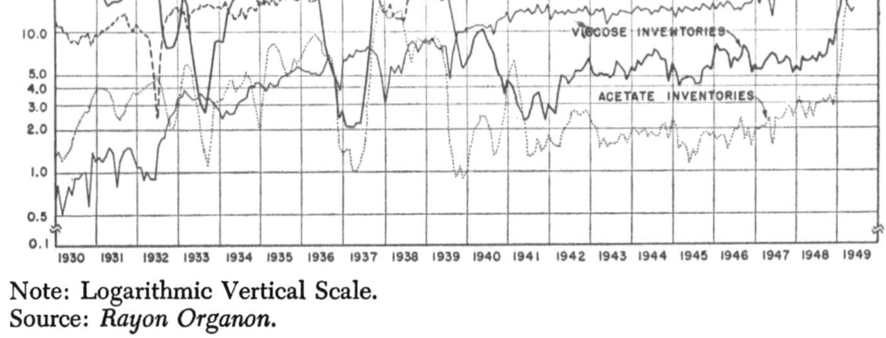

Note: Logarithmic Vertical Scale.
Source: *Rayon Organon.*

progresses along several fairly stable plateaus. The almost total absence of sharp peaks from the series is accounted for by the upward inflexibility of installed capacity and the fact that the industry has not yet suffered from long-run over capacity.

Rayon plants are designed to run at rather rigidly defined machine speeds on a twenty-four-hour-day basis. Any increase in machine speed much beyond optimum speed results in a decrease in value product because of the high percentage of second grade and inferior yarn produced. Hence, a violent shift in the demand curve to the right at a time all plant equipment in the industry is being utilized will induce only a negligible increase in output.[32] Therefore, a smooth line drawn through and connecting the first months of flat segments of the monthly production series would indicate the approximate capacity output for the industry at any given time and, correspondingly, periods in which production dips below such an imaginary line can be viewed as periods of output curtailment.

Hence, a comparison of price and output behavior in the neighborhood of the downward deviations from capacity output should give some insight into rayon producers' price and production policy. Such a comparison will necessarily be of an approximate nature and limited to the periods in which production was unmistakably curtailed on the initiative of producers, that is, decreases in output of a non-purposive nature, such as those which result from strikes, floods, power failures, denier change-overs, etc., should not be included.

Generally, it is not difficult to differentiate between purposive and non-purposive output curtailments of viscose rayon. The latter are much less perceptible by inspection and, for the most part, are identified in the trade literature. Significant curtailments in viscose yarn output due to external causes have been relatively infrequent, consisting chiefly of the April floods in 1936 and labor strikes at several plants in 1935 and 1937. Non-purposive curtailments of acetate yarn output are more pronounced because one firm, which until 1939 had only one plant, accounted for from 80 per cent to 90 per cent of the total acetate yarn output over this period. Hence, any forced shutdown of the Celanese plant which lasted for a reasonable

[32] This is currently more applicable to the viscose than to the acetate plants. Recent experiments in the acetate sector of the industry show that capacity may be increased considerably simply by enlarging the air chambers in which coagulation takes place and by speeding up the spinning machines. This was not true, however, over most of the period covered in this study.

length of time is reflected in the output series. Examples are labor strikes in November and December 1937 and August and September 1939.

The significant periods of purposive production curtailment are readily distinguishable in Chart 8, where appear the price, inventory, and output series for both viscose and acetate rayon yarn. Viscose yarn output was curtailed during 1930 and up to October 1931. The reversal of the inventory swing in September 1931 resulted in a new period of curtailed output that commenced in October 1931 and lasted until about October 1932.

The industry produced at 100 per cent capacity until January 1933, but rising inventories led to a brief, mild reduction in output from February until June. From June 1933 to March 1934, output was again at 100 per cent capacity. In March, production curtailment commenced and lasted until October 1935. Production schedules were increased very gradually, however, after September 1934, and it is difficult to tell precisely when the industry again reached full capacity operations. It was stated in the October 1935 issue of *Textile World* that the industry had reached capacity operations.[33] This seems to agree with the production data but the industry operated, except for a very mild decrease in output in late spring and early summer, close to full capacity during the entire year of 1935.

Production continued at maximum capacity from October 1935 until the 1937–38 depression. Commencing with October 1937, output was sharply curtailed, and capacity operations were not reached again until August 1939. The industry has operated at virtually full capacity since that date with the exception of a 5 to 10 per cent reduction in output in midsummer, 1940, and again in the spring of 1949.

The relationships among the rayon price, output, and inventory series are sufficiently consistent to indicate rather clearly some aspects of the industry's price and output policy. It is apparent that price and output are greatly cushioned by inventory changes from sharp impacts of fluctuating demand. This is evident from the relative stability of the output and price series and the highly cyclical inventory series. Whereas relative fluctuations in inventories in manufacturing industries generally are greater than relative fluctuations in price and output, fluctuations in rayon inventories are considerably greater, in comparison with those in price and especially

[33] *Textile World,* October 1935, rayon section.

output, than would ordinarily be expected. An extreme example may be found in the last half of 1937 and the early months of 1938: Inventories increased from 2.1 million pounds to 63 million pounds, an increase of 3000 per cent; over the same period price fell only 14 per cent and output was decreased 33.5 per cent.

Furthermore, a rise in inventories substantially above the monthly production rate usually heralds a gradual reduction in both price and the rate of output; whereas, when inventories fall substantially below the monthly production rate, full capacity operations are resumed and previously initiated price cuts are partially restored. This tendency is due to the fact that "normal inventories" in the industry are considered to be approximately four or five weeks' supply, based upon deliveries over the preceding twelve months, or approximately one month's production. The time lag between the sustained directional movement of inventories and changes in price and output, however, is usually several months. Moreover, some tolerance for seasonal demand shifts obviously is allowed.

In Table 16 the viscose yarn production series shown in Chart 8 has been broken into segments corresponding to periods in which production was decreased from capacity or near capacity operations to maximum curtailment, and from maximum curtailment back to capacity operations.[34] The percentage change in output and price and the time such changes occurred are shown for periods corresponding to each segment. The production data, of course, permit only the designation of the month in which each turning point is located; although the first day of the month is used when it appears to be a better "guess" than the fifteenth.

In every market recession producers have curtailed output before they have reduced list price. Even in those instances where list-price behavior can be adjusted for known off-list selling, the time lag is

[34] The trade literature does not always make it clear whether 100 per cent "installed capacity" or 100 per cent "operating capacity" is used as a basis for the computation of per cent of capacity operations. The latter is approximately 90 per cent of the former due to routine maintenance, denier change-over, unbalanced plant, etc. One hundred per cent "installed capacity" is based upon continuous production of 150-denier yarn. The percentage change in output in most instances, however, could be checked with per cent of capacity operations reported in the *Rayon Organon*, the *Rayon Journal*, *Textile World*, and other sources. In all cases but one the differences were negligible; the production series shows that output was reduced 33.3 per cent between November 1937 and July 1938, whereas all other sources showed 40 per cent curtailment.

TABLE 16

A Comparison of the Timing and Percentage Change between Production and Price Movements for Viscose Yarn over Several Specific Cycles, 1930–1949

Production Change: Time	Production Change: %	Price Change: Time	Price Change: %	Price Lag Behind Production (Months)	Per Cent Production Curtailed at Time of Price Change
PERIODS OF RECESSION					
Dec. 1, 1929[a] to Dec. 1930	37.5	July 22, 1930 Jan. 9, 1931	34.8	7.75	31.7
Nov. 1, 1931 to July 1932	81.5	May 26, 1932 June 21, 1932	26.7	6.90	31.3
Feb. 1, 1933 to Apr. 1933	28.0	April 3, 1933	16.7	2.10	20.0
Mar. 1, 1934 to Sept. 1934	21.5	May 24, 1934	15.4	2.80	18.5
Nov. 1, 1937 to July 1938	33.3	Jan. 14, 1938 Jan. 21, 1938 May 20, 1938	22.2	2.50	37.0
Apr. 1939 to June 1939	16.2	None	—	—	—
May 1940 to July 1940	13.5	None	—	—	—
March 1, 1949 to June 1949	20.0[b]	May 19, 1949	8.5	2.60	20.0
PERIODS OF RECOVERY					
Jan. 1, 1931 to Oct. 1931	68.8	None	—	—	—
Aug. 1, 1932 to Jan. 1933	500.0	Aug. 29, 1932	9.1	0.90	46.6
May 1, 1933 to Oct. 1933	47.6	Apr. 3, 1933 Apr. 26, 1933 July 27, 1933	30.0	−0.90[c]	24.6
Oct. 1, 1934 to Mar. 1935	31.2	Dec. 13, 1934 Dec. 31, 1934	9.1	2.40	14.3
July 1, 1939 to Nov. 1939	29.6	Sept. 2, 1939	3.9	2.10	17.5
Aug. 1, 1940 to Oct. 1940	15.6	None	—	—	—

[a] Output curtailment was assumed to have commenced in December since deliveries began to decline in November 1929. Monthly production data are not available prior to 1930. The last price change before 1930 was initiated in June 1929.

[b] Estimated. See financial section of *New York Times*, March 5, 1949, and the *Rayon Organon*, April 1949, p. 50.

[c] Led.

significant, varying from 6.75 months to 1.1 months.[35] The lag has diminished considerably, however, since 1932.

Moreover, there appears to be a moderately well-defined limit to the extent producers can curtail output before they reduce price. On the average, after output has been curtailed roughly about 25 per

[35] A comparison of the list prices and actual prices charged by large producers from November 1931 through December 1933 (see Table 9) shows that list-price reductions lagged behind actual price reductions by about one month during the 1930–1932 recession.

cent, a price reduction follows.[36] This varies from 18 per cent to 37 per cent, as would be expected, since the limits would be contingent upon the rate of change in inventory levels and upon factor price behavior over the period, particularly the behavior of wages. The lower limit of about 18 per cent is further indicated, however, by the fact that prices were not reduced when output was curtailed 16.2 per cent between April and June 1939, and 13.5 per cent between May and July 1940. The average price-breaking point, with the exception of one price change in 1932,[37] holds as well for upswings as downswings. Generally, price reductions initiated during a recession are partially restored during the subsequent recovery after the rate of output has been brought up to from 76 per cent to 86 per cent of capacity.

A comparison of the percentages by which output and prices are curtailed under falling demand conditions shows that, in most instances, output is reduced substantially more than list price. The difference is partly reduced, however, when allowances are made for off-list selling. For example, between February and July 1932, low net realized price for 150-denier viscose yarn fell 34.1 per cent whereas the list price fell only 26.7 per cent. Similarly, between December 1932 and April 1933, low net realized price fell 18.2 per cent while list price fell only 16.7 per cent.[38] This does not contradict the relationship between price and production cycles discovered in the annual data earlier in the analysis. The monthly data reveal occasional sharp contractions of output which, since they have been of relatively short duration, have had very little effect upon the annual production data.

The difference between the percentage change in output and the percentage change in price in periods of recovery is even greater. Production schedules are usually stepped up to capacity operations

[36] Since a good theory should yield accurate predictions, it may be of interest to the reader to point out that, by employing the lower limit of the price-breaking point computed in the original study from prewar data, the May 1949 rayon price reduction could have been predicted from the per cent of capacity operations and inventory data.

[37] In August 1932, output was still curtailed 46.6 per cent when price was increased by 9.1 per cent. The insignificance of the magnitude of the price increase ($0.05 per pound) when viewed against the preceding price reductions and the rapidly changing market at the time, which reduced inventories from 30 million pounds to a little over 10 million pounds in less than three months, justifies the omission of this increase as an exception.

[38] See Table 9 for high and low net realized prices from November 1931 through December 1933.

quickly but price increases are initiated cautiously. This tendency has reflected in a downward secular trend in rayon prices. Price decreases have rarely occurred except under the impetus of a declining rayon market. The price reduction initiated in the market decline is practically never fully restored in the following market revival.

The foregoing conclusions concerning price and output behavior for viscose yarn also hold true for the acetate sector of the rayon industry. The data for acetate yarn are shown in Chart 8 for purposes of comparison. It is hardly necessary to repeat the above procedure since the patterns are so strikingly similar. The acetate production series, however, is not, for reasons previously given, as stable as the viscose production series; hence, the purposive and non-purposive reductions in output are more difficult to separate. Moreover, no per cent of capacity operations data are available for acetate yarn with which percentages computed from the production data might be checked. The covariation of the three series between the two types of yarn, however, is apparent.

G. Differences in Output Behavior among Producers

The inadequacy of available firm data has necessitated an industry approach to price-output relationships in the rayon industry. Before such results as those obtained above can be meaningfully interpreted, however, the practices of individual firms must be taken into account. With respect to price, intercompany comparisons were made in the chapter on price leadership.

It has already been pointed out that inventory fluctuations greatly cushion the immediate impact of shifting demand upon price and output. Throughout the expansionary stage of the twenties, however, demand for rayon was equal to supply at prices considerably in excess of a long-run equilibrium price so that fairly healthy profits, near-capacity operations, and "normal" inventories were accepted by the large- and medium-size producers as a matter of course. Consequently, there have been only a few notable contractions of output in the rayon industry.

The first such instance of overcapacity was experienced in the 1929–1932 depression. When the initial impact of the recession was felt in the rayon industry in late 1929 and early 1930 there was a general tendency for large producers to curtail output in order to stabilize price, and for small producers to shade prices and maintain capacity output.[39] These practices are fully and freely discussed in the trade literature and are evident from the available production data. For example, in 1929, output for the industry was over 75 per cent of installed capacity but American Viscose and Du Pont curtailed output by 36 per cent and 32 per cent, respectively.[40] These two companies are the largest producers in the industry. Between December 1929 and July 1930, the industry curtailed output by 35 per cent. Over the same period, however, American Viscose curtailed production by 38 per cent and Du Pont by 50 per cent. Industrial, a medium-size producer, curtailed output by only 22 per cent and both Tubize and Skenandoa increased production (see Chart 9).

In commenting on the market outlook for rayon in the spring of 1930, *Textile World* pointed out that whereas some producers were adopting a cautious output policy, having cut schedules about 15 per cent, this policy was not generally apparent, but limited only to the large producers. The big problem that confronted the industry was how to spread curtailment equitably among producers — there was a great need for an organization.[41] In his editorial directed against prevailing practices in the rayon industry, John Black, Assistant Editor of *Textile World*, stated, "The July price cut [led by American Viscose, July 22] was aimed at price cutting and at those who did not follow production curtailment, but operated at one-hundred per cent capacity and sold at below list-price at the expense of those who followed the curtailment plan." [42] This tendency persisted throughout 1930. In November, the large producers were operating at 75 per cent of capacity or less, but a number of the smaller producers were maintaining capacity output.[43]

Whether through an agreement, as charged by the Federal Trade Commission, or through more subtle means which stem from recognition of the interdependence of firms in an oligopolistic industry, the pattern of behavior altered as the depression deepened. By the last quarter of 1931, the tendency toward output curtailment was much more general. A market survey conducted during the second week of November by the rayon division of the staff of *Textile World* indicated "that small producers are also following the

[39] This practice led to the trade association activity previously discussed and precipitated an investigation by the Federal Trade Commission. See F. T. C. *Decisions*, vol. XXV, Viscose Company *et al.*, Docket No. 2161.

[40] *Textile World*, February 1, 1930, p. 123; and February 1, 1931, rayon section.

[41] *Textile World*, March 15, 1930, p. 81; April 5, p. 89.

[42] *Textile World*, August 2, 1930, pp. 41, 84.

[43] *Textile World*, November 15, 1930, pp. 70–71.

Chart 9

Monthly Viscose Rayon Yarn Production for Five Producers, 1929–1934

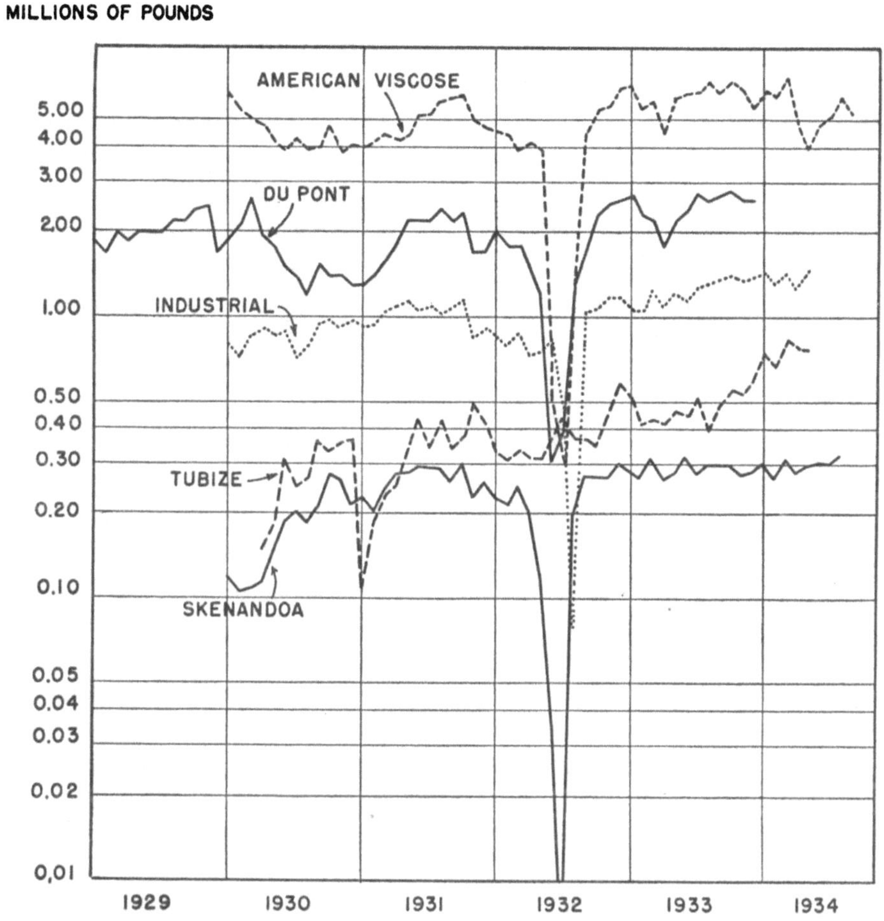

Note: Logarithmic Vertical Scale.
Source: Federal Trade Commission, compiled from various Exhibits in *Hearings*, Docket 2161.

curtailment plan this time and not insisting on one-hundred per cent capacity output — the industry is operating at seventy-five per cent capacity compared with eighty per cent capacity last week." [44] Two weeks later, the division reported that the coöperation of small producers considerably brightened the 1932 outlook. That the small producers became increasingly coöperative is evidenced in Mr. Black's quarterly report on the rayon industry in the early spring of 1932; he stated:

[44] *Textile World,* November 14, 1931, p. 59.

A few weeks ago, the Viscose Corporation announced that production had been cut from eighty per cent to seventy per cent of capacity; this statement had a salutory effect upon output by other companies, and since then the movement toward curtailment has been growing steadily. At the moment, output is down nearly to sixty per cent of capacity — now a new spirit is manifest . . . which explains the prompt response to the lead taken by the Viscose Corporation. The move is practically unanimous . . . it is known that all plants cannot cut by the same percentage, large plants cut more.[45]

The last observation was borne out by individual firms' operation data reported in the same issue. Most large producers operated at the above-mentioned 60 per cent of capacity level; but some smaller firms, for example the Skenandoa Rayon Corporation, reported operations at 80 per cent of capacity.[46]

Thus, in a period of less than two years, the problem of how output curtailment was to be spread among producers in periods of falling demand seems to have been fairly effectively dealt with although certainly not completely solved. The large producers, particularly American Viscose, had nevertheless been accepted as leaders in setting output as well as price policy. Some indication of the extent to which the industry accepted the output policy announced in advance by American Viscose during the latter stages of the depression may be obtained from the data presented in Chart 9. In the spring of 1932, for example, American Viscose announced that it would close down many of its units for June and July to allow demand to catch up with output. All rayon producers except Tubize heeded the announcement with such seriousness that viscose yarn output for the entire industry in July amounted to only 2.5 million pounds. Almost all producers closed down for one or two months.[47] The general feeling of satisfaction over the coöperative spirit among domestic yarn producers was summed up by the rayon editor in the 1934 edition of *Textile World* as follows:

Production control, and through it, price stability, are attributes which rayon possesses to a degree unknown in any other textile division. Add to these advantages a continuance of the present spirit of coöperation and wise leadership, and the industry this year may well make such a showing as would outdistance even its own notable record of 1933.[48]

[45] "New Rayon Curtailment Shows Power of Coöperation," *Textile World,* March 26, 1932, pp. 23, 27.
[46] "New Rayon Curtailment Shows Power of Coöperation," pp. 23, 27.
[47] *Textile World,* July 1932, p. 83; *Rayon Journal,* June 1932, pp. 9, 26.
[48] *Textile World,* 1934 annual edition, p. 122.

Similarity of action, although perhaps not nearly so similar as industry spokesmen would have liked it to be, was evident throughout the 1937–38 depression and the other less severe rayon market recessions which occurred after 1934. When the down-turn in sales became obvious in September 1937, the large producers, after waiting two months, commenced curtailing output in November under the pressure of mounting inventories and a steady decline in orders. It was reported that curtailment was industry-wide by early December and on a 75 per cent of capacity basis.[49] By April 1938, "Because of the growing problem of accumulating stocks of rayon, the leading producers announced last month [March] that they would produce to order only." [50] Presumably, the announcement was to serve (and probably did) as a guide to the rest of the industry. At least the voices of dissatisfaction were not nearly so audible as they were in the 1930–1933 depression. However, the May 1938 list-price reduction to meet price-shading suggests that coöperation was not perfect.

There is some evidence, therefore, that production policy in the rayon industry as well as price policy has been influenced by the action of large producers, that is, that some significance can be attached to the term "output leadership." Similarity of action among rayon producers with respect to output can be accounted for in part, of course, by the fact that all producers were confronted with the same market forces. The colinearity among the monthly production series of individual firms in Chart 9, and among the monthly inventory series of individual firms in Chart 10, strongly suggests that all producers in the industry felt the impact of changing market conditions from 1931 to 1934 at about the same time, and with approximately the same force. This would be expected in an industry that sells to thousands of customers, many of whom buy their yarns from six or seven rayon companies.[51] Hence, the periodic announcements made by American Viscose concerning its production policy might

[49] *Textile World*, December 1937, p. 129. In the initial stages of the recession, however, curtailment varied among producers from almost complete plant shutdowns to capacity operations. See *Rayon Organon*, December 1937, and January 1938.

[50] *Textile World*, April 1938, p. 104.

[51] A tabulation of rayon knitting and weaving companies, which appeared on the customers' lists of leading rayon yarn producers, by month, from November 1931 to January 1934, shows that many of them, particularly the large knitters and weavers such as Beaunit, Raynit, Globe, etc., consistently purchased yarn simultaneously from American Viscose, Industrial, North American, American Enka, and Tubize Chatillon. *Hearings*, F. T. C., Docket No. 2161, vols. IV–VI, Commission's *Exhibits*.

Chart 10

Month End Inventories for Five Viscose Rayon Producers, 1929–1934

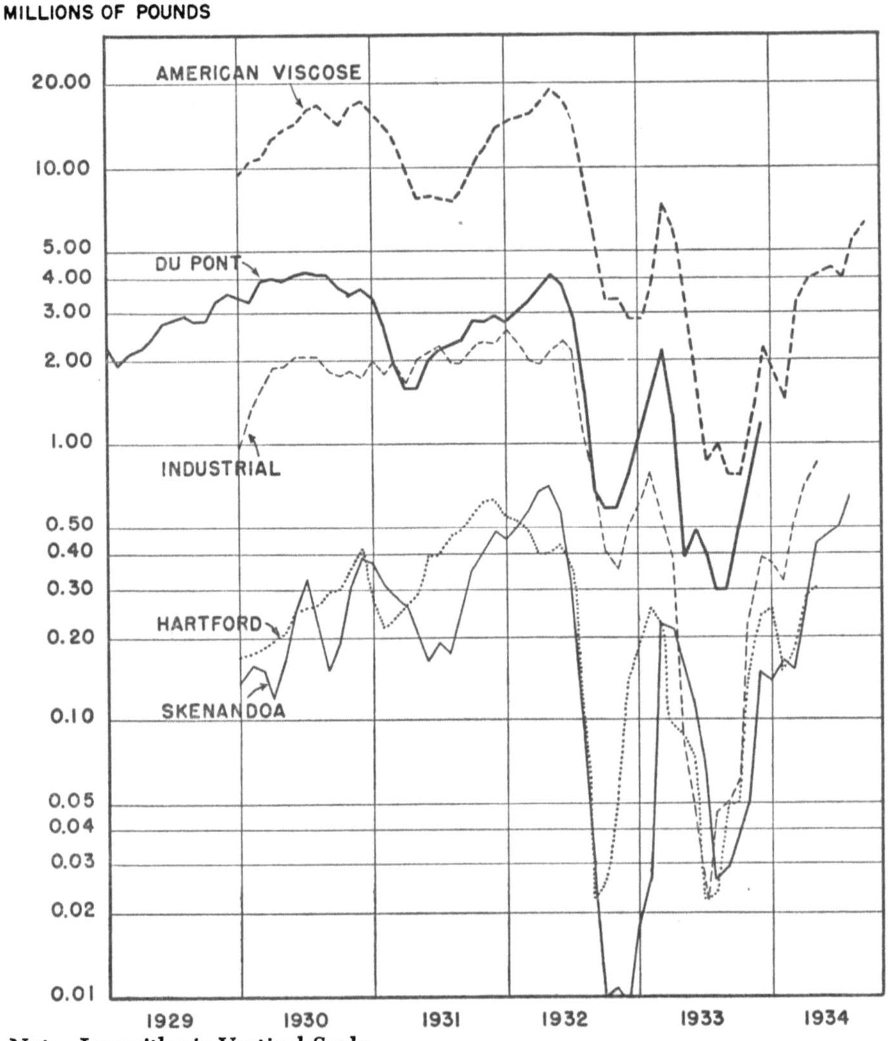

Note: Logarithmic Vertical Scale.
Source: Federal Trade Commission, compiled from various Exhibits in *Hearings*, Docket 2161.

have simply indicated the obvious road to be taken by the rest of the industry anyway.

It would, therefore, be highly misleading to infer that coöperation among rayon firms has been so perfect that the *de facto* behavior of output and price since 1931 has been the same as that which would have resulted had the policies of all producing units been under the absolute control of the largest producer or a tightly organized trade association. Policies initiated by large producers in time of crisis undoubtedly have been conditioned by the expected probability that the rest of the industry would or would not follow a proposed course of action. Moreover, some instances of independent action on the part of individual firms, for example, off-list selling, regrading, etc., have already been discussed. Nevertheless, what the industry itself terms "enlightened leadership" seems to have served as the *modus operandi* among producers when the rayon market was "normal" or, more precisely, when inventories were not much in excess of one month's capacity production and most firms were operating between 75 per cent and 100 per cent of installed capacity. Hence, for such "normal" periods, the policy implied from the price and output behavior of industry data examined in this chapter is probably representative of the price and output policy of each producer. When the rayon market becomes severely depressed, however, tacit parallelism seems to disintegrate into individual action.

H. Summary

By way of summary, the course of rayon prices after 1919 was sharply downward. The downward movement commenced to taper off after the first half of 1932 but was not noticeably interrupted until 1936. The trend for the 1919–1934 period is best approximated by a compound interest rate curve (negative slope). The apparent cause of such secular behavior is that the price reductions initiated in rayon market recessions are seldom fully restored in the subsequent market revivals. After 1934, the price series approximated a horizontal line until price controls were removed in November 1946. From 1911 to 1949, the trend in output has been sharply upward. Between 1919 and 1940 the trend has so closely approximated a Gompertz curve that it is used as a textbook example of the curve's applicability to production series.

An examination of the available monthly data shows that neither price nor output schedules respond to seasonal and other short-run demand shifts. On the whole, short-run disequilibria between production and consumption are completely absorbed by fluctuations in inventories. When the period of observation is extended to include the two-year textile cycle, a phenomenon apparent in all textile consumption data, the output series shows a higher degree of sensitivity to demand shifts than the price series. Annual data, however, do not reveal any noticeable differences between the amplitudes of output and price cyclical swings; both price and output conform to a common cyclical pattern that is synchronized with Professor Mitchell's reference cycles. The monthly data available since 1930, however, disclose several more significant characteristics of price and output behavior, particularly with respect to timing and intensity of change. When supplemented by other historical evidence, they hint at the price and output policy pursued in the industry since 1930.

When confronted with a continuing decline in orders, producers curtail output several months before they decrease price. Since 1932, price reductions, after allowance is made for off-list selling, have lagged output curtailments by from thirty to sixty days. The magnitude of the lag is partially determined by the severity of the recession and, hence, by the rate of change in the level of inventories. On the average, output curtailment to roughly 75 per cent of capacity in the industry forecasts a price reduction. There are two possible explanations for such a breaking point: (1) The large producers who lead list-price changes may suspect small producers of price-shading when the market has declined this severely; accordingly, they take *de jure* recognition of the suspected *de facto* price; and (2) the nature of rayon firms' short-run cost curves, to be explored in the succeeding chapter, makes it imperative that each firm maintain output at 75 per cent of installed capacity or above for cost considerations.

Since rayon is a textile fiber, substitutable for other textile fibers that experience day-to-day price changes, it may well be asked how moderately stable rayon prices are possible, even from season to season? An answer could conceivably be found in the imperfect substitutability among textile fibers. Over short periods of time, silk, cotton, and wool prices may fluctuate inside margins which, only if exceeded, would result in a transference of demand between natural fibers and rayon. When these margins are exceeded, particularly over the business cycle, demand for rayon and, therefore, rayon inventories, are sufficiently affected to bring about rayon price revisions. Hence, the price of rayon may be virtually independent of short-run price fluctuations of natural fibers but considerably influenced by natural fiber prices over the course of a business cycle. If this is true, several features of the rayon industry are conducive to a short-run stable price.

The oligopolistic features of the supply side of the industry may be sufficiently strong to give rise to the kinked demand curve. Much of the force behind the kinked demand curve argument as an explanation of price stability is considerably weakened, however, by the high degree of price leadership in the industry. Nevertheless, historical evidence suggests that price decreases are more readily followed than price increases, and several producers make it a matter of policy to follow announced price increases more cautiously than price decreases. Moreover, it is certain that all producers visualize a discontinuity in their marginal revenue curve when price guarantees are in effect. Hence, the kinked demand curve is offered as one of a number of possible explanations of stable rayon prices.

Perhaps the most significant cause of short-run rayon price stability is to be found in the industry's attitude toward pricing its commodity. Rayon producers have attributed much of their success to the fact that rayon price, unlike the prices of silk, cotton, and wool, is not contingent upon the vagaries of the weather or the productive capacity of sheep or silkworms, but upon their own price and output policy. They have highly advertised the price stability of their commodity to textile fabricators, pointing out that substitution of rayon for other fibers obviates such nuisances as hedging and eliminates the risk of inventory losses and the uncertainties of future raw material costs. They have, moreover, given every indication that immediate gains for the rayon producer may profitably be sacrificed for the sake of a stable price.

Furthermore, rayon is produced by large corporations. Once the existence of a pricing "policy" is admitted, there are reasons to believe that market forces are translated into price changes much more slowly in large corporations than in small owner-controlled corporations and simple proprietorships.[52] The compromising of conflicting interests among financial, production, and sales representatives is frequently time-consuming, once it has been generally agreed upon that a price change is necessary. The validity of this argument with respect to price and production policy in the rayon industry is illus-

[52] The reasons have been adequately discussed elsewhere so they will not be repeated here. Cf. R. A. Gordon, *Business Leadership in the Large Corporation*, Washington, The Brookings Institution, 1945, pp. 81–85; Edward S. Mason, "Price and Production Policies of Large-scale Enterprise," *American Economic Review*, 1939 (March) Supplement; pp. 66–68, and others.

trated by the problems which confronted decision-making bodies in July 1931: A market recovery had substantially reduced inventories but all producers were still operating below capacity output; *Textile World* commented: "Low rayon stocks may cramp fall sales. Many producers see strength in present inventory position with production curtailed, but also see loss of business from lack of stock. In several companies there is a clash between financial and sales departments, the former insisting on no output increases while the sales outfit want production to fill orders." [53] In a previous issue of *TextileWorld* it had been intimated that a tight fall market might be conducive to a price increase.

Another factor which contributes to short-run price stability in the rayon industry is the stability of the prices of factors which enter variable costs. For example, the price of a standard grade of sulphuric acid, one of the principal chemicals used in producing viscose yarn, has changed only once since 1928. Most other chemicals consumed by the rayon industry have very stable prices. Chemical wood pulp, which accounts for almost one-half of total material costs in rayon production, has been subject to infrequent price changes. Also, average hourly earnings in the industry have been quite stable. Cost-price relationships, however, will be taken up in the following chapter.

[53] *Textile World,* July 18, 1931, p. 52.

8

SHORT-RUN AND LONG-RUN
Rayon Price Determinants

Up to this point the behavior of price and output in the rayon industry has been examined in the light of fluctuations in demand and such phenomena as rising or falling inventory levels. Obviously, however, corporation officials charged with formulating price policy translate shifts in demand for their product into certain causative forces such as changes in price or quality of competing products, favorable or adverse product publicity, etc.

Indeed, the process of unraveling the multiplicity of causative forces behind shifts in demand for one's product, and the subsequent reshuffling of variables over which the firm exercises a fair amount of control, are distinguishing features of an imperfectly competitive market. A single cotton grower, for example, need not think in terms of adjusting the price of his cotton so that it will be more in line with the price of silk. This adjustment has already been made for him in the competitive market. He either accepts the market price or stores his cotton. Under more imperfect market conditions, the range of choice is considerably wider, and the freedom to exercise choice between alternatives renders admissible the use of such terms as price or output "policy." It has already been demonstrated that rayon producers (behind the leadership of the large firms) are free, within limits, to maintain short-run price and output stability in the face of fluctuating demand, and to adjust output several months before they adjust price. Rayon yarn producers have exercised their freedom of choice between alternative lines of action with sufficient consistency to imply a "policy."

It is also obvious, however, that there are forces which limit, and hence partially determine, the rayon producer's pricing policy. Even if it could be assumed that the largest producer could rely upon the rest of the firms in the industry to follow his own course of action, there would still be variables that must enter into his price and production formula over which he exercises little if any control.

For analytical purposes, short-run price determinants may be treated under two classifications: (1) Cost elements and (2) non-cost elements, such as the prices of competing products. It cannot be assumed, of course, that rayon producers exercise no control over any of these factors. They probably have some influence on wage rates and their own price policy influences the price of silk and perhaps, in recent years, the prices of cotton and wool. Yet the extent to which they can control factor prices and the competitive prices of natural fibers is considerably limited.

Rayon producers have, since the introduction of rayon into the United States, consistently given costs or competing fiber (including foreign-produced rayon) price movements as the principal reasons for rayon price revisions. For instance, Samuel A. Salvage, President of the American Viscose Corporation, stated on June 26, 1926, in reference to an announced price reduction, that:

> As there is too wide a difference between our prices and the rates quoted for European yarns, we feel it necessary at this time to depart from the policy endorsed in April — to maintain present prices. The low wages that prevail in Europe, and the greatly depreciated foreign currencies with which we have to compete, have compelled us to make drastic reductions in our prices effective July 1, and we hope that our action will fully restore confidence in the rayon market.[1]

The July 1, 1926 price revision was an attempt to curb a twofold increase in rayon imports for the fiscal year ending June 30, 1926. Such statements were made frequently throughout the twenties.

Rayon producers, in their zealous attempts to impress consumers with the distinctive features of their product, occasionally have been reluctant to admit that intertextile price and consumption cross-effects have bordered upon anything that resembles close competition. Much of their publicity has been directed toward the acceptance of rayon by fabricators as a style leader and as a stabilizing factor in the textile industry.

[1] *Rayon Journal,* June 30, 1926, p. 4.

Nevertheless, they have given ample evidence that natural fiber prices, particularly silk and cotton prices, have significantly influenced rayon pricing decisions: For example, when silk prices commenced to recover in June 1930, after they had declined steadily over the previous eight months, thereby exerting a downward pressure upon rayon prices, *Textile World* commented: "Rayon producers take hope in the rise in silk prices, which has put tremendous pressure on finer deniers of rayon, but silk prices will have to rise considerably before the present pressure is off." [2] After silk prices declined further in July, President Salvage of American Viscose announced a price reduction on July 22 "to restore price parity between chemical yarns and raw silk." [3] This downward pressure had become so great by the depths of the depression in 1932 that American Viscose, Du Pont, Industrial, American Enka, Glansztoff (now North American), Tubize, and Skenandoa jointly petitioned Congress for a $0.75 per pound import duty on raw silk for the purposes of increasing federal revenue (*sic*) and protecting rayon sales.[4]

Again, in April 1933, "The lowering price of raw silk had brought about indications that weavers and knitters were planning to substitute silk for rayon in their late spring and summer period, therefore American Viscose announced new prices on rayon to put them on parity with silk prices." [5] Three weeks later, American Viscose restored half of this price cut because "Stocks had dwindled to a two-week supply, sharp gains in cotton and silk prices are causes also." [6]

Rayon producers have been considerably less hesitant to admit the adverse effects of falling silk and cotton prices than they have the beneficial effects of rising natural fiber prices. For example, after the textile yarn market had revived in 1933, rayon producers stated that, although rising silk prices had had some bearing on the rayon boom, it was a highly overrated factor.[7] Four months later, *Textile World*, speaking for the rayon industry, stated that a price rise was unlikely, and that "Although profit margin is slim, volume makes return on investment 'satisfactory.' An increase in silk and cotton prices may bring about a price change, but rayon producers

[2] *Textile World*, July 19, 1930, p. 49.
[3] *Rayon Journal*, August 1, 1930, p. 3.
[4] *Textile World*, May 28, 1932, p. 81; see also *Rayon Organon*, June 1932.
[5] *Rayon Journal*, April 1933, p. 32.
[6] *Textile World*, May 1933, p. 106.
[7] *Textile World*, June 1933, p. 104.

view demand arising from high fashion and quality fields more significant than the price differential between synthetic and natural fibers." [8]

There is little evidence that factor prices have significantly influenced short-run rayon price movements. Industry spokesmen stated, however, that the November 1946 price increase was due to the . . .

> rise in average hourly labor rates from October, 1941, to December, 1946, from $0.77 to $1.10 or a 43 per cent increase, and the rise in price of such basic raw materials as caustic soda, sulphuric acid, woodpulp and cotton linters; woodpulp prices went from $85.00 per ton in October, 1941 to $118.50 per ton in December, 1946, or a rise of 39 per cent. Production efficiency and maximum capacity operations kept the price rise in rayon as low as 10 per cent.[9]

Rayon producers usually attribute the *level* of domestic prices, as compared with foreign rayon prices, to the high cost of labor in the United States. They also attribute much of the downward secular trend in domestic prices to the secular decline in total unit costs which has resulted from technological change and larger scale operations. Factor price changes, however, have rarely been considered as causes of price changes. A simple explanation for such a lack of emphasis on factor price movements is that factor prices are more stable than the price of rayon. Consequently, factor prices are to be associated more with rayon price stability than with rayon price fluctuations.

A. Costs, Price, and Output

Costs, for purposes of analysis of cost-price and cost-output relationships, may be approached through: (1) The shape of the firm's short-run cost curve; (2) factor price behavior; (3) variation in unit cost with size of plant and with technological change; and (4) secular movements in factor prices. (1) and (2) bear significantly upon short-run price and output behavior, and the more stable the prices of factors in the short-run, the more relevant is the shape of the short-run cost curve to price and output behavior. (3) and (4) relate essentially to long-run price characteristics of rayon in that they allow for change in installed capacity, which results from altera-

[8] *Textile World*, October 1933, p. 112.
[9] *Rayon Organon*, December 1946, pp. 187–188.

tions in plant size and technology, and for factor secular price movements.

It is recognized at the outset that an interpretation of the behavior of time series in terms of the foregoing short-run and long-run economic concepts is mildly Procrustean and open to several objections on theoretical grounds. For example, the general shape of the short-run cost curve, once indicated, will be assumed, in the following analysis, to hold over a significant period of time. That is, given a short-run cost curve for a particular plant, it will be used in the analysis of price and output behavior removed in time from the instant in which the producer visualized the given cost curve. Moreover, the available cost curve is for a specific plant. Except where there is evidence to the contrary, such as differences in slope between curves for large and small plants, it is necessary to assume that all plant cost curves are similarly shaped.

There are obvious objections to this procedure since cost curves vary in shape with respect to time and firm. There are reasons to believe, however, that the short-run "fixed capacity" of rayon plants, the similarity of equipment among plants, and the absence of radical change in production techniques since 1935[10] leave the analysis that follows less open to criticism than would otherwise be admissible on strict theoretical grounds.

The curves in Chart 11 show the relationship between unit cost and per cent of installed capacity operated (curve B) and unit cost and size of plant (curve A). They were prepared for this study by members of the industrial engineering and cost accounting staffs of one of the multi-plant rayon producers. Curve B is expressed in index form for the maximum size plant operated by the company. Since the computation of total unit cost at each per cent of installed capacity operated is based upon constant factor prices but allows for the most economical adjustment of variable factors, the curve approximates the short-run cost curve of economic theory.[11] The

[10] Since 1935 the industry's capacity has been increased chiefly through gradual technological change and enlargement of existing facilities. The only radical change in production technique took place in Industrial Rayon Corporation's Painesville plant in 1939. See Chap. 2.

[11] "The relationship which we are submitting to you assumes that periods of curtailment will be sufficiently long to justify a practical contraction of overhead organization. Similarly, in the case of variation due to plant size, we have assumed an overhead organization which would be in agreement with this Company's policies and practices." Taken from a letter from the company official who directed the preparation of the chart, March 10, 1948 (name withheld by request).

period of curtailment has to be of moderate duration, however, before the company releases any of its direct labor, and of still longer duration before overhead organization is contracted. Hence, the curve that would represent the relationship between average total unit costs and output in the immediate short-run would rise more rapidly with decreases in output.

Some of the features of curve B are quite helpful in explaining the price and output behavior discussed in the preceding chapter.

Chart 11

Variation in Unit Cost (A) with Size of Plant and (B) with Per Cent of Installed Capacity Operated

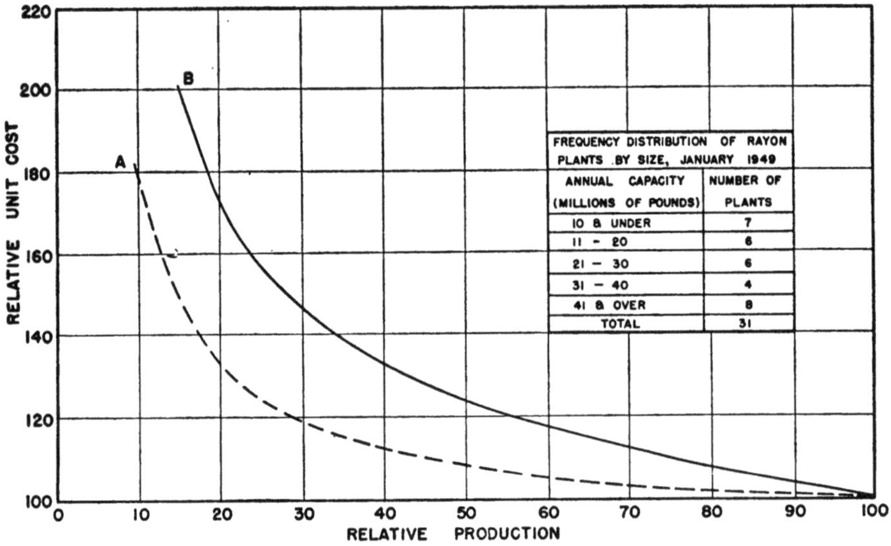

Source: See text.

Unit costs rise at an increasing rate as output is curtailed and commence to increase immediately with curtailment below 100 per cent of installed capacity. The shape of the curve is attributable for the most part to the high proportion of overhead costs and the relative inflexibility of operations. In 1940, a year in which nearly all firms maintained capacity output, fixed costs exclusive of management and supervisory salaries amounted to 22.1 per cent of cost of goods sold.[12] When the relatively fixed charges of management and supervision and a portion of maintenance are included, fixed costs are

[12] *Hearings.* H. R., Project V, p. 47. Based upon the operating reports of ten rayon companies.

increased to about 33 per cent. Although overheads vary among companies, it is generally estimated that total costs per unit of output may be roughly divided into one-third labor, one-third materials, and one-third depreciation, research, and other overhead costs.[13]

In addition to the relatively high ratio of fixed to total costs, the increase in cost per unit as output is curtailed is considerably aggravated by the relative inflexibility of operations. Although technological advancement has increased the speeds at which spinning machines may be operated, variation from optimum or designed speed in the short-run is extremely limited and accompanied by production diseconomies. In fact, fairly small increases in machine speeds above designed speed result in a decrease in value product due to the higher percentage of second grade and inferior yarns produced. This accounts for the fact that the short-run cost curve is not extended beyond 100 per cent operating capacity. Producers do not appear to think in terms of producing beyond designed capacity since the cost curve, if extended, would be almost a vertical straight line.[14]

The principal features of the price and output pattern discovered in the preceding chapter were as follows: (1) Price and output are extremely stable in the short-run but inventories fluctuate over a wide range; (2) price revisions usually lag production schedule revisions by about two months; and (3) curtailment to approximately 75 per cent of installed capacity is usually followed by a price reduction.

The stability of the output series and the consequent violent inventory fluctuations undoubtedly are accounted for in part by the increase in unit costs that accompanies operations short of capacity. Unless there are compensatory price changes in variable cost factors, a 25 per cent curtailment in output increases total unit costs 10 per cent; 35 per cent curtailment increases total unit costs 15 per cent, and the rate of increase in unit costs is considerably greater as output is further reduced. Based upon the one-third relationship among labor, materials, and overhead, in order for total unit costs to remain

[13] Schwarz and Mauersberger, *Rayon and Synthetic Yarn Handbook* (2nd ed.; 1936), p. 29.

[14] This explains the absence of peaks in the industry's output series. After all plants have reached designed capacity, no price can immediately induce further increases in output since several years are required to increase plant. For a rough estimation of average total and average marginal unit costs beyond designed capacity operations, see Fig. 2.

unchanged as output is curtailed from optimum capacity to 65 per cent of capacity, the price of all materials and wage rates would have to decline approximately 22.5 per cent. Since overhead would constitute over one-third of total costs at this rate of output, and since producers do not adjust labor and supervision to contracted operations until a moderately long period of curtailment is certain, the reduction in factor prices necessary to leave unit costs unchanged would probably be around 33 per cent for the immediate short-run. Hence, there is considerable pressure upon producers to maintain full capacity output and allow inventory fluctuations to cushion consumption and production disequilibria.

Moreover, because unit costs commence to rise rapidly after operations have been decreased to 75 per cent of capacity, there is pressure upon producers to reduce prices and stimulate sales to avoid further reductions in output once 65 to 75 per cent of capacity operations has been reached. This follows from a line of reasoning that is consistent with both the usual price models of economic theory and the empirical data for the rayon industry.

The demand curve confronting each rayon firm, of course, cannot be determined, but in view of the number of firms in the industry and the number of fibers for which rayon is substituted, it is obvious by now that each producer must consider his own demand curve to be highly elastic. It was suggested in Chapter 6, in fact, that it would not be unrealistic to assume the demand curves confronting very small producers to be identical and of almost infinite elasticity. This is particularly true over the range of secret downward price revisions.

Therefore, according to the shape of the average total unit cost and average marginal unit cost curves shown in Figure 2, at least all small producers would, under equilibrium prices, produce in the vicinity of rated capacity. The mere fact that inventories commence to accumulate, however, means that the price leader's price does not permit the current rate of output to clear the market. Minor reductions in the rate of output, say of from 5 per cent to 15 per cent, to reduce the rate of inventory accumulation may not affect unit costs sufficiently to induce any producer to challenge the price leader's price. As output is further curtailed, however, unit costs commence rising at a more rapid rate. Even for the large plant represented by Curve B, the unit costs index increases by 3.7 points between 100 per cent and 90 per cent of capacity; by 4.0 points between 90 per cent and 80 per cent of capacity; by 4.5 points between 80 per cent and 70 per cent of capacity, and by 5.1 points between 70 per cent and 60 per cent of capacity. The rate of increase in the unit cost index is higher at lower rates of output. Hence, if the price leader has not reduced prices by the time most producers have curtailed by approximately 25 per cent, producers commence to shade prices to avoid high-cost rates of output. It was demonstrated in Chapter 7 that this has been the usual range of operations over which downward price revisions have occurred, in spite of the apparent concerted effort of rayon yarn producers to give textile fabricators a stable price. Ordinarily, unit costs rise so rapidly as curtailment proceeds below 50 per cent of installed capacity that it is less costly to close down plants completely than to operate.[15]

The 70 to 75 per cent of capacity price-breaking point for reasons of costs is further supported by profits and per cent of capacity operations data. In 1931, for example, the industry as a whole operated at 86 per cent of capacity and made profits which amounted to a 3.35 per cent rate of return on total capital. In 1932 the industry operated at 69 per cent of capacity and made a rate of return of only 1.47 per cent, and most small firms, in spite of their slightly higher rates of operations, incurred losses (see Table 7). In 1933, under lower than 1932 prices, the industry operated at 93 per cent of capacity and made a rate of return of 12.16 per cent, and none of the ten firms for which profit data are available incurred losses. For the years 1934–1937 the industry operated at slightly over 90 per cent of capacity and made an average rate of return of about 9 per cent. In 1938, however, when operations were reduced to 80 per cent of capacity, the rate of return fell to 2.52 per cent. When rates of return based on accounting profits, which impute no interest to equity capital, fall to between 1.5 per cent and 2.5 per cent when the industry operates between 69 per cent and 80 per cent of capacity, it is hardly unrealistic to conclude that economic profits disappear somewhere around these rates of output.

Again referring to Curve B in Chart 11, the foregoing profit and rate of output behavior suggests that a price which permits a fairly high unit profit margin when all firms operate at capacity does not cover full costs at rates of output below 75 per cent of capacity. However, if each firm views his demand schedule as highly elastic,

[15] Cf. *Textile World*, May 7, 1932, p. 47; and May 21, p. 50; and *Rayon Organon*, June 1932.

he has a better option in the form of a lower price and a higher rate of output open to him. Moreover, as evidence presented later will show, there are good reasons for believing that the total demand schedule for rayon becomes more elastic as it shifts to the left, thereby giving each producer, regardless of his size, an incentive to reduce prices when the quantity demanded at prevailing prices falls short of a fairly high rate of output.

Another important feature of the industry's cost structure, for purposes of explaining price behavior, is related to the flexibility of plants and of firms of various sizes. Large and small rayon firms alike accept the proposition that large producers can curtail output by a given per cent of capacity and incur a lower percentage increase in total unit costs than small producers. Although the proposition cannot, in a mathematical sense, be proved, it is supported by a considerable amount of evidence. For example, when the industry resorted to collective action to reduce rayon output in the 1930–1933 depression, it was generally recognized that small firms could not be expected to curtail output in proportion to large producers because of cost considerations.[16] In the subsequent hearings before the Federal Trade Commission, small producers frequently referred to the high costs which resulted from substantial reductions in their output.[17]

It is difficult, however, to determine whether the greater flexibility of large producers is principally a phenomenon of the multi-plant firm or of the large plant. It is possible, because of the greater number of options open to them, to visualize a number of reasons why multi-plant firms are more flexible than either large or small single-plant firms: They can curtail output at their higher cost plants but maintain near-capacity production at their lower cost plants. Two multi-plant firms, for example, have fairly consistently curtailed output in their older northern plants before they curtailed output in their newer southern plants. Moreover, to the extent that flexibility may be varied among plants, multi-plant firms can curtail output where curtailment costs are the least.[18] Small producers, all of which

[16] Cf. pp. 135 ff., esp. p. 138.

[17] F. T. C., Docket No. 2161, *Record,* see esp. pp. 491 and 1383.

[18] It is of interest from both a theoretical and an empirical point of view to note that the more flexible plants and the plants having the highest total unit costs at designed capacity operations are likely to be the same. See George J. Stigler, "Production and Distribution in the Short Run," *Journal of Political Economy,* vol. XXVII, no. 3 (June 1939), pp. 310–311.

have operated a single small plant, have a much narrower range of choice.

There is evidence of a more substantive nature, however, that small plants are less flexible than large ones. Although the entire family of short-run cost curves from which curve A was derived was not made available to the author, the industrial engineer who took charge of the cost study did submit to the author a report which set forth the techniques used, and the general pattern of the derived statistical relationships. According to the report, if cost indexes for a plant one-half the size of the plant represented by Curve B were plotted on the same chart, with the unit cost for each plant at 100 per cent of capacity equaling 100, the short-run cost curve for the smaller plant would diverge from Curve B from above. This means that unit costs for small plants increase more percentage-wise than those for large plants with corresponding percentage reductions in rates of output.

The relative slopes of curves A and B in Chart 11, in view of the empirical data from which they were constructed, confirm this relationship. Curve A, as previously pointed out, was obtained by connecting the minimum costs points of short-run plant cost curves for various size plants. All points, according to the cost report, on all the short-run plant cost curves, except the minimum cost points, lie above the derived envelope curve.[19] Hence, from inspection, it would seem that the short-run cost curves for plants smaller than plants of the size represented by Curve B, particularly the short-run cost curves for very small plants, have greater absolute slopes than short-run cost curves for plants approximately as large as the plant represented by Curve B, that is, unit costs increase more rapidly with curtailment of output for very small than for very large plants. If, for example, a plant one-fifth the size of the maximum size plant shown in Chart 11 were to curtail output 50 per cent, total unit costs would be increased by more than 42.6 per cent (estimated from Curve A), whereas a 50 per cent reduction in output by the

[19] Several economists who read and criticized the manuscript have warned the author that this is likely to be construed by some as a perpetuation of the well-known "Viner" error. The reader is reminded, therefore, that the above envelope curve is an empirical relationship and must be evaluated as such. Because of the shape of short-run cost curves for rayon plants, tangents to their low-cost points may have considerable slope. Hence, even without the benefit of the derived curve, it is easy to visualize an envelope curve connecting the low-cost points of a family of short-run plant cost curves.

maximum size plant would result in only a 23.5 per cent increase in total unit costs.

The usefulness of the relative slopes of curves A and B, as empirical evidence that unit costs increase more rapidly with decreases in output for small than for large plants, is confined to the area where the slope of Curve A increases at least as rapidly with equal percentage reductions in output as Curve B. Hence, they show only that plants roughly one-quarter the size of the largest plant, or smaller, are less flexible downward than the largest plant. Moreover, it should be reiterated that even this evidence is limited to the experience of one multi-plant firm. Nevertheless, for purposes of analyzing price behavior in the rayon industry for the 1930–1949 period, during which time large producers operated plants more than five times the size of those operated by small producers, the curves are quite useful, particularly when considered along with the other evidence of a less quantitative nature.

It was previously pointed out that small producers have been less hesitant in selling rayon at off-list prices than large producers in a declining rayon market but have been more hesitant in curtailing output. This pattern of behavior is in part a product of the composition of the rayon industry. Each small producer feels that he controls such an insignificant percentage of total rayon output that his own production policy can have little if any effect upon the industry's price or excess inventories problem. Moreover, since he knows that most large- and medium-size producers will reduce prices only after the price leader has announced a price reduction, he can usually obtain a momentary advantage in the market by selling at less than list price and thereby maintain his output. This line of reasoning is amply supported by the testimony of producers and consumers of rayon before the Federal Trade Commission, by the Commission's and Defendants' exhibits contained in the *Hearings,*[20] and by frequent statements in the trade literature.

It is of interest to point out also, however, that this aspect of price and output behavior in the rayon industry is consistent with the cost structure of the industry described above. If output curtailment is more costly for small than for large producers, there are impelling economic reasons why small producers should try to maintain near-capacity output. Since they have some assurance that

[20] *Hearings,* F. T. C., Docket No. 2161; see esp. pp. 750–752, 848, 947, 1206, 1337, 1476, and 5315 of the *Record.*

most large producers will maintain prices until the price leader announces a list-price reduction, the best means open to them is off-list selling. Hence, one of the best reasons for accepting the proposition that large firms, and perhaps even large plants, are more flexible downward than small ones, is that the industry's price and output behavior supports it. At the same time, the cost structure can be offered as one reason why *de facto* rayon price reductions, in contrast to *list* price reductions, are usually initiated by small producers.

Such a difference in cost behavior among firms could, moreover, largely account for the breaking down of price discipline in the industry during periods of severe depression. The large firms may be quite willing to coöperate to keep from spoiling the market, but small firms are compelled to shade prices in order to maintain a fairly high percentage of capacity output. For example, price-shading by small producers was particularly prevalent from 1930 to 1932, when no firm could sell a high percentage of its capacity output at the then prevailing list prices.

It should be reiterated that all the foregoing conclusions are predicated upon the shape of short-run cost curves as conceived at a given instant of time and, therefore, no allowance is made for price changes in variable factors as production schedules are altered. If factor prices remain relatively stable in the short-run, the above conclusions seem to be fairly well founded. To the extent that factor prices are flexible in the short-run, however, compensatory shifts in short-run plant cost curves will modify the foregoing conclusions.

B. Short-Run Factor Price Behavior

Among the principal variable cost factors in rayon production are labor, chemical wood pulp and cotton linters pulp, caustic soda, carbon bisulphide, sulphuric acid, corn sugar or glucose, acetic anhydride, acetic acid, acetone, fuel, power, and water. Historically, labor, pulp, and chemicals have accounted for slightly over two-thirds of total variable costs per pound of rayon produced.

Published monthly prices for most of the materials used in rayon production are not entirely satisfactory indicators of factor cost behavior for two reasons: First, published prices on wood pulp and chemicals are taken largely from sellers' price lists; there are good reasons for believing that the ratio of list price to transaction price for these materials fluctuates over the course of the business cycle. Secondly, most published prices are spot market prices, whereas rayon producers obtain some of their materials on a fairly long-term contract basis. For example, in 1930 a fifteen-year contract was negotiated between Du Pont and Ranier Pulp and Paper Company (now Rayonier, Inc.), which provided for the coöperation of Du Pont's technical staff in the development of improved wood pulps for rayon and other cellulose products.[21] Furthermore, Du Pont, Celanese, and Tennessee Eastman produce some of their own chemicals, and Celanese and American Viscose are currently making preparations to produce their own wood pulp.[22]

The difference between published list prices on certain materials and the actual prices paid by rayon manufactures cannot be determined but in some instances it is known to be significant. For example, between 1929 and 1947 a standard grade of sulphuric acid sold for from $0.0077 to $0.0082 per pound, in tank-car lots at works,[23] whereas over the same period a large rayon manufacturer reported delivered costs of from $0.005 to $0.006 per pound at one of its plants.[24] Rayon producers collectively account for only 5.4 per cent of total sulphuric acid consumption in the United States,[25] while they account for as much as 20.6 per cent of total caustic soda consumption[26] and 37.0 per cent of total cotton linters consumption.[27] Hence, the difference between list and contract prices on these and other raw materials may be even greater than the difference on sulphuric acid.

The published prices of most materials used in rayon production show an extremely high degree of stability. It is highly probable that prices paid by rayon producers for many of these materials are subject to even less frequent changes than are published list prices. For example, while the price of a standard grade of unbleached wood pulp often remains unchanged for over a year, the price of chemical wood pulp used in rayon production remained virtually unchanged from the latter part of 1932 to 1938 at $0.035 to $0.036 per pound,[28]

[21] *Hearings*, H. R., Project V, p. 17.

[22] *Notes on The Chemical Fiber Industry*, January 1948; no. 2 in a series of informative bulletins to stockholders of the Celanese Corporation; and *Rayon and Synthetic Textiles*, September 1948, p. 47.

[23] *Survey of Current Business*, 1947 Supplement.

[24] *Hearings*, H. R., Project V, p. 48.

[25] *Chemical and Metallurgical Engineering*, January 1946, pp. 99–101.

[26] *Chemical and Metallurgical Engineering*, pp. 99–101.

[27] *Weekly Cotton Linters Review*, Production and Marketing Administration, United States Department of Agriculture, for March 29, April 12, and July 3, 1946.

[28] *Hearings*, H. R., Project V, p. 50.

and changed only twice between February 1939 and April 1944.[29] The price paid for caustic soda, as reported by one large producer, changed only $0.001 per pound between 1933 and 1937, and remained unchanged at $0.017 per pound from 1937 to October 1946.[30] The price paid for carbon bisulphide changed only 3 per cent between 1933 and 1937 and between 1938 and 1940; it remained unchanged from 1941 to October 1946.[31] The price paid by rayon producers for sulphuric acid has been between $0.005 and $0.006 per pound since 1929.[32] Whereas the prices of most materials essential to rayon production decreased between 1929 and 1933, they have been highly insensitive to economic fluctuations less severe than the 1930–1933 depression.

Moreover, wages in the rayon industry appear to be relatively insensitive to most economic disturbances, the only wave-like movement apparent in wage data having occurred in the 1930–1933 depression. The Bureau of Labor Statistics has published average hourly earnings, based upon nearly full coverage of the rayon and allied products industry, since October 1932.[33] The Bureau also published each month the number of rayon establishments reporting wage changes for the two-year period following October 1931.[34] In 1932, twenty-three establishments, or the approximate number then comprising the industry, reported wage decreases, most of which were reported between February 15 and March 15 and between June 15 and September 15. Practically all wage increases reported between October 1931 and October 1933 occurred between May 15 and August 15, 1933. These are reflected in the average hourly earnings series (see Chart 12). Between May and August 1933, average hourly earnings increased 20 per cent; between April 26 and July 27 of the same year, the price of rayon increased 30 per cent. This is the only cyclical price movement that can be associated with a similar movement in the average hourly earnings series, and this one

[29] *Rayon Organon*, March 1947.
[30] *Hearings*, H. R., Project V, p. 50.
[31] *Hearings*, H. R., Project V, p. 50.
[32] *Hearings*, H. R., Project V, p. 50.
[33] *Monthly Labor Review*, United States Department of Labor, Bureau of Labor Statistics, 1932 and following issues.

Rayon waste, staple fiber, and cellophane account for most of the allied products; these are produced almost entirely by rayon companies as an integral part of their rayon yarn operations.

[34] *Monthly Labor Review*, United States Department of Labor, Bureau of Labor Statistics, 1931 to 1933 issues.

was principally a reflection of the provisions of the National Industrial Recovery Act.

A further indication of the relative insensitivity of wage rates to recessions in the rayon industry is the strong inverse relationship between output and unit labor cost[35] (see Chart 12). This is particularly noticeable in periods of obvious production curtailment such

Chart 12

Wage Earner Employment, Average Hourly Earnings, Production, Labor and Wood Pulp Costs, and Prices in the Rayon Industry, January 1930–December 1941

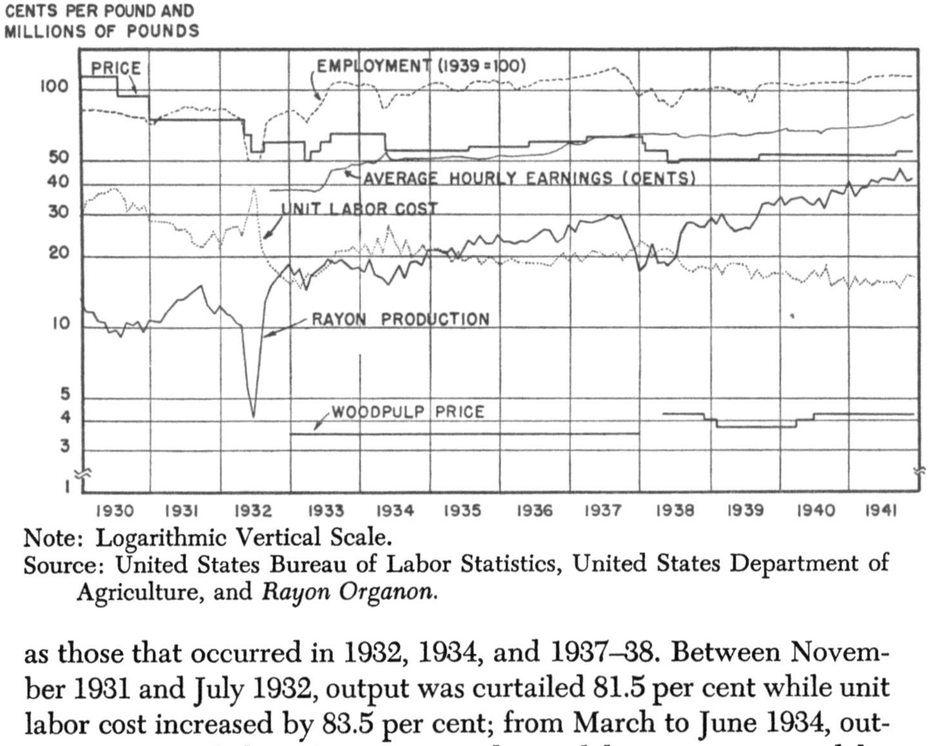

Note: Logarithmic Vertical Scale.
Source: United States Bureau of Labor Statistics, United States Department of Agriculture, and *Rayon Organon.*

as those that occurred in 1932, 1934, and 1937–38. Between November 1931 and July 1932, output was curtailed 81.5 per cent while unit labor cost increased by 83.5 per cent; from March to June 1934, output was curtailed 21.5 per cent and unit labor cost increased by

[35] The monthly unit labor cost series was computed in the following manner: The Bureau of Labor Statistics publishes a monthly wage earner payroll index for rayon and allied products which is adjusted to Census data. The indexes were converted back into actual wage-earner payrolls and checked against dollar wage-earner payrolls as reported by the Bureau of the Census. Actual production was adjusted so that one pound of staple fiber was counted as one-third of a pound of yarn (the industry considers one pound of yarn the labor equivalent of three pounds of staple fiber). Payrolls were divided by production to obtain unit labor cost. Since rayon yarn and staple fiber do not account for the total of rayon and allied products, unit labor cost is somewhat overstated and there is a slight upward bias in the unit labor cost series.

32.5 per cent; from November 1937 to July 1938, output was curtailed 33.3 per cent and unit labor cost had increased 23.4 per cent by January 1938. Over these periods of production curtailment there are no perceptible fluctuations in the average hourly earnings series.

The computations presented in Table 17 show the behavior of output, unit labor cost, wage-earner employment, average hourly earnings, and rayon price over several fairly noticeable rayon market depressions. Two factors account for the sharp rise in unit labor cost as output is curtailed: (1) Employment does not decrease proportionately with output, and (2) there is no compensatory decrease in average hourly earnings. The slight increase in average hourly earnings over the periods of production curtailment is the secular wage movement which, apparently, is not seriously interrupted even

TABLE 17

Percentage Change in Output, Unit Labor Cost, Employment, Average Hourly Earnings, and Price in the Rayon Industry During Four Market Recessions

Period of Output Curtailment	Per Cent Change in Output	Per Cent Change in Unit Labor Cost	Per Cent Change in Wage Earner Employment	Per Cent Change in Average Hourly Earnings	Per Cent Change in Price of 150-Denier Rayon Yarn
Nov. 1931–July 1932	−81.5	+83.5	−38.3	Not available	−26.7
Feb. 1934–Sept. 1934	−21.5	+32.5	−19.2	+6.3	−15.4
Nov. 1937–June 1938	−33.3	+23.4	−22.3	+2.7	−22.2
Mar. 1939–June 1939	−16.2	+9.5	−6.1	+0.5	none

by such fairly severe rayon market recessions as the one which occurred in 1937–1938.

Hence, since factor costs in the rayon industry are so obviously stable, the foregoing analysis based upon the shape of the short-run cost curve for the individual plant is subject to no significant modification; that is, the curves are not subject to violent shifts which would vitiate conclusions based upon their shape. The increase in total unit costs which results from higher unit overhead and labor costs as output is curtailed limits the extent to which rayon yarn price stability may be maintained in periods of general business recession. Attempts to maintain stable prices have been futile after plants have reduced operations to 75 per cent of capacity. Stable factor prices have undoubtedly contributed considerably toward the maintenance of rayon price stability, but in fairly protracted textile slumps, rayon price has been forced downward to stimulate demand after production has been curtailed by about 25 per cent of installed capacity. The shape of the short-run cost curve for the rayon plant is offered as one explanation for such price behavior.

C. Non-Cost Factors and Short-Run Price Behavior

The relationships among fiber prices, even in those market areas where price largely determines which fiber will be used, is difficult to determine. For a number of years the International Statistical

Chart 13

Monthly Rayon, Silk, Cotton, and Wool Prices, 1923–1949

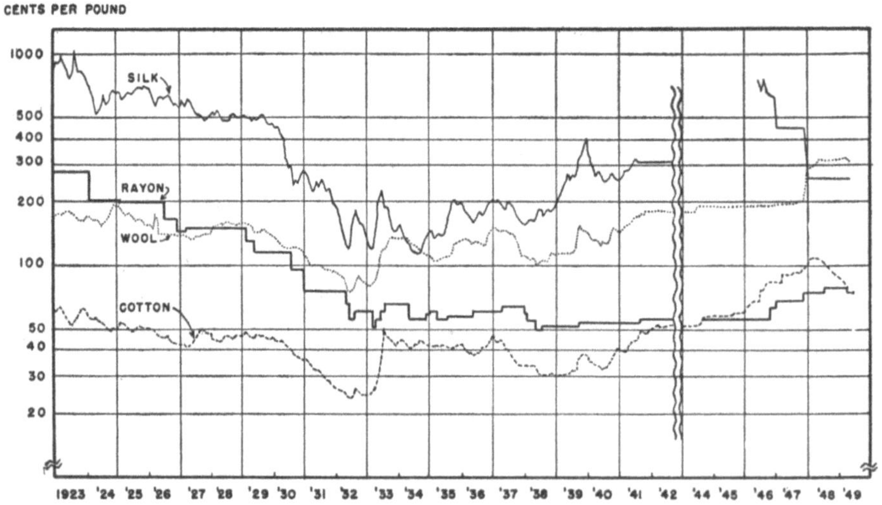

Note: Logarithmic Vertical Scale.

Source: Rayon Prices from *Rayon Organon;* all others from United States Bureau of Labor Statistics. Silk, raw Japan white 13/15 denier spot price, New York; cotton, single warp 40/s at mill; wool, 2/32's white crossbred stock worsted at mill.

Bureau, by employing multiple correlation analysis, published estimated or "parity" prices for each of the four fibers concurrently with actual prices.[36] Although the estimated price series is a smoothed version of the actual series, there is a remarkably high degree of colinearity between the two series for each fiber. From 1923 to 1935 the Bureau found that a high estimated price for rayon (which meant that the actual price of rayon was low relative to other fibers, particularly silk, which at that time was weighted heavily in

[36] See International Statistical Bureau, Inc., *International Textile Apparel Analysis,* February 24, 1934 and September 28, 1935 issues.

the rayon price equation) invariably resulted in the substitution of rayon for silk and, to a lesser extent, other fibers.

Moreover, the analysis showed that once rayon and silk prices were in balance ("parity" and actual prices equal for each fiber), a greater than 10 per cent change in the price of silk was always followed by a rayon price change in the same direction.[37] Such a relationship is fairly well indicated by the behavior of monthly rayon and silk prices shown in Chart 13. The rayon price series is considerably less oscillatory than the silk price series, but when silk price changes exceed 10 per cent, the price of rayon changes in the same direction. The two rayon price changes in the first half of 1929 are the only exceptions.

Between 1923 and 1931 it was generally accepted among rayon producers that rayon price could not vary substantially from one-third the price of silk. Over this period, the ratio of average yearly silk price to average yearly rayon price varied within the limits 3.24 and 2.69, or almost exactly 10 per cent either side of the 3.00 indicated in the studies made by the International Statistical Bureau.

After the depths of the 1930–1933 depression, rayon producers commenced to question the usefulness of the three-to-one ratio as a guide in setting rayon yarn prices. The position of rayon in the textile market had changed a great deal during the preceding ten years. In 1919 rayon consumption was only one-eighth of silk consumption; by 1927 rayon consumption had exceeded silk consumption, and, by 1932, was twice that of silk. Moreover, constant research had greatly improved the quality of rayon and, hence, had increased the number of uses to which the yarn could be put. It was estimated by the Textile Economics Bureau, Inc. in 1932 that rayon had developed its own markets to such an extent that only 20 per cent of total rayon production was in extremely close competition with silk.[38]

For the 1932–1934 period, the price of rayon was slightly less than one-half that of silk. After 1934, silk prices gradually increased while rayon prices remained near the 1934 level until, by 1940, the ratio of silk to rayon price had increased to 4.75. Over this period silk consumption declined by 50 per cent while rayon consumption almost doubled. In the process of probing the demand possibilities for their product, rayon producers had, with an improved product

[37] *International Textile Apparel Analysis,* February 24, 1934.
[38] *Rayon Organon,* April 1932, p. 13.

at relatively lower prices, driven silk from all but a few special markets. Since silk consumption in the United States has decreased to where it is currently less than 1 per cent of total rayon consumption,[39] silk price movements obviously have less influence upon rayon prices and consumption than they had prior to 1935.

It was pointed out in Chapter 2 that the area of competition between rayon and cotton has grown considerably in recent years. As an inferior silk substitute, rayon possessed few of those highly desirable qualities that gave cotton its dominant position in markets representing literally thousands of end uses: It was not durable, possessed little dimensional stability, was not easily laundered or dyed, and adverse publicity and its glossy appearance gave it little style appeal. Moreover, until 1929 the price per pound of rayon yarn was over three times that of cotton. Hence, until the thirties there were physical as well as economic barriers to competition between cotton and rayon. These barriers were gradually removed as the price and quality pattern of filament rayon yarn shaped itself toward the price and quality pattern of cotton, and as the production of rayon staple fiber, which possesses many of the physical properties of baled cotton, rapidly increased.

A complete quantitative analysis of the extent to which rayon and cotton have competed with each other in recent years would envisage at least rough calculations of the cross-elasticities of demand for the two fibers for selected points in time. The complexities of the textile industry and the multitude of end uses to which each fiber is put, however, make such calculations virtually impossible.[40]

Until about 1927, the boundaries between the broad silk industry (which included broad woven rayon goods), the cotton weaving industry, and the woolen and worsted industry were fairly well defined. Although each of these three industries used small quantities of all the other textile fibers for their mixtures, there was little doubt from year to year as to the branch of the industry with which a particular firm was associated. While the intermediate stages of fabrication were so clearly delineated, substitution among fibers was most likely to be initiated by end-product fabricators. By the time fabrics constructed of each type of fiber had proceeded this far along the production pipeline, however, the initial cost of the yarn

[39] *Rayon Organon*, February 1948; statistical supplement.

[40] See Daniel Vandermuelen, "Intertextile Competition" (MS.), Claremont College, for some of the definitional problems associated with the textile industry.

had become a relatively insignificant percentage of the total cost of the fabric.[41] Hence, only large changes in the relative prices of fibers would have led to perceptible substitution among the various types of fabrics. Moreover, the actual substitution of one type of fabric for another in substantial quantities required a shift in investment away from the intermediate capital equipment employed to produce the fabric for which demand had decreased to the intermediate capital equipment employed to produce the fabric for which demand had increased. Under these conditions, the cross-elasticities of demand among textile fibers were probably very low.

As rayon output increased and as rayon producers incorporated the more desirable physical attributes of silk, cotton, and wool in rayon yarn and staple fiber, sharp boundaries between the various sectors of the textile industry began to disappear. Rayon acquired some of the softness of natural fibers after 1926 when technical improvements permitted an increase in the filament count of 150-denier yarn from 18 to 60 filaments. Between 1921 and 1945 the tenacity of 150-denier textile rayon yarn was increased by 65 per cent. Elongation on a dry basis was increased from 15 per cent in 1921 to 25 per cent by 1930, but has subsequently been gradually reduced to 22 per cent as producers found yarns having lower elongation than 25 per cent more desirable. In 1937, Du Pont introduced a high-tenacity yarn having over twice the dry strength of 150-denier textile yarns and possessing a high degree of resistance to deterioration under heat and repeated flexing. These features make high-tenacity rayon yarn particularly adaptable to automobile tire production. Other less measurable but nonetheless tangible improvements which have made rayon a better substitute for, or superior to, natural fibers, were the introduction of staple fiber, dull and semi-dull yarns, and a much wider range of deniers and filament counts, all in the late twenties, and sustained progress in crimping, draping, and dyeing qualities since 1920.

With the evolution in the physical properties of rayon yarn, weavers gradually adopted more flexible equipment so that they could weave all rayon, all cotton, or rayon and cotton mixed fabrics. Similarly, rayon staple fiber, designed to be spun equally as well on cotton, woolen, worsted, and silk spinning systems, added much

[41] For mill margins at the various levels of fabrication in the textile industry, see L. D. Howell, *Marketing and Manufacturing Margins for Textiles*, United States Department of Agriculture, Technical Bulletin no. 891, March 1945.

flexibility to textile operations,[42] so much flexibility, in fact, that some spinning and weaving firms, classified by the Census according to the principal fibers consumed in terms of linear yards, are frequently included among rayon woven goods producers one year and among cotton woven goods producers the next.

These developments in the textile industry have eliminated many of the obstacles to substitution among fibers and have shifted the point at which substitution is most likely to be initiated away from end-products to intermediate stages of fabrication closer to the fiber and yarn markets. In the process, one would logically expect the cross-elasticities of demand between cotton and rayon, and to a less extent the cross-elasticities of demand between rayon and wool, to have been significantly increased. In fact, some idea of the extent to which spinners and weavers have substituted rayon for natural fibers in recent years can be obtained from the following data: Between 1939 and 1947, the quantity of rayon yarn spun on the cotton system in the United States increased by 130 per cent and the quantity of mixed yarns, chiefly cotton and rayon mixtures, increased by 240 per cent; over the same period, the quantity of cotton spun on the cotton system increased by only 21 per cent. Similarly, between 1939 and 1947 the quantity of cotton broad woven goods produced in the United States increased by only 15 per cent and the quantity of woolen and worsted broad woven fabrics by only 27 per cent, whereas rayon and related broad woven fabrics increased by 47 per cent, 100 per cent rayon filament broad woven goods by 24 per cent, 100 per cent spun rayon fabrics by 88 per cent, synthetic and natural fiber blends by 37 per cent, and filament and spun rayon mixed fabrics by 790 per cent.[43]

The most comprehensive treatment, from the standpoint of coverage, of markets in which rayon competes with cotton appears in 1167 pages of hearings before the House Committee on Agriculture, in a study of agriculture and economic problems of the cotton belt.[44] After an exhaustive study of 127 end-use cotton markets and the intermediate markets between them and rayon and cotton fiber markets, the Committee estimated in 1947 that, under conditions of full employment, cotton consumption in 1950 would equal 3.67

[42] For a fairly detailed treatment of the rise of the multi-fiber firm, see the author's article "Integration in the Textile Industry," *Harvard Business Review*, vol. XXVIII, no. 1, January 1950, pp. 74–88.

[43] All data from 1947 *Census of Manufactures*, textile products section.

[44] *Hearings*, H. R., see esp. Project IV, pp. 255–374.

billion pounds if cotton prices remained at $0.25 per pound, if the prices of rayon yarn and staple fiber remained unchanged, and if cotton maintained its 1947 relative position with respect to quality characteristics. Under the same conditions, if the price of cotton were increased to $0.40 per pound, cotton consumption could be expected to decline by 1.19 billion pounds to only 2.48 billion pounds, nearly all of which would be reflected in increased rayon consumption.[45]

Although an analysis of the effects of smaller cotton or rayon price changes would have been much more meaningful, the Committee's findings indicate a high positive cross-elasticity of demand for rayon in terms of cotton prices. If, for example, "nearly all" of the 1.19 billion-pound decrease in cotton consumption could be construed as an increase in rayon consumption ranging somewhere between 0.8 and 1.0 billion pounds, the arc cross-elasticity of demand for rayon in terms of cotton prices is somewhere between 1.24 and 1.44.[46]

The substitution between rayon and cotton caused by changes in the relative prices of cotton and rayon, however, varies greatly among end-use markets. For example, the Committee's report shows that an increase in cotton prices from $0.25 to $0.40 per pound or, presumably, a corresponding decrease in the price of rayon, would give rayon producers the entire automobile tire cord and fabric market. Similarly, with a corresponding change in relative prices cotton would lose all of its thermal insulation market, 66 per cent of its tablecloth and napkin market, 62 per cent of its women's underwear market, and about 50 per cent of its curtain fabric, domestic thread, and men's pajama markets. On the other hand, it would lose only insignificant percentages of its sheet, diaper, pillowcase, belt, and bed-ticking markets.[47] The wide variation among markets in the effects of changes in relative prices is due primarily to differences in the physical attributes of cotton and rayon. For some of the above end-uses, rayon is virtually a perfect substitute for cotton; for others,

[45] *Hearings,* p. 273. The analysis was made at a time when, for all practical purposes, rayon and cotton, in both yarn and fiber form, sold at the same price per pound. Throughout the report, no allowance was made for the time required to install the additional rayon capacity and bring it into operation.

[46] From the formula $\eta_{xpy} = \frac{Q_O - Q_1}{Q_O + Q_1} \Big/ \frac{P_O - P_1}{P_O + P_1}$, where the Q's are quantities of rayon and the P's are prices of cotton.

[47] *Hearings,* H. R., Project IV, pp. 267–268, 271–272. See also Table 3 for data showing the extent to which rayon has already been substituted for cotton in the production of tire cord and fabric.

such as the sheeting and diaper markets, it is a very poor substitute.

In spite of the serious inroads which rayon could make in cotton consumption with a change in relative prices in favor of rayon, the Committee concluded that the greatest threat to cotton was the rayon industry's aggressive research program. With rayon prices having already declined to where they are about equal to cotton prices, the Committee estimates that, if this price equality continues, and if rayon research proves to be as fruitful in the future as it has been in the past, cotton could easily disappear from domestic textile markets altogether. Their forecasts along these lines are as follows: If cotton continues to hold all of its present quality advantages, the United States, again assuming full employment, will consume about 3.8 billion pounds of cotton in 1955. If, however, rayon should become as launderable as cotton, cotton consumption would be reduced to 3.2 billion pounds; if rayon should become as launderable and as durable as cotton, cotton consumption would be reduced to only 1.3 billion pounds; and if rayon should become as good as cotton in all qualities, cotton consumption would be reduced to only 0.38 billion pounds or might disappear from textile markets altogether.[48]

Rayon producers, therefore, probably consider quality competition between rayon and cotton to be at least as significant as price competition, now that rayon prices have fallen approximately to the level of cotton prices. In the immediate past, however, changes in the relative prices of cotton and rayon have probably had immediate impact upon the relative consumption of the two fibers. The above evidence indicates that this is still, and at least in the immediate future, will continue to be, true.

Competition between wool and rayon filament yarn, as pointed out in Chapter 2, has been limited to a few special markets that account for only a small percentage of total rayon consumption. Because of the quick-drying features of acetate rayon yarn, however, it has been substituted in considerable quantities for wool in the production of such commodities as swim suits and beach wear. Rayon staple fiber, on the other hand, which bears a remarkable resem-

[48] *Hearings*, H. R., Project IV, p. 270. The Committee, in keeping with the traditional arguments advanced by textile experts, contend that other features of rayon give it an advantage over cotton when the two fibers possess the same basic physical qualities and sell for approximately the same price, i.e., rayon is more uniform in quality, rayon staple fiber contains less waste than baled cotton, and rayon prices are less erratic.

blance to wool when spun on the woolen system, has recently been a strong competitor for traditional woolen markets. Possessing both the worsted appearance and some of the warmth-giving quality of wool, its lower price has resulted in a substitution of spun rayon yarns for wool yarns in the production of spring and fall wear, upholstery, men's socks, top coats, rugs, and other commodities formerly made exclusively of wool. Moreover, large quantities of spun rayon and nylon are used in the production of woolen and worsted mixtures.

Accordingly, it is not likely that producers have regarded wool prices as a significant determinant of their filament yarn prices, although in recent years there has probably been a good deal of price interdependency between rayon staple fiber and wool. Rayon staple fiber, and the new synthetic textiles such as spun nylon and orlon, all of which are products of rayon chemical research and production techniques, show much more promise of offering stiff competition to the woolen industry in the future than rayon filament yarn has in the past.

The cross-elasticities of demand for rayon in terms of each of the natural fiber prices, therefore, have probably increased considerably as rayon has improved in quality, and as prices for the four principal fibers have shifted their relative position. Until recent years, the price of silk was always from two to three times that of rayon; since 1940 rayon has sold for about one-fourth the price of silk. Until 1928 the price of rayon was higher than the price of wool yarn; since 1928 the price of wool yarn has been higher. The two price series have gradually diverged until the current price of wool yarn is three times that of rayon. In the early twenties the price of rayon was four times that of cotton yarn; in 1944 cotton yarn price rose above rayon price for the first time and has remained at the approximate level of rayon price since 1946. The price of rayon, therefore, has experienced a tremendous decline relative to natural fiber yarn prices. This secular price movement and the sustained technological improvement in rayon have accounted for a substantial part of the inverse secular trends in consumption of the four fibers.[49] Correspondingly, since many of the present markets for rayon were, until recent years, exclusively silk, cotton, or woolen markets, the demand for rayon should be considerably more elastic now than in the early twenties.

Moreover, in view of the short-run price behavior of the four

[49] Cf. Chart 1, and *infra*, this chapter.

fibers and the role played by expectations, it seems fairly safe to conclude that the elasticity of demand for rayon increases as it shifts to the left during textile market recessions. Accordingly, both cost and demand conditions are such as to encourage price reductions in a declining textile market. In the long-run, competition between rayon and natural fibers can be conducted on either a price or quality basis or both. In the short-run, however, competition must be conducted purely on a price basis. Stated another way, when rayon producers see inventories piling up, the most pressing problem is to sell "current" rayon. Since rayon prices lag behind natural fiber prices, a downward revision in rayon prices during a textile market recession can be expected to recapture some of the old markets which were lost to natural fibers before the price gap was closed. Sales of "current" rayon, however, can be stimulated only through price reductions. On the other hand, an invasion of new markets by rayon presents the problems of both price and quality. Since price reductions alone are more likely to be effective in regaining old markets than in opening up new ones, and since regaining old markets is essentially a recession problem for the rayon industry, there are good reasons for suspecting that the elasticity of demand for rayon increases during a textile market recession.

Furthermore, reductions in natural fiber prices lead to expectations of a decrease in rayon prices; but since rayon list prices are not frequently revised, knitters and weavers probably view rayon price changes as being much more permanent than natural fiber price changes. Hence, a downward revision of rayon prices during a textile market recession can also be expected to stimulate buying to replenish inventories of knitters and weavers who have engaged in only hand-to-mouth buying in anticipation of a price reduction. Rayon producers, cognizant of the effects of price expectations on sales, have occasionally offered guarantees against price changes to offset them, particularly the effects of expected price reductions, but large producers have preferred to rely upon their reputation for maintaining stable prices.[50]

In addition to the price effects of inter-fiber competition, rayon prices have also been influenced by competition from rayon produced in other countries. The extremely favorable tariffs which domestic producers have been able to obtain in Washington, however, have greatly reduced foreign competition since the Tariff Act

[50] See Chap. 4 and fn. 31, Chap. 5.

of 1930. On a strictly competitive basis, the domestic rayon industry would never have flourished as it has without tariff protection; it is even doubtful that it would have survived. Comparative costs of production of one pound of rayon for the five leading rayon producing countries, for the year 1934, are shown in Table 18. These data show that the cost of producing rayon in the United States in 1934 was 177 per cent higher than production costs in Japan, 93 per cent higher than in Italy, 40 per cent higher than in Germany, and almost 20 per cent higher than in Great Britain. Although all factors of production in terms of 1934 dollar equivalents cost more in the United States than elsewhere, much of the cost differential is accounted for by higher labor costs. This has been the chief argument advanced by domestic producers for keeping high import tariffs in force.[51]

TABLE 18

Costs of Producing a Pound of Viscose Rayon Yarn in Five Leading Rayon-Producing Countries, 1934

(Units are in Cents per Pound at 1934 Exchange Rates and Per Cent)

	Pulp and Chemicals		Wages and Power		Business Expense		Total
	Cost	%	Cost	%	Cost	%	
United States	14.3	32	22.1	50	8.1	18	44.5
Great Britain	13.8	36	17.4	45	7.2	19	38.4
Germany	12.3	37	15.1	45	6.0	18	33.4
Italy	10.6	46	9.7	43	2.7	11	23.0
Japan	8.0	50	6.0	37	2.1	13	16.2

Source: *Report of the Japanese Cellulose Industry Reporters, Ltd.*, January 1935. Reprinted in *Rayon Organon*, April 1935, p. 61.

From 1913 to 1922 the tariff on all imported rayon was 35 per cent *ad valorem;* from 1922 to 1930 the tariff was $0.45 per pound but not less than 45 per cent *ad valorem.* Over the period in which these two tariff rates were in effect, the average price per pound of foreign yarn plus duty in the United States, in all years, was below the domestic price of 150-denier viscose yarn. Although there was a secular decline in the proportion of total domestic yarn consumption imported, imports still accounted for about 12 per cent of total United States consumption as late as 1928 and 1929.

[51] See "American Rayon and the Tariff," *Rayon Journal,* October 27, 1925, p. 14; "Rayon in the New Tariff," *ibid.,* July 1, 1930, p. 77; "Hasty Tariff Revision Fostered by Coalition," *ibid.,* August 1931, p. 9; "Wages and Tariffs," *ibid.,* August 1932, p. 24; and others.

The Tariff Act of 1930, which froze or increased the previous high tariff rates in the face of rapidly declining domestic prices, effectively eliminated foreign competition from the domestic yarn market until January 1, 1948.[52] The new comprehensive act called for a 45 per cent *ad valorem* tariff (but a minimum duty of $0.45 per pound) on standard yarns, and a 45 per cent to 50 per cent *ad valorem* tariff plus $0.45 per pound (but a minimum duty of $0.90 per pound) on all high-twist yarns. The height of the tariff wall and the decline in domestic prices in 1930 and 1931 placed the domestic market completely out of reach of foreign producers. For most high-twist yarns, domestic prices have been below the $0.90 per pound minimum duty since 1930. Declining world rayon prices made the $0.45 per pound minimum duty effective for all standard

TABLE 19

Domestic Yarn Price[a] Less Effective Minimum Duty, 1930–1949

Year	Price	Price Less Duty	Year	Price	Price Less Duty	Year	Price	Price Less Duty
1930	$1.05	$0.60	1937	$0.62	$0.17	1944	$0.55	$0.10
1931	0.75	0.30	1938	0.52	0.07	1945	0.55	0.10
1932	0.66	0.21	1939	0.52	0.07	1946	0.55	0.11
1933	0.61	0.16	1940	0.53	0.08	1947	0.67	0.22
1934	0.59	0.14	1941	0.54	0.09	1948	0.76	0.535
1935	0.57	0.12	1942	0.55	0.10	1949	0.75	0.525
1936	0.57	0.12	1943	0.55	0.10			

[a] Price and duty are for 150-denier viscose yarn.

yarn imported after 1930. In most years the domestic price has not been substantially above the minimum duty.

The impossibility of even the lowest cost foreign producer competing in the domestic market between 1930 and 1948 is indicated by the data shown in Table 19. In order to absorb the tariff and meet prevailing domestic prices for most years in this period, foreign producers would have had to have produced and transported their yarn to the United States at a total cost of less than $0.20 per pound. Even Japan, the lowest-cost foreign producer, could not compete in the United States market when confronted with such formidable duties as those imposed by the Tariff Act of 1930.

[52] The Tariff Act effective January 1, 1948 was worked out under the recent Geneva tariff agreements. The new Act calls for the reduction of duty on virtually all rayon products by 50 per cent. Although the effect the new tariff will have on rayon imports cannot be appraised at this early date, rayon imports have increased noticeably since the new tariff rates became effective. See 1948 and 1949 issues of the *Rayon Organon*.

Hence, prior to 1930, domestic producers constantly encountered the downward pressure exerted by foreign competition upon their prices. The tariff, though quite high, did not completely close the gap between foreign and domestic prices.[53] Except for the war years, which interrupted normal trade relations, the domestic price was roughly 5 per cent to 15 per cent above import price.[54] Until 1930, therefore, domestic price moved in close consonance with foreign

Chart 14

Average Annual Foreign and Domestic Rayon Yarn Prices, 1913–1948

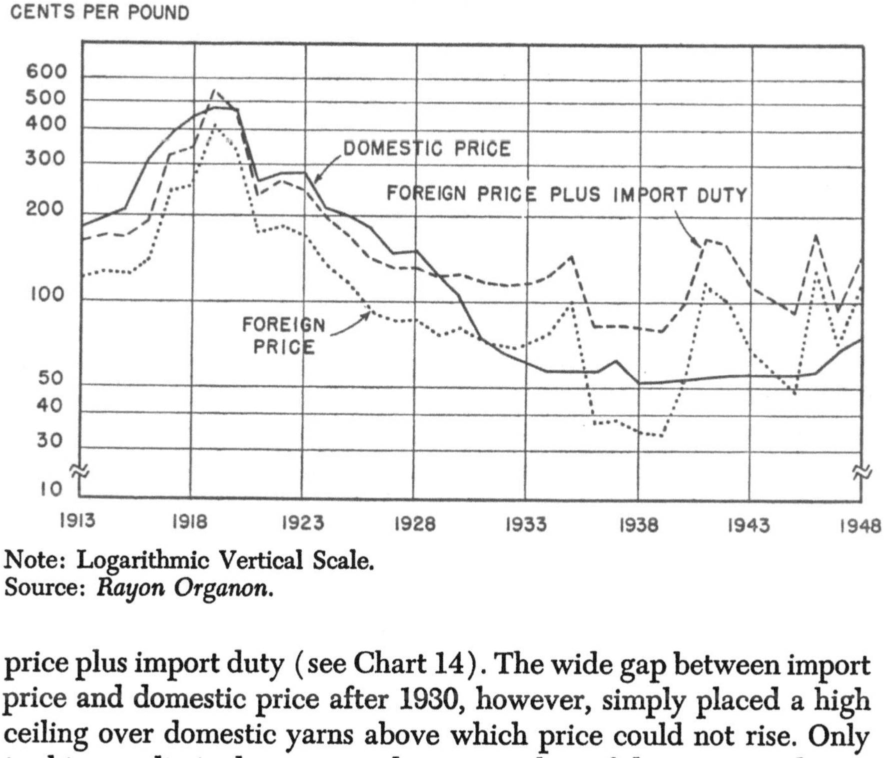

Note: Logarithmic Vertical Scale.
Source: *Rayon Organon.*

price plus import duty (see Chart 14). The wide gap between import price and domestic price after 1930, however, simply placed a high ceiling over domestic yarns above which price could not rise. Only in this very limited sense was the price policy of domestic producers appreciably influenced by the price of foreign yarns between 1930 and 1947.

[53] On the basis of 1934 cost data, however, the duty more than closed the gap between costs of production in the United States and all other countries.

[54] The two price series are not strictly comparable. Import price is an average price based on all rayon yarn imported, whereas domestic price is for 150-denier viscose yarn only. It was demonstrated in Chap. 4, however, that the price of 150-denier viscose yarn is very close to the average domestic price.

D. Causal Factors in Rayon Price Trend, 1920–1947

Prior to 1930, domestic rayon price moved in such consonance with foreign rayon and silk prices and, to a less extent, with the price of cotton yarn, that the directional movement, as well as the cyclical fluctuations, in the rayon price series may be linked causally with the price behavior of these fibers. To explain fully the trend in rayon price before 1930, would entail the task of explaining price trends for the entire textile yarn market.

Since 1930, however, high tariff walls have isolated domestic prices from the effects of price movements abroad and silk prices have had increasingly less influence on domestic rayon price movements.[55] Furthermore, since 1920 all natural fiber prices have increased considerably relative to the price of rayon. The shifting in the relative prices of textile yarns, which has been particularly apparent since the depression, has taken place concurrently with an inverse shift in relative fiber consumption. Prior to 1920, rayon accounted for only 0.2 per cent to 0.3 per cent of total fiber consumption, whereas wool accounted for 8.0 per cent; silk, 1.2 per cent; and cotton, 89.0 per cent. By 1939 rayon accounted for 10.4 per cent of total fiber consumption, and by 1948 it accounted for 18.0 per cent, whereas silk accounted for only 0.1 per cent; wool, 8.5 per cent; and cotton, 75.6 per cent. From 1920 to 1941 the proportion of total rayon consumption imported declined from over 50 per cent to a fraction of 1 per cent. Hence, the largest gains in consumption of domestically produced rayon have been made at the expense of foreign rayon, silk, and cotton.

Although much of the downward rayon price trend after 1920 was undoubtedly a result of similar directional movements in the prices of imported rayon and natural fiber yarns — or perhaps a common economic force which precipitated the price movement of all textile yarns — there is reason to believe that much of it was due to the rayon industry's rapid rate of technological change and plant expansion. Particularly, these phenomena may account for the secular decline in rayon prices relative to natural yarn prices.

Patently, from the very nature of the rayon producer's, *ceteris paribus*, long-run cost curve, substantial decreases in unit costs have resulted from the expansion of plants to benefit from economies of

[55] While silk consumption greatly exceeded rayon consumption, rayon price was tied closely to the price of silk. After silk consumption declined to a small fraction of rayon consumption, the price dependency was probably reversed.

TABLE 20

Essential Materials and Labor per Pound of Rayon, 1923–1945

	1923	1925	1927	1929	1931	1933	1937	1938	1940	1942	1944	1945
Labor Hours	1.111	1.025	0.922	0.856	0.571	0.429	0.328	0.299	0.228	0.184	0.184	0.173
Pounds per lb. of Viscose Yarn[a]												
Linters Pulp	—	—	—	0.56	—	0.53	0.05	—	—	—	—	—
Wood Pulp	—	1.30[b]	—	0.58	—	0.56	1.05	1.12	1.15	1.13	1.12	1.12
Caustic Soda	—	—	—	1.30	—	1.20	1.00	0.90	0.90	0.90	0.90	0.90
Carbon Bisulphide	—	—	—	0.38	—	0.35	0.34	0.35	0.34	0.35	0.35	0.35
Sulphuric Acid	—	—	—	1.70	—	1.60	1.60	1.70	1.40	1.30	1.30	1.30
Corn Sugar	—	—	—	0.80	—	0.40	0.45	0.45	0.19	0.17	0.13	0.13

Source: Labor hours per pound computed from output per man-hour data published by the Bureau of Labor Statistics in *Productivity and Unit Labor Costs in Selected Manufacturing Industries, 1919–1940* (Washington, 1942). A special mimeographed release takes the series through 1945.

[a] Materials consumed are based upon operations at one plant of a large rayon manufacturing corporation. See *Hearings*, H. R., Project V, p. 48.

[b] Varies with quantities of linters pulp used.

scale; furthermore, technological changes have shifted the long-run cost curve to a lower level. Production economies that have been effected through the operation of these two forces are reflected in the data presented in Table 20. Between 1923 and 1945 the quantity

Chart 15

Average Annual Price and Unit Costs per Pound of Rayon, 1923–1945

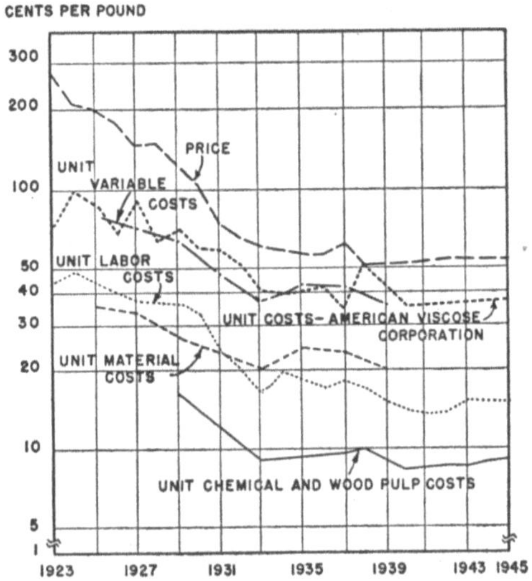

Note: Logarithmic Vertical Scale.
Source: Prices from *Rayon Organon;* data for the American Viscose Corporation from *Investment, Profits and Rates of Return for Selected Industries* and *Hearings,* H. R., Project V; other data computed from *Census of Manufactures* and *Monthly Labor Review.*

of labor required to produce one pound of rayon was reduced by 84.5 per cent (or output per man-hour was increased from 0.9 pounds to 5.8 pounds). Although there has been little change in the quantity of pulp used in the production of a pound of rayon, the development of more efficient recovery systems has considerably reduced the quantities of chemicals and other materials used. Between 1929 and 1945, for example, caustic soda consumption per pound of viscose yarn was reduced by 31 per cent, carbon bisulphide by 8 per cent, sulphuric acid by 24 per cent, and corn sugar[56] by 84 per cent.

The combined effect of larger-scale operations and technological change has more than offset the secular movement of factor prices, particularly the secular increase in average hourly earnings (see Chart 15). Although rising factor prices reversed the downward trend in unit costs between 1933 and 1934,[57] unit costs for the largest producer were reduced from $0.98 to $0.36 between 1927 and 1940. Hence, much of the downward trend in rayon yarn prices relative to the prices of other textile yarns can be explained in terms of technological changes which have reduced unit costs.

[56] The decrease in the quantity of corn sugar consumed per pound of rayon is probably due in part to the substitution of glucose, but no data on glucose consumption are available.

[57] Very few additions were made to fixed capital in the industry in the first half of the thirties; the scale of operations at individual plants being virtually at a standstill. See installed capacity, Chap. 3, and investment series, Appendix C.

9

PROFITS, INVESTMENT, and Prices

There are no well-developed methods for appraising the social performance of a particular industry. It is generally agreed upon, however, that the more competitive an industry is the better it serves society; but competition, except for the atomistic or pure variety, is not a very precise concept. Moreover, conceptual measures of competition such as the relationship between price and marginal costs have two very serious drawbacks when carried into the field of empirical industrial studies: (1) they assume static conditions, and (2) they are susceptible to very limited statistical application.

Less precisely formulated but more practicable indexes to the social performance of an industry may be obtained through an examination of its structural characteristics and its over-all performance. That is to say, although it may be impossible to state precisely *how far* an industry falls short of fulfilling all of the conditions of perfect competition at a given instant of time, it is both possible and useful to examine the conditions conducive to competition which have prevailed in an industry and the effectiveness with which they have brought about competitive behavior. For purposes of public policy, however, the all-important question becomes "Are the conditions conducive to competition *sufficient* and have they played their role effectively *enough,* that is, can the industry be said to be 'workably competitive'?" An attempt to answer this question as it relates to the rayon industry will be deferred to the final chapter; a more limited picture of the over-all performance of the domestic rayon industry is presented here.

One criterion for judging the effectiveness of competition in an industry is the secular behavior of prices, profits rates, and rate of investment. An important precept of competitive theory is that the abnormally high rate of return which accrues to the innovator be

Chart 16

Average Annual Price, Investment, and Rate of Return in the Rayon Industry, 1915–1948

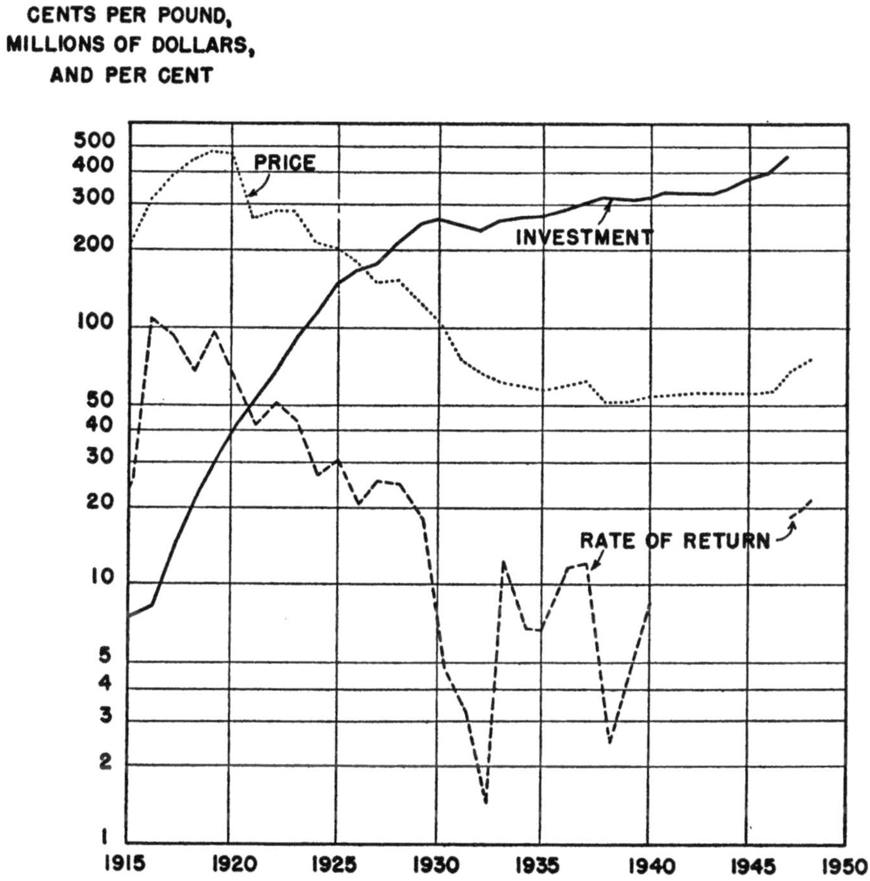

Note: Logarithmic Vertical Scale.
Source: See Investment, Profits, and Rate of Return, Appendix C.

finally bid down to a level that approaches the competitive rate of return through increased investment and lower prices. A supplementary condition is that the increase in investment and the decline in prices occur at as rapid a rate as could be expected when due consideration is given to the nature of the production process.

Generally, the relationships among investment, the rate of return, and prices in the rayon industry approximate those which would have been expected under highly competitive conditions (see Chart 16).[1] Average investment for 1947 was fifty-seven times that of 1915. Between 1915 and 1920, the last five years American Viscose monopolized the production of rayon in the United States by virtue of its patent holdings, the company increased investment in rayon plant by 422 per cent. Between 1920 and 1925, investment in the industry increased by 268 per cent; and between 1925 and 1930, by 72.6 per cent. The first interruption to this staggering rate of increase in investment came during the early thirties when the industry suffered a few years of excess capacity. Investment in the industry declined in 1931 and 1932, but increased slightly in 1933 and increased 28.8 per cent between 1933 and 1941. Wartime demand for rayon for the national defense program and postwar demands for textile and automobile tire yarns led to a 37.2 per cent increase in investment in the industry between 1941 and 1947. Moreover, between 1920 and 1930 the number of rayon producers in the United States increased from one to twenty.

Rapid expansion of capacity has been accompanied by an equally rapid secular decline in price and the rate of return on investment. It has been previously demonstrated that the price of rayon fell at a rate of 12.8 per cent per year between 1919 and 1935. Return on investment in the industry has declined at approximately the same rate. For the period 1915–1919, investment earned an average annual rate of return of 80 per cent. This rate fell rapidly as investment increased during the twenties. The average annual rate of return for the 1920–1924 period was 45 per cent; for the 1925–1929 period, 24 per cent; and from 1930 to 1941, the average annual rate of return was only 6.9 per cent. The only comparable data available for the postwar period show that the rate of return on investment in the industry was 18.7 per cent in 1947 and 21.4 per cent in 1948.[2] High rates of return after the war had attracted three new entrants to the industry by 1948.

In spite of the high premium placed upon industrial "know-how" and the shortage of trained rayon technicians, no evidence can be

[1] See Appendix C for a description of the investment and rate of return series.

[2] F. T. C., *Rates of Return for 528 Identical Companies in 25 Selected Manufacturing Industries, 1940, 1947 and 1948,* mimeographed release (December 1949), p. 14.

found to indicate that bookkeeping profits have been understated because a large percentage of net returns was drained off in the form of high administrative salaries. No separate data for top-management salaries are available but, historically, total administrative and distribution expense has averaged from 3 per cent to 5 per cent of manufacturing expense (exclusive of depreciation).[3] On the basis of 1940 financial statements for twelve rayon yarn producing companies, administrative expense alone accounted for only from 1 to 2 per cent of total manufacturing expense.[4] Payments to salaried employees in the industry other than central administrative officers but including corporation salaried officers ranged from 4 to 11 million dollars per year for the period 1927–1937, or from $2000 to $3000 per salaried employee.[5] The range of salaries cannot be ascertained.

Although the above secular behavior of prices, investment, and the rate of return in the rayon industry is consistent with that which would have been expected under highly competitive conditions, it is obvious that the trends themselves can serve only as a basis for qualitative analysis. They do not prove the absense of monopoly restraint; they merely indicate a performance that bears a strong resemblance to the results one would expect from competition. For this reason, it is necessary to examine more closely the behavior of prices, profits, and investment for evidence of monopoly power. Before making such an examination, however, some of the more important features of the rayon industry deserve a brief review.

It is quite obvious that no rayon producer, or any group of rayon producers, has possessed sufficient power over the market to restrict directly the entry of new firms to the industry. This is adequately demonstrated by the increases in the number of firms in the industry which have occurred during periods of abnormally high profits such as the twenties and the postwar period. If, on the other hand, it could be assumed that all rayon producers have been tacitly in agreement on both price and investment policy, they conceivably would also have possessed the power to restrict the entry of new firms indirectly through their pricing policy.

It has been fairly well demonstrated historically that a considerably higher rate of return is required to attract new entrants to the

[3] F. T. C., *Investments, Profits, and Rates of Return for Selected Industries*, pp. 17999–18002; from the income statements of American Viscose and Du Pont.

[4] *Hearings*, H. R., Project V, p. 47.

[5] 1939 *Census of Manufactures*, rayon and allied products section.

TABLE 21

Per Cent of Total Rayon Yarn Capacity Controlled by Each Producer and Per Cent of Combined Yarn Capacity Controlled by Each of the Ten Viscose Rayon Producers Charged with Price Collusion by the Federal Trade Commission, 1931–1949[a]

	Per Cent 1931	Per Cent 1933	Per Cent 1935	Per Cent 1938	Per Cent 1942	Per Cent Capacity Expanded 1931-1942	Per Cent 1945	Per Cent 1949	Per Cent Capacity Expanded 1945-1949
American Viscose						86.0			29.5
Total Yarn Capacity	43.7	33.0	34.3	28.7	30.8		29.3	26.2	
Ten Viscose Producers' Capacity	50.0	40.7	44.4	36.8	42.0		39.5	35.0	
Du Pont						186.7			34.9
Total Yarn Capacity	15.3	15.9	17.0	14.9	16.6		17.0	15.8	
Ten Viscose Producers' Capacity	17.5	19.7	22.0	19.1	22.6		22.9	21.1	
Tubize[b]						35.1			—
Total Yarn Capacity	7.5	7.0	3.6	5.6	3.9		3.7	—	
Ten Viscose Producers' Capacity	8.6	8.6	4.7	7.2	5.2		5.0	—	
North American						114.3			25.0
Total Yarn Capacity	7.1	7.4	7.2	7.0	5.8		5.1	4.4	
Ten Viscose Producers' Capacity	8.2	9.2	9.3	9.0	7.9		6.9	5.9	
Industrial						192.3			24.6
Total Yarn Capacity	7.0	7.2	6.1	9.0	7.3		10.4	9.0	
Ten Viscose Producers' Capacity	7.6	8.8	7.9	11.6	10.0		14.0	11.9	
American Enka						500.0			75.7
Total Yarn Capacity	2.5	6.4	4.7	8.4	5.8		5.9	7.2	
Ten Viscose Producers' Capacity	2.9	7.9	6.1	10.8	7.9		8.0	9.6	
Skenandoa						100.0			(c)
Total Yarn Capacity	1.8	1.5	1.4	2.0	1.4		(c)	1.1	
Ten Viscose Producers' Capacity	2.0	1.9	1.9	2.5	2.1		(c)	1.5	
Delaware						50.0			(c)
Total Yarn Capacity	1.0	0.9	1.1	0.8	0.6		(c)	0.4	
Ten Viscose Producers' Capacity	1.2	1.1	1.4	1.1	0.8		(c)	0.5	
Acme						0.0			(c)
Total Yarn Capacity	0.5	0.5	0.4	0.3	0.2		(c)	0.2	
Ten Viscose Producers' Capacity	0.6	0.6	0.5	0.4	0.3		(c)	0.2	
Hartford						60.0			(c)
Total Yarn Capacity	1.3	1.2	1.4	1.1	0.8		(c)	0.7	
Ten Viscose Producers' Capacity	1.5	1.5	1.9	1.4	1.3		(c)	1.0	
Celanese						672.7			96.4
Total Yarn Capacity	5.6	9.4	12.6	10.4	16.4		17.9	24.3	
Tennessee Eastman						3300.0			77.0
Total Yarn Capacity	0.5	2.4	3.6	5.9	6.6		5.6	6.9	
American Bemberg						180.0			25.0
Total Yarn Capacity	2.5	3.4	2.9	2.8	2.7		1.9	1.7	
Rest of the Industry									
Total Yarn Capacity	3.6	3.8	3.6	3.1	1.3		3.2	2.1	

[a] Percentages computed from capacity data presented in Table 5. Capacities of several producers for 1942 estimated from 1938 data.

[b] Merged with Celanese in 1946.

[c] Exact capacities in 1945 unknown.

rayon industry than is required to induce old firms to expand.[6] While no new firms entered the rayon industry during the decade of the thirties when the average rate of return was around 6 per cent, old firms continued to expand capacity, some having doubled or trebled their 1931 capacity by the outbreak of the war (see Table 21). During the twenties and in the postwar period, however, rates of return ranging upward of 10 per cent attracted new entrants. Hence, rayon producers collectively could, through their price policy, conceivably keep profits suppressed below the attraction rate and thereby limit the number of producers.

Such a price policy could hardly have been effective, however, if not supported by collusion, either tacit or overt, on investment policy as well. The suppression of rayon prices by concerted action or through oligopolistic rationalization would have created the attendant problem of how to deal with the resultant rayon shortages. Rayon producers could have met this problem in one of two ways: they could have forestalled or met the shortage by expanding their own capacities at a sufficiently rapid rate, or they could have agreed not to expand and thereby have forced textile consumers to commence substituting cotton, silk, and wool for rayon. Since the latter course would have been patently unwise in that it would not have been an effective measure for suppressing profits rates in the short-run and, in the long-run, would have been unprofitable for the industry as a whole, it is not surprising that all the evidence supports a contrary course of action.

Rayon producers have consistently shaped their research programs and their price and production policies to encourage the substitution of rayon for natural fibers and, as has been demonstrated elsewhere in this study, they have been extremely successful in accomplishing their purpose. Moreover, except for the war and postwar periods, when plant construction was restricted, the history of the rayon industry reveals only two brief instances when the effective demand for rayon could not be filled out of current production and accumulated rayon stocks.[7] Rayon producers were forced to ration available stocks during the months of August and September 1932,

[6] The reasons why a fairly high attraction rate is necessary in the rayon industry were suggested in Chap. 3.

[7] Because inventory fluctuations are permitted to cushion short-run disequilibria between production and consumption in the rayon industry (see p. 131 ff.), consumption has frequently exceeded capacity production without creating a rayon shortage. Hence, capacity or near capacity operations in the industry over fairly long periods of time are entirely consistent with the complete absense of severe rayon shortages.

after monthly sales had increased sharply from 10.5 million pounds to 23.5 million pounds between March and May, and again in March, April, May, and June 1937, after monthly sales had increased sharply from 20.2 million pounds in May 1936 to a new all-time high of 30.5 million pounds by August, and remained substantially above capacity production until December 1936 (see Chart 5).

Although it is impossible to state conclusively why, in these two instances, the price of rayon did not increase rapidly enough to equate short-run supply and demand, the brevity of the shortages would suggest that the rayon producers' penchant for stable prices could be offered as a more plausible explanation than concerted action to suppress prices and profits in order to keep new firms out of the industry.

It would seem fairly safe to conclude, therefore, in view of the pronounced upward trend in rayon consumption since its introduction in the United States, that rayon producers have not only refrained from restricting capacity, but have in fact expanded capacity in anticipation of increased future demand.

If rayon producers have conspired on investment policy, then, it seems obvious that they have conspired to expand capacity rapidly enough to provide for expected increases in rayon consumption. There are reasons for believing, however, that the rate of investment under oligopolistic conditions will more nearly approach the rate of investment under highly competitive conditions when each producer formulates his own decisions to invest, than when investment decisions are subject to the restraining force of a collusive agreement.[8] Hence, an analysis of the social performance of an industry cannot be entirely complete unless some answer can be given to the question of whether or not the rate of investment has been subject to a collusive agreement at all.

It is not entirely clear as to what the outward manifestations of collusive action with respect to investment policy among oligopolists would be, even if it could be assumed that collusive action of some

[8] The arguments in support of this point of view have been cogently set forth by Professor Donald H. Wallace in his *Market Control in the Aluminum Industry*, Harvard Economic Studies, vol. LVIII (Cambridge, Mass.: Harvard University Press, 1937). See especially pp. 337–352. Although Professor Wallace advanced most of his arguments in comparing the incentives of a single-firm monopoly to invest with those of a single oligopolist, many of the forces which restrict investment when a single firm controls the entire output of an industry are partly or wholly applicable to an oligopoly under a collusive agreement.

sort were, from the standpoint of each oligopolist, both desirable and possible. Since, however, the rest of the industry has relied upon the large viscose rayon producers, particularly the American Viscose Corporation, to establish the list price for rayon, it is highly probable that if producers have conspired at all on investment policy, they have conspired by tacitly observing the investment policy of the same large producers.

It is patently inconceivable that oligopolists could rationalize their decisions to invest independently of their decisions with respect to pricing policy. Since the price leader's list prices have not withstood the intense competition which develops among producers when demand for rayon has greatly decreased, it obviously would not be expected that large rayon producers have possessed more control over investment in the industry than enough to insure other than a modicum of parallel action on investment policy.

Nevertheless, if there has been any collusion on investment policy at all, an analysis of the capacity series for each of the rayon producers should reveal certain indications of parallel action. If, for example, a mutual understanding among producers with respect to investment policy has been in effect, it would logically have precluded the possibility of wide discrepancies among firms, particularly the large firms, with respect to expansion programs and, hence, a shifting in the relative positions held by individual firms in the industry.

If rayon producers have ever tacitly observed a mutual agreement in formulating their investment decisions, they would most likely have done so between 1931 and the outbreak of World War II. Throughout the twenties new firms were entering the industry at the rate of two per year; by 1931, however, those firms that were to constitute the rayon industry until 1948 had already become firmly established. Moreover, ten of the viscose rayon producers were subsequently found by the Federal Trade Commission to have entered into a collusive agreement between October 1931 and May 1932, for purposes of fixing prices and output. Hence, it is an established fact that by 1931 viscose yarn producers had recognized certain advantages in coöperation and, although the evidence suggests that the Association was ineffective and was voluntarily dissolved because producers could not reach an agreement, were willing to explore the possibilities of sacrificing individual for collective action. Furthermore, by 1931, tariff barriers and precipitous domestic rayon price movements had effectively placed the United States rayon market out of the reach of foreign producers.

In spite of these factors conducive to concerted action, however, an analysis of the capacity series for individual firms over the period 1931–1942, presented in Table 21, suggests little evidence that rayon producers either conspired to control investment or even tacitly followed the investment policy of the price leader. Between 1931 and 1942 total installed rayon capacity in the United States increased from 196.6 to 519.0 million pounds, an increase of 164 per cent. The variation in increases in installed capacity among firms over the same period, however, is quite large, ranging from 35.1 per cent to 672.7 per cent (ignoring the absolute reductions in the installed capacities of some of the smaller producers and the tremendous 3300 per cent increase in the installed capacity of the Tennessee Eastman Corporation). Du Pont, for example, expanded capacity more than twice as rapidly as the American Viscose Corporation, but only at about one-fourth the rate of the Celanese Corporation and at slightly over one-third the rate of American Enka.

Differences in rates of expansion resulted, quite naturally, in a reshuffling of the relative positions of firms. Whereas the Tubize Corporation had been the third largest producer of rayon yarn in the United States in 1931, by 1942 the company ranked as only the eighth largest producer. Over the same period, the Celanese Corporation changed its relative position in the industry from the sixth to the third largest producer; Tennessee Eastman from the fourteenth to the fifth; Industrial Rayon from the fifth to the fourth; Skenandoa from the ninth to the tenth; and North American and American Enka from the fourth and seventh largest producers respectively to a tie for the sixth. The relative positions of even the ten viscose yarn producers who had attempted to fix prices and output by concerted action in the depths of the 1929–1932 depression changed several times over the eleven-year period. The only systematic features to be found in the data are (1) all rayon yarn producers except one expanded capacity, (2) the American Viscose Corporation and Du Pont retained their respective ranks as the first and second largest producers in the industry, although the per cent of total capacity controlled by the former was, in the meantime, considerably reduced, and (3) Du Pont appears to have followed an investment policy that would at all times keep about 16 per cent of total domestic rayon capacity under its control or, stated alternatively, the company appears to have either followed closely the average rate of expansion for the industry as a whole or has anticipated with remarkable accuracy what the rest of the industry was going to do.

It can be fairly concluded, therefore, that rayon yarn producers have not only expanded their capacities in anticipation of the higher rate of substitution of rayon for natural fibers, toward which much of their research has been aimed, but they have also exercised a considerable amount of independence in doing so.

Hence, the available evidence indicates that the relationships among investment, prices, and rate of return in the rayon industry have been compatible with those which would have been expected under conditions of competition: High profits have induced rapid expansion and, in the process, prices and the rate of return have sharply declined. In fact, unless an average annual rate of return of 6.9 per cent on investment (1930–1941) is considered abnormally high for a still new and rapidly growing industry, it can be concluded that profits have been bid down close to a competitive level. At least, between 1931 and World War II, the average rate of return to large producers was not sufficiently high to induce other large firms to enter the industry, and the rate of return to small producers was not sufficiently high to prevent their exit.

The course of investment in the rayon industry, however, can be distinguished from that of a highly competitive industry of the atomistic variety by the fact that virtually all investment between 1930 and 1948 was undertaken by the large successfully entrenched firms instead of new entrants, and nearly all disinvestment can be traced to the financial collapse of small, unsuccessful producers. Accordingly, the number of producers in the industry decreased between 1930 and the end of the war while the size of the successful firms tremendously increased. The economic reasons why the industry has, perforce, been limited to a few producers have already been discussed. Considerable emphasis was placed upon the shape of the long-run cost curve for the plant and for the firm, and upon the highly technical processes employed in production.

A Note on Full-Cost Pricing. It would not be expected a priori that a price largely dependent upon the price of closely competing commodities would be related to costs of production, or to rigid profit margins, for each accounting period in such a way as to imply full-cost pricing. Moreover, the rayon industry has experienced, and still experiences, a rapid rate of growth and technological change. Hence, it is neither the type of industry nor has the period covered in this study been the historical stage of development that would be likely to give rise to a full-cost pricing policy. Neither costs nor de-

TABLE 22

Per Cent Price of Variable Costs and Total Costs for the American Viscose Corporation, 1915–1945

Year	Manufacturing Cost per Pound (exclusive of depreciation)	Total Costs per Pound	Average Annual Price	Price Less Cost	Per Cent Price of Unit Manufacturing Cost	Per Cent Price of Total Unit Cost
1915	$0.69	$0.76	$2.13	$1.37	309	280
1916	0.73	0.81	3.11	2.30	426	384
1917	0.80	0.90	3.86	2.96	485	429
1918	1.10	1.26	4.40	3.14	400	349
1919	0.98	1.09	4.77	3.68	487	437
1920	0.74	0.84	4.66	3.82	630	555
1921	1.01	1.18	2.67	1.49	264	226
1922	0.72	0.84	2.80	1.76	389	333
1923	0.60	0.73	2.80	2.07	467	384
1924	0.85	0.98	2.11	1.13	248	215
1925	0.82	0.95	2.00	1.05	244	211
1926	0.60	0.70	1.81	1.11	303	259
1927	0.82	0.92	1.49	0.57	182	162
1928	0.54	0.65	1.50	0.85	278	231
1929	0.60	0.70	1.24	0.54	207	177
1930	0.48	0.60	1.05	0.45	219	175
1931	0.51	0.59	0.75	0.16	147	127
1932	0.43	0.52	0.66	0.14	154	127
1933	0.35	0.41	0.61	0.20	174	149
1934	0.35	0.40	0.59	0.19	169	148
1935	0.36	0.41	0.57	0.16	158	139
1936	0.37	0.42	0.57	0.15	154	136
1937	0.30	0.35	0.62	0.27	207	177
1938	0.45	0.53	0.52	−0.01	116	98
1940	0.31	0.36	0.53	0.17	171	147
1945	0.33	0.38	0.55	0.17	167	145

Note: Pounds produced by the American Viscose Corporation not available for 1939 or for 1941–1944.
Source: 1915 to 1938 data from reprints of income statements of the American Viscose Corporation in *Investments, Profits, and Rates of Return for Selected Industries,* pp. 18001–18002. Annual pounds produced were obtained by dividing profit per pound produced into profits. Data since 1938 from Moody's *Manual of Industrial Investments.* Price is list price published by the American Viscose Corporation.

mand, even if the cyclical aspects of both could be ignored, have reached a sufficiently stable level to base price exclusively upon current or expected costs. Conditions conducive to full-cost pricing, however, are stable factor prices and fairly predictable operations.

Since the pricing policy of the industry has been greatly influenced by the largest producer, the problem of testing the historical behavior of prices relative to costs and profit margins can probably best be approached through the data available for the American Viscose Corporation. A possible argument against such an approach might be that the largest producer, if he wishes to preserve his position as price leader, would not set his price on the basis of his own costs but on the basis of what he thinks unit costs for the industry will be. Even if this argument were valid, however, there should be a relationship between price and the price leader's unit costs unless there is some reason for believing that his costs have behaved differently over time from costs in the industry generally.

Costs and price data for the American Viscose Corporation are presented in Table 22. As far as it is possible to do so, items not connected with the principal operation of the company are eliminated.[9] Manufacturing expenses are chiefly labor and materials (75 per cent to 80 per cent), social security (12 per cent), repairs and maintenance (8 per cent), and taxes other than income and excise. These items constitute the variable costs of production.[10] Total costs of production are obtained by adding depreciation and administrative and distribution expenses to manufacturing expense.[11] The price series used is list price as issued by the American Viscose Corporation.[12]

If the American Viscose Corporation had employed a policy whereby price was set according to total or variable unit costs, some

[9] Mainly, financial expenses incurred in the investment business. The company has invested quite heavily in government securities from time to time. Until recently, all operating expenses related to production of rayon, since this was the company's only manufacturing activity.

[10] Taxes and a portion of maintenance and repair are fixed charges, but they cannot be sifted from the other expenses. The total fixed charges included in variable costs is probably quite small.

[11] Similarly, all distribution expense is not fixed. The fixed portion, such as the maintenance of sales offices, etc., cannot be separated from selling expenses that vary with the volume of sales.

[12] Net realized price would be more appropriate, but data for pounds sold per year by the company are not available for all years. Over the period for which net realized prices on the various types of rayon may be checked against list prices, the two are practically identical. The following is a comparison of American Viscose Company's list price and net realized price per pound as reported in *Moody's Manual* for the period 1937–1940. For a similar comparison of monthly prices from November 1931 to December 1933, see Table 9.

	Viscose Yarn		*Acetate Yarn*		*Staple Fiber*	
	Net Realized Price	List Price	Net Realized Price	List Price	Net Realized Price	List Price
1937	$0.61	$0.62	$0.67	$0.67	$0.25	$0.27
1938	0.51	0.52	0.61	0.62	0.23	0.25
1939	0.52	0.53	0.62	0.63	0.23	0.25
1940	0.53	0.53	0.62	0.63	0.23	0.25

evidence of a constant dollar or percentage relationship between price and total unit cost or price and unit variable cost should appear in the data. The very magnitude of the price to cost ratios in many years, however, would seem to deny the employment of such a pricing formula. It is inconceivable, for example, that the company could have rationally decided upon profit margins per pound that sometimes ran as high as 455 per cent of total unit costs. Also, profit margins have been highly cyclical — timed quite closely with the cycles which appear in the price and output series. Between 1920 and 1921, profit per pound of rayon declined from 455 per cent to 126 per cent of total costs; between 1926 and 1927, from 159 per cent to 62 per cent; between 1930 and 1931, from 75 per cent to 27 per cent; and between 1937 and 1938, from 77 per cent to —2 per cent (loss). Between 1915 and 1920, profit per pound of rayon rapidly increased from 180 per cent to 455 per cent of total unit costs; between 1921 and 1922, from 126 per cent to 233 per cent; between 1927 and 1928, from 62 per cent to 131 per cent; between 1932 and 1933, from 27 per cent to 49 per cent; between 1936 and 1937, from 36 per cent to 77 per cent; and between 1938 and 1940, from —2 per cent (loss) to 47 per cent. The percentage relationships between price and unit variable costs conform to a similar cyclical pattern.

Hence, there is no evidence in the statistical data or in the trade literature that price per pound of rayon results from a cost plus profit margin calculation. There is much more evidence that the price of domestic rayon has been a function of natural fiber yarn and foreign produced rayon prices, but this functional relationship has been considerably tempered over time by American tariff policy, rapid technological change, plant expansion to benefit from economies of scale, research policy, and long-run demand considerations.[13]

[13] Most of the evidence offered throughout this study that rayon producers, as a matter of policy, try to give fabricators a stable rayon price is, of course, the same evidence that would be offered against any hypothesis that short-run profit maximization motives can fully explain rayon price movements. There have been obvious cases where rayon price could have been higher and maximum capacity production still clear the market. An excellent example is the postwar price experience. Manufacturers' list price for 150-denier rayon from December 1947 to August 1948 was $0.74 per pound. In the resale market, the same yarn sold for from $1.80 to $2.75 per pound. Baker, Weeks, and Harden, *Strength of the Textile Industry* (New York: March 1948), p. 10.

10

THE WORKABILITY OF Competition in the Domestic Rayon Industry

It is probably unnecessary to point out that no theoretical schema, however logically conceived and applied, can be expected to explain the price of a commodity at any given instant of time.[1] Nevertheless, it is possible to examine the structure and the price and output behavior of a particular industry against a background of explanatory hypotheses, and to reach certain conclusions concerning the degree to which they respond to market forces. That is to say, the theory of competitive markets might be quite helpful in indicating whether one should logically expect prices, output, and the number of firms to increase or decrease under given conditions, although it cannot explain why prices, output, and the number of firms are precisely what they are.

Evidences of competitive behavior, however, can be found in many markets in which competition is neither perfect nor pure. Since competition of these varieties is not frequently encountered in the highly industrialized economy of the United States, economists have recently endeavored to define a more realistic standard of economic performance — "workable" or "effective" competition.[2]

[1] Some conflicting views on this score have been discussed in recent economic writings. See Richard A. Lester, "Short Comings of Marginal Analysis for Wage-Employment Problems," *American Economic Review*, XXXVI, no. 1 (March 1946), pp. 63–82; Fritz Machlup, "Marginal Analysis and Empirical Research," *ibid.*, no. 4, Part 1 (September 1946), pp. 519–554; R. L. Hall and C. J. Hitch, "Price Theory and Business Behavior," *Oxford Economic Papers*, no. 2 (1939), pp. 12–45.

[2] The term "workable competition" was first used by Professor John M. Clark in his article "Toward a Concept of Workable Competition," *American Economic Review*, vol. XXX, no. 2, Part 1 (June 1940), pp. 241–256.

Since the concept of workable competition owes its creation to a public policy need and not to the logic of abstract theory, it can, at best, be divorced only in part from value judgments. To the unswerving socialist nothing short of complete government ownership and control of all economic activity may make for a workable society; to him, no economy is workably competitive if it is privately competitive. Yet, a proponent of unlimited free enterprise would probably view any economy not subject to governmental intervention as workably competitive. Again, thoroughgoing antitrust sympathizers may reject any definition of the concept that falls noticeably short of pure competition. On the other hand, economists who subscribe to the Schumpeterian theory of creative destruction may willingly accept, in fact insist upon the acceptance of, far less. Hence, there may be wide differences of opinion among economists as to whether or not a particular industry is workably competitive.

Another obstacle to the formulation of a precise definition of workable competition becomes evident when one attempts to define the "industry" to which the concept is to be applied. Concentration ratios are frequently employed as measures of monopoly in specific industries, but concentration ratios in themselves might be quite meaningless unless they relate to well-defined markets. For example, E. I. du Pont de Nemours & Co., Inc. is the sole producer of nylon, but Du Pont accounts for little over 17 per cent of the total synthetic yarn production and for an infinitesimally small percentage of total domestic yarn production of all kinds. Obviously, therefore, a measure of Du Pont's monopoly power is dependent upon whether one has in mind the domestic nylon market, the synthetic yarn market, or simply the yarn market.

These obstacles, however, by no means preclude the possibility of developing a more workable definition of competition. In their search for a standard of performance more applicable to a highly industrialized society than the one implied in the definition of perfect competition, economists might reach — or certainly hope to reach — a point at which they find themselves in substantial agreement. However, since the concept of workable competition finds its origin in a public policy need and, accordingly, partakes of value judgments, it is worth while to point out that agreement probably will not be — in fact, need not be — unanimous.

It is the purpose of this chapter (1) to summarize the significant characteristics of the domestic rayon industry and its observable pattern of price and output behavior, and (2) to set forth the author's conclusions concerning the workability of competition in the industry. In light of the foregoing discussion of the concept of workable competition, however, it is highly probable that other economists, given the same empirical findings, might reach entirely different conclusions.

A. Characteristics of the Industry — Summary

The most important conclusions reached in this study may be summarized as follows:

1. The rayon industry is an oligopoly. At different times the number of producers has varied from one to twenty. Currently, the nominal number of firms is sixteen but, if cognizance is taken of intercompany affiliations, the actual number of completely independent producers is reduced to twelve. Perhaps the chief limitation to the number of firms is an economic one: The shape of the long-run cost curve for the firm, at least to the extent that it is indicated by available plant cost curves and other data, places the rayon industry among the natural oligopolies. Rapid expansion of plant capacity by entrenched firms to obtain economies of scale and concurrent precipitous declines in rates of return seem to have been the principal deterrents to entry after 1930, by which time most basic patent rights had expired, and a gradual dissemination of "know-how" had commenced. Concentration of control, although still moderately high, has declined rapidly since 1920. From 1911 to 1920 one firm monopolized the industry; this single company now accounts for about 30 per cent of total installed capacity and the four largest firms account for 75 per cent of installed capacity.

2. The industry has experienced a spectacularly rapid rate of expansion. During the ten-year period between 1920 and 1930, increases in installed capacity were largely due to the entrance of new firms; between 1930 and 1946, increases in capacity resulted wholly from the expansion of existing firms; and since 1946 all firms have expanded their capacity and two new firms have entered the industry. Generally, only the large- and medium-size companies weathered the great depression. A number of small-scale producers failed during the 1930–1933 depression or before they reached a stage of commercial production. A sharp secular decline in prices and the rate of return has accompanied the rising secular trend in investment. Profit rates for the industry ranged from 1.5 per cent to 12.0 per cent

throughout the thirties and for twelve years averaged about 6.9 per cent. In view of the demonstrable wide differences among firms with respect to the rate of expansion, it seems fairly safe to conclude that rayon producers have observed no agreement, either tacit or overt, on investment policy. Trends in prices, profits, and investment in the rayon industry, therefore, are consistent with what would have been expected under competitive conditions.

3. The price relationship among producers has varied somewhat with respect to particular phases of the business cycle but there is almost conclusive proof of list-price leadership by the largest producer, the American Viscose Corporation having been the first to announce all but a few list-price changes. In periods of severe depression, however, such as 1930–1932 and, to a less extent, 1934 and 1938, it is abundantly clear that list-price changes announced by the largest producer merely took *de jure* recognition of *de facto* market prices. When the rayon market becomes severely depressed, small producers shade prices in order to maintain output rather than adhere to list prices and accumulate abnormally high inventories or drastically curtail operations. Quantity discounts were frequently the vehicle of such price cutting until 1936, at which time they were discontinued by all producers to avoid possible conflicts with the Robinson-Patman Act. Extremely tight rayon markets, on the other hand, have occasionally given rise to premiums above list price and, since World War II, there has been some variation among producers with respect to quoted price. Market conditions intermediate to an acute yarn shortage and a severe depression, however, appear to be characterized by close agreement between list price less industry-wide allowances and net realized price.

As the proportion of total yarn produced by the acetate process has increased, price leadership in the entire rayon industry has manifested itself in the following manner: A list-price change announced by the largest viscose producer is usually followed by other viscose yarn producers, acetate yarn producers, and the single cuprammonium yarn producer, in less than two weeks. The industry is slightly more hesitant in following list-price increases than decreases: Whereas most firms meet an announced price decrease in a day or two, whether they publish new price lists or not, they usually wait from ten days to two weeks before following a price increase.

There are several reasons, aside from theoretical considerations, why some *modus operandi* such as price leadership might have been expected to develop in the domestic rayon industry: (1) Most domestic firms started as subsidiaries of established European companies; hence, they were loosely knit together through the European cartels. (2) The same European firms had established subsidiaries in Great Britain before and concurrently with those they established in the United States. In Great Britain, Courtaulds, Ltd. was the accepted price leader until 1938, at which time price leadership gave way to a formal price and market-sharing agreement among producers. The acceptance of American Viscose (a wholly owned subsidiary of Courtaulds until 1943) by the rest of the industry as the price leader in the United States may have been a logical consequence of previous experience in Great Britain. (3) Rayon producers in the United States have maintained several points of contact that conceivably could have eliminated some of the uncertainty as to what rivals' reactions would be to a proposed price change. The Rayon Institute was organized by rayon producers in 1927 for joint advertising purposes; a yarn producers' trade association was formed in 1929; ten rayon producing corporations attempted, through a collusive agreement, to maintain price and restrict output from October 1931 to July 1932; the two largest producers occupy central offices close to each other in Wilmington, Delaware, and practically all rayon producers have a central administrative office or sales office in or around the Empire State Building in New York City.

Moreover, until 1931 the American Viscose Corporation possessed most of the attributes of a theoretically conceived dominant firm; the company produced about 50 per cent of the total output of an industry composed of only a few producers, all of which were small by comparison with American Viscose. Throughout the thirties the company lost those attributes usually associated with the dominant firm type of price leader, but retained many of the features of a price leader of the barometric type.

Since all other firms usually wait for American Viscose to initiate a list-price change and, since their off-list selling usually produces a comparable list-price change by American Viscose, price differentials among rayon producers, when they occur, are short-lived. Hence, the list-price series of American Viscose is a fairly good indicator of *de facto* rayon prices except for the period of violent price cutting which occurred in the years 1930–31.

4. By the usual definition, rayon prices are administered — they do not move to equate short-run demand and supply. The seasonal

demand pattern for rayon yarn contains fairly high peaks and low troughs but there is no corresponding seasonal response observable in the rayon price series. Since 1920, the rayon deliveries series (as well as all other textile deliveries series) shows a very noticeable two-year "textile cycle" — deliveries are high in odd-numbered years and low in even-numbered years. There is very little price response to these two-year cyclical swings in demand.

Over most of the period covered in this study the rayon price series has had a sharp downward secular trend. Between 1919 and 1935 the trend may be represented by a negatively sloped compound interest rate curve with an annual rate of decline of 12.8 per cent. When the trend is eliminated, rayon price shows a moderately high degree of sensitivity to the business cycle. The resulting price cycles are timed in almost perfect consonance with some acceptable business cycle bench mark such as Professor Mitchell's reference cycle.

5. Similarly, output is quite stable in the short-run. Generally, seasonal and irregular fluctuations in deliveries are absorbed by inventory fluctuations. This is partly due to the fact that rayon is produced by a continuous process. Minor shutdowns are costly, and several weeks are usually required to get plants back to top operational efficiency. Moreover, unit costs increase when output is contracted below capacity. This is true when all variable factors may be adjusted to the new production schedule. The increase in unit costs is aggravated in the immediate short-run that would probably include seasonal and irregular fluctuations in demand. When the period of observation is lengthened to include the two-year "textile cycle," output appears to be more sensitive than price to demand fluctuations. In all but a few years, a weak two-year cycle is apparent in the output series.

Annual domestic rayon output has been increased substantially in all years since 1910 except in the years 1932, 1934, and 1938. The annual production series (1919–1942) has so perfectly followed a Gompertz curve that the series is frequently used as a textbook example of the curve's applicability. Production trend ratios computed from the fitted trend line are usually lower than price trend ratios in even-numbered years; the reverse is true in odd-numbered years. This tendency alone suggests that producers customarily contract output before they lower price but, in the 1919–1942 series limited to annual data, there is no evidence that output fluctuates more violently than price over the business cycle. Both the price and output series yield similar cyclical patterns and both series have peaks and troughs that correspond closely with the peaks and troughs of the reference cycles.

An analysis of the monthly data available for the period 1930–1949 yields more significant features of the price-output pattern. Usually, output for the industry is curtailed from one to two months before price is reduced, but the price lag has varied from about one to five months. Even production schedules, however, are left unaltered until inventories have reached a high level. After output has been curtailed approximately 25 per cent of installed capacity, a price reduction usually occurs. If the recession is sufficiently severe to call for output curtailment below 70 to 75 per cent of installed capacity, several more price reductions may occur after output has been further curtailed. Price reductions which have been initiated in periods of recession have usually been restored in part in periods of market recovery, but only after the rough vicinity of 70 to 75 per cent of capacity operations had been reached. This price breaking-point is further indicated by the absence of price reductions when, in mild recessions, output curtailment has not exceeded 20 per cent of installed capacity.

Nearly all price changes in the industry have occurred after a sustained directional movement in inventory levels. The downward secular trend in price has been effected through price reductions in periods of recession that have not been fully restored during periods of recovery.

The foregoing characteristics of the rayon industry can be fairly well explained in terms of the behavior of factor costs, the shape of the firm's short-run and long-run cost curve, the rate of technological change, the price behavior of competing products, the organization of the industry, and certain long-run objectives common to most rayon producers which give rise to discretionary practices that may be called "price policy."

Rayon producers' factor costs are extremely stable, having shown little if any sensitivity to economic fluctuations since 1932. Chemical and wood pulp prices and average hourly earnings are considerably more stable than rayon prices. Such stable factor prices are conducive to a stable rayon price.

Moreover, stable factor prices over the business cycle make it possible to analyze the cyclical price behavior of rayon in terms of the shape of firms' cost curves, that is, cost curves do not shift radically because of factor price changes. According to the shape of the individual plant's short-run cost curve, average and marginal unit costs rise with output curtailment, particularly as curtailment proceeds below 75 per cent of installed capacity. Furthermore, there are good reasons for believing that the elasticity of demand for rayon increases during a textile market recession. Accordingly, when inventories continue to increase in a declining market, thereby indicating to all producers that the present price does not equate the present rates of output and sales, there is pressure upon the price leader (if small producers have not already done so) to reduce the price of rayon in order to recapture any part of the market temporarily lost to natural fibers, and thus to enable firms to operate at higher rates of output. The combination of flexible natural fiber prices and negatively inclined plant cost curves up to capacity output, therefore, severely limit the extent to which rayon prices can be stabilized by arbitrary entrepreneurial decisions.

The family of short-run cost curves for plants of various sizes also explains in part why the usual close adherence to the price leader's published price has been forsaken in periods of severe depression. All the evidence indicates that the short-run average and marginal cost curves for a small producer rise more rapidly when proceeding to the left from the point of lowest average total cost than do those for a large producer such as the price leader. Furthermore, small producers obviously view their individual demand curves as being more elastic than larger producers view theirs. There is considerable incentive, therefore, for small producers to shade price and maintain output, particularly when sales volume at list price calls for sharp curtailment. Such price-shading was patent around 1930 and 1931 and has been noticeable in subsequent recessions.

Perhaps the most logical explanation of the greater short-run stability of rayon prices when compared with natural fiber prices is to be found in the positive policy of the leading firms in the industry. Corporation officials have frequently voiced their belief that a stable price — in the long-run — is the most profitable price. They have reasoned that the supply (and hence the price) of rayon, unlike that of silk, cotton, and wool, is not contingent upon the vagaries of the weather or the productive capacities of sheep or silkworms, and that fabricators of rayon, given a stable price, would not have to engage in hedging or risk the uncertainties of fluctuating inventory valuations. Hence, in the long-run, rayon producers should, simply by building up a reputation for short-run price stability, capture a sizable proportion of the textile market. By following such a policy, rayon producers have sometimes sold their entire output at lower prices than the short-run equilibrium price. For example, for over a year after the end of World War II the resale price of 150-denier rayon yarn was approximately $1.80 to $2.75 per pound, whereas manufacturers' list price was only $0.74 per pound. This type of pricing policy strongly suggests, moreover, that rayon producers place a higher premium upon short-run price stability than they do upon short-run profit maximization.

Other frictional forces are present in the domestic rayon market which undoubtedly contribute to price stickiness. All rayon producers, regardless of their relative size in the industry, are fairly large corporations. It is generally conceded that the large corporate form of enterprise responds to given market stimuli more sluggishly than small owner-controlled corporations and simple proprietorships. Moreover, rayon price is communicated to consumers in the form of published lists. A certain amount of expense is involved in the printing and mailing of new price lists, particularly where an industry serves thousands of fabricators scattered over the Western Hemisphere. Another self-imposed restriction that has operated against downward price revisions is the price guarantee. On several occasions producers have guaranteed their price lists against future revision for from sixty to ninety days. When such guarantees are effective, a price reduction not only affects the revenue from future sales, but also necessitates refunds on sales consummated over the past sixty or ninety days. Finally, the kinky oligopoly demand curve may also contribute to short-run price rigidity. The strong evidence of price leadership, however, considerably weakens, although it does not completely invalidate, the rationale of the kinky demand curve argument.

B. Conclusions on the Workable Competitiveness of the Rayon Industry[3]

Several serious attempts have been made to define the term "workable competition." In no case, however, has an author set forth conditions so completely devoid of value judgments or so all-embracing that he feels free to acclaim the universal applicability of

[3] Approximately five pages of the following discussion, with only minor changes, appear in my article "The Concept of Workable Competition: An Alternative Approach," *American Economic Review*, vol. XL, no. 3 (June 1950), pp. 349–361. I am indebted to the American Economic Association for permission to reproduce them here.

his definition. Professor J. M. Clark, the creator of the term, places much emphasis upon rivalry among selling units and the "Free option of the buyer to buy from a rival seller or sellers of what we think of as 'the same' product." [4] Professor Clark concedes, however, that the "specific character of competition in any given case depends on a surprisingly large number of conditions — so many, in fact, that the number of mathematically possible combinations runs into the hundreds of thousands — and suggests the possibility that every industry may be in some significant respect different from every other, or from itself at some other stage of development." [5]

On a number of counts, the domestic rayon industry would be workably competitive under Professor Clark's definition. He himself would probably place the industry under the following caption in his classification of competition scheme:[6]

II Modified, intermediate or hybrid competition.
- A. Standard products, few producers. The most important cases involve formally free entry, but no exit without loss.
  - 3. Quoted prices, sloping individual demand curves.
    - b. Demand schedules indefinite (limited freight absorption).

There is room for little doubt concerning the existence of rivalry among the producers of rayon. In times of depressed markets rivalry has taken the form of fairly vigorous price-cutting and price-shading. Even during normal market periods when the price leader's list price seems to have prevailed throughout the industry, however, there has been intense rivalry among producers in the form of cost-cutting and quality competition.

And, except for the brief interval between October 1931 and May 1932, it can be fairly concluded that rayon purchasers have generally had a real option before them as to their source of supply. Sometimes, optional sources have been distinguished by price differentials; at other times, when all producers have rigidly adhered to the price leader's quoted price, the buyer's option has been limited pretty much to small quality and grading differences among producers. However, to the extent that buyers regard rayon, nylon, silk, cotton, and wool yarns as "the same" commodity, they have always had, in addition to the above, a real price option. Hence, on

[4] John M. Clark, "Toward a Concept of Workable Competition," p. 243.
[5] Clark, p. 243.
[6] Clark, p. 245.

most counts the rayon yarn industry would qualify as workably competitive under Professor Clark's definition. At least any disagreement with this conclusion would evolve from placing a different construction upon such terms as "rivalry," "option," and "the same" commodity.

According to Professor Stigler, "An industry is workably competitive when (1) there are a considerable number of firms selling closely related products in each important market area, (2) these firms are not in collusion, and (3) the long-run average cost curve for a new firm is not materially higher than that for an established firm." [7]

Any conclusion concerning the workability of competition in the rayon industry under Professor Stigler's definition would depend largely upon the interpretation given to the term "closely related products." If all textile yarns are in some sense to be considered as closely related, an interpretation which would seem justifiable in light of the degree of competition among fibers in specific market areas, the rayon industry (as a small segment of the total yarn market) would patently be classified as highly competitive under the above definition. If, on the other hand, the product of one rayon producer were to be considered as closely related only to other rayon, other features of the definition would come into play and the above conclusion would not be so evident. The workable competitiveness of the rayon industry would then depend upon how Professor Stigler would answer the following questions: Do sixteen producers constitute "a considerable number of firms"? Do sporadic price-shading and price-cutting so counteract the acceptance of price leadership in normal periods that it could be fairly concluded that rayon producers neither tacitly nor explicitly avoid price competition? Unless both of these questions could be answered in the affirmative, there would be some doubts about how workable competition has been in the rayon industry. Under the more restrictive interpretation of the term "closely related products," competition in the industry would probably be considered as workable only in those periods when the rate of sales is low relative to installed capacity. In instances where all firms operate somewhere between 80 and 100 per cent of installed capacity, however, and seem passively to adhere

[7] George J. Stigler, "Extent and Bases of Monopoly," *American Economic Review*, Annual Supplement (June 1942), pp. 2–3.

to the price leader's price, the industry may not qualify as workably competitive because of the second provision of Professor Stigler's definition.[8]

Dr. Corwin Edwards has also defined workable competition in terms of the structural characteristics of a particular market. They are as follows:[9]

1. There must be an appreciable number of sources of supply and an appreciable number of potential customers for substantially the same product or service. Suppliers and customers do not need to be so numerous that each trader is entirely without individual influence, but their number must be great enough that persons on the other side of the market may readily turn away from any particular trader and may find a variety of other alternatives.
2. No trader must be so powerful as to be able to coerce his rivals, nor so large that the remaining traders lack the capacity to take over at least a substantial portion of his trade.
3. Traders must be responsive to incentives of profit and loss: that is, they must not be so large, so diversified, so devoted to political rather than commercial purposes, so subsidized, or otherwise so unconcerned with results in a particular market that their policies are not affected by ordinary commercial incentives arising out of that market.
4. Matters of commercial policy must be decided by each trader separately without agreement with his rivals.
5. New traders must have opportunity to enter the market without handicap other than that which is automatically created by the fact that others are already well established there.
6. Access by traders on one side of the market to those on the other side of the market must be unimpaired except by obstacles not deliberately introduced, such as distance or ignorance of the available alternatives.
7. There must be no substantial preferential status for any important trader or group of traders on the basis of law, politics, or commercial alliances.

The structural characteristics of the rayon market since 1932 would seem to fulfill Dr. Edward's requirements for workable competition, even under the more rigid definition of an industry. Dr. Edwards states that there must be an appreciable number of sources of supply but neither suppliers nor customers need to be so numer-

[8] This would depend upon whether Professor Stigler considers the temporary acceptance of a price leader's price as a "tacit avoidance of price competition for fear of retaliation of close rivals." See his footnote, *loc. cit.*, p. 3.

[9] From Corwin Edwards, *Maintaining Competition,* pp. 9–10, copyright, 1949. Reprinted by permission of McGraw-Hill Book Company, Inc.

ous that each trader is entirely without individual influence. However, there must be no agreement among rivals with respect to commercial policy.

It would appear, therefore, that oligopolistic markets are ruled out under the above set of conditions only when individual firms act in concert to an extent that implies either an agreement or the possession of coercive power by a large producer. The off-list selling by individual rayon producers in periods marked by a noticeable decline in demand, the differential premiums for quick delivery when yarn shortages appear, and the quoted price differentials among producers since the war would probably be sufficient evidence to show that rayon prices are not set by collusive agreement. Although American Viscose has generally led the industry in effecting list-price changes, on several occasions the admitted purpose of the price revision was to bring list price more in line with the *de facto* price. Also, several other producers have occasionally taken the initiative in revising price schedules. These features of rayon price behavior would seem to be compatible with the structural characteristics required of a particular competitive market as set forth above. There is evidence that each firm considers the effect his actions will have upon his rival's behavior, but there is a sufficient amount of independent pricing over the period of a business cycle to give buyers a variety of options among sellers. When this type of price behavior appears in a market, sixteen producers probably constitute an "appreciable number of sources of supply."

It is obvious, however, that the rayon industry would not have qualified as a workably competitive industry from October 1931 to May 1932, during which time a collusive agreement among ten rayon producers was in effect. Nor is it likely that Dr. Edwards would have considered the industry to be workably competitive during the twenties. From 1920 to 1928 the American Viscose Corporation was sufficiently large relative to its rivals to exert a substantial amount of coercive power. Moreover, and this logically follows, the remaining producers did not collectively control enough productive capacity to be able to take over a substantial portion of the trade that usually went to the American Viscose Corporation.

Although it is possible to classify the domestic rayon industry among the workably competitive industries by an application of any one of the above three definitions, it should be reiterated that results obtained from the application of each involves a value judgment.

Hence, it is unlikely that any prescribed set of market characteristics would either obtain the approval of all economists or could uniquely determine the workable competitiveness of all industries. Those who reject any set of conditions that falls noticeably short of the classicists' ideal of perfect competition would probably find few workably competitive markets. Those who place much reliance upon the dynamics of creative destruction would find many more.

A possible alternative approach to the concept of workable competition, therefore, is one which shifts the emphasis from a set of specific structural characteristics to an appraisal of an industry's over-all performance against the background of possible remedial action. A first approximation to the concept of workable competition when viewed along these lines might be as follows: An industry is workably competitive when, after its market characteristics and the dynamic forces which shaped them have been thoroughly examined, there is no clearly indicated change that can be effected through public policy measures which would result in greater social gains than social losses.

Admittedly social gains and social losses, when viewed in the light of possible remedial action, are not easy terms to define with precision. There is, however, a strong presumption that so long as American society shows a preference for a political and economic system that permits a maximum of individual action consistent with present welfare objectives, it will also prefer to have its markets regulated by the free play of economic laws until they demonstrably no longer regulate effectively. Hence, public policy measures which encourage, maintain, or restore open channels through which the benefits of competition accrue to society represent social gains.

Obviously, however, a distinction must be made between the benefits of competitive behavior and the structural features usually associated with theoretical models of purely competitive industries. The former relate to the dynamics of industrial development and embrace, among other things, such activity as the introduction of completely new products, close substitutes for existing products, improved processes and new technology. The latter relate to long-run equilibrium conditions which, at any given time, a few industries may substantially fulfill, a larger number may be approaching, but many, for technological or other reasons, may never fulfill. Yet, industries which fall in the latter two groups would be workably competitive under the above definition if there were no public policy measure which could clearly make a free enterprise society better off.

A definition of workable competition centered upon social gains and losses therefore, stems from three major premises: (1) The public prefers regulation by competitive forces to other forms of regulation so long as they regulate or show promise of regulating effectively; (2) it is not to be expected that at any given instant of time many industries in a dynamic industrialized economy will conform to the conditions of theoretically pure competition; hence, public policy should be more concerned with preserving the dynamics of competitive behavior than with effecting approximations to theoretical long-run equilibrium conditions associated with the definition of pure competition; and (3) a society which prefers a free enterprise economy is benefited by all public policy measures which increase competition in a given industry at no social cost or which result in benefits from increased competition that clearly outweigh the social costs involved.

If it is not at all clear, therefore, that the definitional conditions of a competitive industry can be attained by public action without some sacrifice in the benefits which are derived from competitive behavior, they obviously should not be sought after as ends in themselves. For example, to impose limitations upon the size of firm or the per cent of total output each firm may control in an industry may conceivably result in more firms and hence, a closer approximation of the industry, structurally, to purely competitive conditions. If on the other hand, however, the imposition of such limitations could be expected to retard or eliminate technological development and the introduction of new products, or result in losses in economies of scale, the social costs of the more competitive structural features might well prove to be prohibitive.

However difficult the problems associated with measuring social gains and losses might be, the above first approximation to a definition of workable competition at least avoids the pitfall of listing specific market conditions that can have very limited general applicability. Moreover, it ascribes paramount importance to that which should be uppermost in the minds of those who formulate public policy toward industry — the possibility of prescribing appropriate remedial action. Adopting this line of approach, it is worth while to see whether or not competition in the rayon industry would appear to be workable. In the process, some of the implications of the definition may be brought out more clearly.

Concentration of control in the rayon industry has gradually declined since 1920 as the number of surviving firms has increased from one to sixteen. As new firms have entered the industry, prices and rates of return have rapidly declined and productive capacity has rapidly increased. These results would be the aims of an enlightened public policy oriented toward the preservation of competitive private capitalism. Moreover, since the industry was transformed from a monopoly by a single producer to an oligopoly of twenty firms in the short span of ten years, the destruction of monopoly power probably proceeded at a sufficiently rapid rate. Hence, with respect to these desirable results, competitive forces have already provided the remedy for monopoly that would presumably be envisaged by those concerned with public policy toward industry.

Although rayon prices over short time intervals are considerably more stable than those of natural fibers, there is a high degree of interdependence among all textile yarn prices. Rayon competes closely with silk, cotton, and, more recently, nylon and other new synthetic yarns; and in some market areas, rayon competes with wool. Since natural fiber prices are usually accepted as highly competitive, it follows that prices geared closely to them partake of their competitive aspects. Moreover, there is every indication that rayon producers have thoroughly explored and exploited the long-run demand possibilities for their product by carrying competition to the natural fibers through the introduction of numerous new types of yarn. In some respects, therefore, rayon producers have increased competition in the already highly competitive textile yarn market. Furthermore, it follows that competitive forces would severely limit the power of rayon producers, should they agree to act in concert, to impose an arbitrary pricing policy upon rayon consumers. Under price leadership not invulnerable to a declining market, arbitrary pricing is even more closely circumscribed.

On the other hand, the differences between the domestic rayon market and a perfectly competitive market are fairly clear. For purposes of analysis, however, it is both convenient and necessary to differentiate between two types of phenomena which have distinguished the rayon industry from a perfectly competitive one, namely, (1) economic phenomena such as the number of firms in the industry, pricing practices, etc., most of which seem to stem directly or indirectly from the nature of rayon firms' cost functions, and therefore relate principally to conditions of supply; and (2) those phenomena primarily of political origin such as tariff policy and cotton price support programs which condition the demand side of the domestic rayon market.

Quite obviously, these two types of phenomena do not operate upon the rayon market independently of each other. Tariff policy has patently had considerable influence upon the number of firms in the industry and upon the behavior of rayon prices; correspondingly, the voices of producers of rayon have probably not gone completely unheeded when the question of tariffs on foreign-produced rayon was raised. Nevertheless, from the standpoint of formulating public policy toward the rayon industry, the two types of phenomena present fundamentally different problems: The latter are completely subject to control by policy-making bodies; the former, to the extent they in fact are attendant features of cost functions, must be accepted by policy-making authorities as data.

With respect to the economic features of the rayon industry, as distinct from the political environment in which it has grown, stable prices over moderately long time intervals, the acceptance of a price leader in relatively prosperous periods, and a fairly small number of large producers appear to be the most obvious differences between the rayon industry and a purely competitive one. In an industrialized society in which the conditions of pure competition are never encountered, are these departures sufficiently inimical to the public welfare to conclude that competition in the rayon industry is "unworkable"? An answer to this question involves an examination of the changes that an enlightened public policy would envisage in order to eliminate them.

Since both short-run price stability and periodic leadership stem largely from the oligopolistic features of the rayon market, the only obvious way to eliminate such price behavior is to eliminate the foundations of the oligopoly market, that is, increase the number of independent producers in the industry. This could conceivably be accomplished by limiting the size of the rayon firm or by redistributing existing rayon plants.

That the largest *plants* currently producing rayon are the most efficient plants, however, can be satisfactorily established. It can be fairly safely concluded, therefore, that nothing could be gained at present by placing a limitation upon their size. Short-run price flexibility, if indeed it could be obtained by invoking this limitation, is hardly worth the social costs involved. The thirty rayon plants, however, are controlled by sixteen firms. Hence, rayon prices might conceivably be made more flexible by limiting each firm to one plant. Whether or not such a measure would make society better off, however, depends largely upon the interpretation of all the available evidence. Case studies made by rayon engineers and the financial statements of individual firms indicate that substantial production and distribution economies have also been obtained by increasing the size of the firm. Moreover, there is no evidence that any firm in the rayon industry has yet expanded beyond the point where further economies are impossible. To limit each producer to a single plant would, assuming that buyers could be found, entail considerable duplication in overhead (research, physical and chemical testing laboratories, management, sales offices, etc.) and thereby raise costs. On the other hand, it is quite likely that an increase in the number of rayon producers from sixteen to thirty (again assuming that buyers for all plants could be found) would eliminate some short-run price inflexibility by making price leadership more difficult.

Strong competition from other yarns, however, already limits the amount of control the price leader may exercise over rayon price. Moreover, since rayon producers have continued to maintain a high level of output in the short-run because of cost considerations, a number of arguments against short-run price inflexibility are rendered inadmissible — there are no resultant short-run fluctuations in employment attributable to the "administered" rayon price. Hence, at the present stage of development of the rayon industry, it would probably be unwise to place legal limitations upon the size of the firm, particularly since the number of firms is still increasing.

It is extremely doubtful, therefore, that society could be made better off by altering the present structure of the rayon industry. Even if it could be assumed that society would benefit measurably from more flexible rayon prices, there is certainly no assurance that the expected increase in price flexibility would yield benefits that would clearly offset expected increases in costs. Hence, it would seem that the only practicable public policy measures which could be applied directly to the rayon industry would follow the lines of those which have already been and, presumably, are now also, employed; namely, to keep a watchful eye on the industry to insure a continuation of competition consistent with the economic forces that shape the industry's structure and development.

An appraisal of the effects which those forces largely of a political origin have had upon competition in the domestic rayon industry raises several questions relevant to a broader problem than that of workable competition in a particular industry. It is difficult, for example, to discuss the total effects which tariff barriers erected against foreign-produced rayon have had upon domestic consumers of rayon without, at the same time, airing the whole question of the United States' tariff policy. Obviously, however, a treatment of such broad questions as those which relate to the efficacy of our historical policy toward patents or tariffs, however relevant to a discussion of competition they might be, lies beyond the scope of this study. Hence, the following analysis will be addressed to the much narrower problem of pointing out only the more apparent direct effects which governmental action has had upon the domestic rayon market, and will be confined to a discussion of (1) tariffs on imported rayon, (2) the cotton price support program, (3) the Government's disposition of foreign-owned rayon plants taken over during World War II, and (4) the allocation of rayon plants constructed by the Government during the war.

The domestic rayon industry quite clearly would never have flourished as it has, if indeed it would have ever been born, had it not been protected from the competition of foreign rayon. Between the years 1910 and 1930, rayon yarn produced in Germany, France, England, and Italy could have been shipped to the United States and sold at prices, exclusive of import duty, substantially below domestic prices and, in most years, below the costs of the oldest and largest domestic producer. Over this period technology was considerably more advanced in European countries than in the United States, so much so that only those domestic producers who had access to European technology could enter the industry with any hope of surviving. Moreover, most of the domestic firms which were established before 1930 were loosely associated with each other through a network of European cartels.

As rayon technology in the United States reached the level of that in Europe, however, domestic firms commenced to break away from their parent or affiliated European companies and, in the process, became more independent of each other. By 1930, the domestic rayon industry had grown from a single Courtaulds' subsidiary to nineteen firms of which only three were bound together through the European cartel, and domestic prices had been reduced to the approximate level of those on foreign yarns not including import duty. Hence, tariff policy toward foreign rayon producers up to 1930 could be supported by all the arguments usually raised in defense of protecting infant industries.

From 1930 until the outbreak of World War II, import duties on foreign-produced rayon were considerably higher than those necessary to protect domestic producers from competition from Europe and probably just about high enough to protect them from competition from Japan. Since the rayon produced in the United States after 1935, however, is generally considered to be of higher quality than that produced elsewhere, international price and costs comparisons over the past fifteen years are not very meaningful. Nevertheless, for the years 1935–1939 the price of foreign yarn delivered to the United States, not including the duty, was around $0.35 per pound, whereas domestically produced rayon for the same period sold at an average price of $0.55 per pound.

Hence, from 1935 to 1939, under the rather questionable assumption that foreign yarn prices would have remained the same, domestic consumers could have bought a slightly lower quality rayon yarn at substantially lower prices had import duties on rayon been eliminated. It is highly doubtful, however, that the domestic market would, as a consequence, have been made more competitive. Since the variable unit costs of the oldest and largest domestic producer for the years 1935–1939 averaged around $0.42, an elimination of all import duties would probably have eliminated all the domestic producers as well. In such a case domestic consumers of rayon would simply have been substituting either the European or Japanese cartel for a domestic oligopoly. Moreover, much of the synthetic yarn capacity vital to the war effort would never have materialized.

Since 1940, because of the war and the resultant destruction of European and Japanese rayon plants, tariffs against foreign-produced rayon have been virtually inoperative. As late as 1947, rayon output in Germany was only about 10 per cent, in Japan slightly over 6 per cent, and in Italy about 40 per cent, of prewar levels. It is estimated, however, that the output of rayon in all three countries will have been increased substantially by the end of 1950.

As these foreign producers regain their prewar position in the world rayon market, it would seem that the duties on rayon imports should gradually be reduced at least to the point where foreign companies could compete in the domestic market without driving domestic producers out. If European producers do not renew their prewar cartel agreements, such a tariff policy would give domestic rayon consumers approximately six additional alternative sources of supply and, hence, increase competition in the domestic market. An added incentive for carrying out such a tariff proposal, completely aside from the question of whether competition in the rayon industry would be made more workable, is that it would enable foreign countries to build up their stocks of much-needed dollar exchange. Accordingly, the Tariff Act made effective on January 1, 1948, which provides for a reduction in the duty on rayon imports by 50 per cent, is a step in the right direction.

Just as tariff barriers have served to protect the rayon industry from free competition from abroad, the cotton price support program has served to insulate the industry from a free interplay of price competition between cotton and rayon. In more recent years the research programs of rayon producers appear to have been successfully directed toward making rayon a better substitute for cotton. Consequently, parity prices on cotton have given rayon producers many of the advantages but none of the disadvantages of a supported price: Cotton price supports also support indirectly the price of rayon but, unlike the demand for cotton, demand for rayon is, as a consequence of the price support program, increased. Obviously, therefore, one of the means for obtaining more flexible rayon prices would be to eliminate the present rigidities in cotton prices.

Public policy toward tariffs and agricultural commodity prices has affected the rayon industry principally by altering the natural conditions of demand for rayon which would have existed in the absence of regulation. The Government has, moreover, directly influenced the structure of the domestic rayon industry through its wartime construction program and its disposition of the assets of enemy countries through the Office of Alien Property.

During World War II, the Government, through the Reconstruction Finance Corporation, constructed rayon tire yarn plants having a total annual capacity of 213 million pounds. Of that portion of total capacity leased to rayon firms, 99 per cent was leased to American Viscose and Du Pont, the two largest viscose rayon producers, and is still under their control. Although exigencies of the war probably gave the Government no other alternative, this interrupted the prewar trend toward a decrease in the concentration of control in the industry.

Moreover, at the outbreak of hostilities with Germany, the United States Government took over the plants of the North American Rayon Corporation, the American Bemberg Corporation, and the American Enka Corporation, and operated them during the war through the Office of Alien Property. When hostilities ceased, American Enka, in accordance with an agreement with The Netherlands Government, was turned over to its former owners. In December 1948, a controlling interest in American Bemberg and North American was sold to the Beaunit Company, a small producer of rayon which had entered the industry in 1948. The net effect of the two transactions was to divorce three fairly large firms from the control of the Dutch-German cartel, thereby adding one new independent firm to the domestic industry, and to make one small producer, Beaunit, considerably larger. As a consequence, the structure of the rayon industry was probably altered to more nearly resemble that of a competitive industry.

For the most part, therefore, competition in the rayon industry, except for those restrictions on competition which have been imposed by public authorities, would appear to be workable. At least there is no positive remedial action which shows promise of making the rayon industry serve better the interests of society. Since the restrictions imposed on competition by tariffs and cotton price supports are not wholly of the rayon producers' own making, the public can hardly expect them to provide the necessary remedy. In concluding that the domestic rayon industry is workably competitive, however, the author is well aware of having indulged in making value judgments and, hence, would be among the first to agree that others might reach different conclusions. Unfortunately, until the concept of workable competition has been more thoroughly explored, conclusions as to the workability of competition in particular areas of the economy must be appraised almost exclusively on the basis of their consistency with whatever definition of workable competition the author adopts.

APPENDICES

APPENDIX A
Recent Developments in the Domestic Rayon Industry

With but few exceptions, rayon companies produced a fairly homogeneous product until about 1935. This is particularly true if the rayon-producing subsidiaries of such individual giants as Du Pont and Eastman Kodak be viewed as entities in the rayon industry apart from their respective corporate families. More recently, the product of individual producers has become less homogeneous for two reasons: (1) New types of rayon which differ considerably from continuous filament textile yarn have been developed, and (2) rayon producers have demonstrated some tendency toward vertical integration, extending the scope of their activities back to the raw material field and forward to the fabricating field.

In 1935 the output of the rayon industry was over 98 per cent filament textile yarn. Of this total, 78 per cent was produced by the viscose process, 20 per cent by the acetate process, and 2 per cent by the cuprammonium process.[1] The increase in output of staple fiber, the introduction of high-tenacity and semi-high-tenacity industrial yarns in 1937, and the growing importance of the acetate process have greatly changed the nature of the rayon commodity matrix since 1935. In 1947 total rayon output for the domestic industry was slightly over 975 million pounds, of which 76.6 per cent was filament yarn and 23.4 per cent was staple fiber. Of the 747 million pounds of filament yarn, 70 per cent was viscose, 29 per cent acetate, and 1 per cent cuprammonium.[2] Only 56 per cent of the viscose yarn was textile yarn; nearly one-half of all the yarn produced by this process was of the high-tenacity or tire rayon type.[3] Hence, in 1935 viscose process textile yarn accounted for about 78 per cent of total rayon output; currently it accounts for only 31 per cent.

The new types of rayon products differ from textile yarns with respect to both physical structure and market outlet. Rayon textile yarn, regardless of the process employed in production, is a continuous thread closely

[1] *Rayon Organon*, February 1950.
[2] *Rayon Organon*.
[3] Only viscose yarns can be used in tire fabric construction, acetate yarns disintegrate when subjected to heat.

resembling silk. It is used chiefly in the knitting and weaving of textile fabrics. Staple fiber is rayon cut into short staple lengths and put up in bales that, in appearance and stage of fabrication, are much like bales of raw cotton. Staple fiber can be spun into "spun-rayon" thread on either the cotton or woolen system. High-tenacity yarns are classified as industrial rather than textile yarns since virtually all of the current output is used in automobile tire fabric construction. They are from ten to twenty-five times as coarse as 150-denier rayon yarn. An indication of the extent to which product diversification had progressed by the end of 1945 can be obtained from the data presented in Table A-1. American Bemberg, the only company using the cuprammonium process, is the single remaining

TABLE A-1

Approximate Quantities of Designated Types of Rayon Produced in the United States, by Firm, 1945[a]

(UNITS ARE MILLIONS OF POUNDS)

	VISCOSE				ACETATE			
Producer	Filament Yarn Textile	Filament Yarn Tire	Staple Fiber	Total	Filament Yarn	Staple Fiber	Total	Grand Total
American Viscose	85	65	100	250	17	1	18	268
Du Pont	53	61	29	143	26	3	29	172
Celanese	—	—	—	—	92	20	112	112
Industrial Rayon	28	37	—	65	—	—	—	65
Tennessee Eastman	—	—	—	—	36	15	51	51
American Enka	18	19	—	37	—	—	—	37
North American	19	13	—	32	—	—	—	32
Tubize	19	—	—	19	4	—	4	23
American Bemberg[b]	12	—	—	12	—	—	—	12
Others	20	—	—	20	—	—	—	20

[a] Partially estimated. Based on data in annual reports of rayon companies, on information given in the trade periodicals, and on estimates of individuals familiar with the industry. Totals for the industry are from *Rayon Organon*, February 1946. See *Hearings*, H. R., Project V, p. 10.
[b] Cuprammonium.

large- or medium-size producer that has not extended its activities beyond the manufacture of textile filament yarn.[4]

In addition to products listed in Table A-1, some rayon producers have recently acquired or constructed plants that produce other synthetics by processes similar to those employed in the production of rayon. In 1936 the Du Pont Rayon Company was dissolved and made a department of E. I. du Pont de Nemours & Company, Inc. In the administrative reorganization, the Du Pont Cellophane Company was made a division under the rayon department. In 1939 Du Pont introduced the non-

[4] Nearly all producers included under "others" are subsidiaries of large parent weaving and knitting companies.

cellulosic fiber, nylon; and since 1949 the company has announced two new synthetic yarns, orlon and dacron. The nylon plants at Seaford, Delaware, Martinsville, Virginia, and Chattanooga, Tennessee, and the projected orlon and dacron plants have also been placed under the rayon department. In 1940 the American Viscose Corporation introduced vinyon, a vinyl-resin fiber having numerous industrial uses because it is impervious to water and most chemicals. Also, on September 12, 1946, the American Viscose Corporation formally acquired the Sylvania Industrial Corporation, a manufacturer of cellophane.[5]

Moreover, a tendency toward vertical integration has recently become apparent in the rayon industry. Vertical integration has been confined principally to an extension of operations forward to the knitting and weaving industry, but there is some indication that rayon producers are making preparations for owning their sources of supply of essential raw materials.[6] Until 1931, only the Celanese Corporation owned any knitting or weaving equipment. In 1932 the Industrial Rayon Corporation commenced knitting a small percentage of its yarn output. In 1934 the Tubize Corporation bought out a Brooklyn knitting mill and moved the equipment to Hopewell, Virginia, to knit some of its yarn output. By 1938 Celanese had extended its operations to include both weaving and knitting, Industrial was knitting a much higher percentage of its total viscose yarn production, and the North American Rayon Corporation had constructed a knitting mill on its plant site near Elizabethton, Tennessee.

Integration was given considerable impetus by the war and the introduction of tire yarn. The American Viscose Company was assigned much of the tire fabric capacity (40 million pounds per year) built by the Reconstruction Finance Corporation. These fabric mills are currently leased to the company at a rental of 1 per cent of investment per month on an interim basis.[7] In July 1943 the company acquired ownership of the Collins Loom Works of Amsterdam, New York. In March 1944 the company bought out the American Rayon Company and also established a subsidiary, the Aveco Company.[8] The facilities of both are used for chemical and rayon research and developmental work. Early in 1948 American Viscose, jointly with the Puget Sound Pulp and Timber Company, organized the Ketchikan Pulp and Paper Company to explore the possibilities of producing chemical wood pulp in Alaska.

Celanese has recently enlarged upon its fabricating facilities and now operates a spun-rayon plant at Burlington, North Carolina, knitting mills at Cumberland, Maryland and Bridgewater, Virginia, and weaving mills

[5] *Hearings,* H. R., Project V, p. 11.

[6] Du Pont, Eastman Kodak, and Celanese have always produced some of their own chemicals.

[7] *Hearings,* H. R., Project V, p. 61.

[8] *Hearings,* p. 11.

at Williamsport, Pennsylvania and Staunton, Virginia.[9] Celanese is currently constructing a cellulose plant and has recently completed a modern chemical plant at Bishop, Texas.[10] The merger of the Tubize Corporation with Celanese in 1946 brought the rayon plants and the knitting and finishing mills of Tubize under the control of Celanese. Industrial Rayon also enlarged upon its fabricating facilities during the war. Currently the company has extensive facilities for weaving and twisting the yarn produced at its Cleveland plant. About two-thirds of the total output of its rayon plant at Covington, Virginia is consumed in integrated operations of knitting, dyeing, and finishing of fabric.[11]

The most significant postwar development in the rayon industry is the addition of several new producers. Beaunit Mills, Inc. commenced production at its plant near Childersburg, Alabama in 1949. The plant's initial annual capacity was ten million pounds of viscose yarn.[12] Also, the United Rayon Corporation of New York has made public its plans to construct a viscose plant in the near future.[13] Present plans call for an annual capacity of four million pounds of viscose yarn and eight million pounds of viscose staple fiber. The Fair Haven Rayon Company, another new firm, has recently been reported to have commenced producing rayon by the viscose process.

Practically all rayon producers announced large expansion programs immediately after the war but many were shelved because of the rapid rise in construction costs and the postwar wood pulp shortage. The latter deterrent is probably the most pressing problem confronting the domestic rayon industry. Much research has been directed toward the discovery of new sources of cellulose but as yet no substitute for cotton linters and high-grade chemical wood pulp has been found. The future course of the rayon industry in the United States will probably be shaped as much by the availability of high-grade cellulose as by any other single economic factor.

[9] *Hearings,* p. 12.

[10] *Notes on the Chemical Fiber Industry,* no. 2 in a series of informative bulletins to stockholders of the Celanese Corporation of America, January 1948.

[11] *Hearings,* H. R., Project V, p. 14.

[12] *Rayon Organon,* April 1948.

[13] *Rayon Organon,* April 1948.

APPENDIX B
Organizations and Associations Jointly Sponsored by Domestic Rayon Yarn Producers

The Rayon Institute: The Institute was launched in 1927 with an initial appropriation of $500,000 by the Viscose Company, Du Pont, Industrial, Belamose (now Hartford Rayon), and American Glanzstoff.[1] In late 1929 three other companies, Delaware Rayon, American Enka, and New Bedford, joined the organization.[2] "The initial campaign of the Institute was not to increase immediate sales but to build prestige for the industry for the years to come; rayon producers were oversold in 1927, but the large producers believed that the future course of the industry depended upon its goodwill."[3] A breakdown of expenditures of the Institute for its first six months is as follows:[4]

Magazine	Insertions	Cost:[a]
Vogue	6	$19,200.00
Harper's Bazaar	6	17,600.00
New York Times Rotogravure	2	9,221.44
Delineator	4	29,200.00
McCall's Magazine	4	40,000.00
Good Housekeeping	6	45,000.00
Ladies' Home Journal	6	75,000.00
Butterick Quarterly	2	12,000.00
McCall's Quarterly	2	7,500.00
Pictorial Review Quarterly	2	7,500.00
Total		$262,221.44

[a] Trade advertisement to inform retail stores of the merits of rayon amounted to $25,000. Expenditures upon style shows (the chief promotional work of the Institute), booklets, maintenance of the publicity department, etc., are not known.

[1] Mois Avram, *The Rayon Industry* (2nd ed.; New York, 1929), pp. 286 ff.
[2] *Textile World,* January 11, 1930, p. 83.
[3] Avram, *The Rayon Industry,* pp. 286 ff.
[4] Avram, p. 286.

Members of the Rayon Institute were at liberty to continue their own advertising, which, for the most part, was directed toward textile mills. A few producers not members of the Institute did some direct-to-consumer advertising.[5]

The Rayon Institute is no longer listed among the trade and professional associations of the United States.[6]

Rayon and Synthetic Yarn Association: The first real association formed by the domestic rayon producers was organized in 1929. The Association was severely crippled in 1930 by the withdrawal of the two largest producers, American Viscose and Du Pont.[7] The objectives of the Association, as set forth in the *Rayon Journal,* were as follows:

> The main purpose of this association is to form a point of contact between the various factors in the rayon and synthetic industry. This is indeed an essential function of every trade association. There is no question that such contact redounds to the mutual advantage of all concerned. It is particularly valuable in an industry like the rayon industry, which has been developing at such a rapid rate and in which important new developments are looked for in the future. An association of this character can also function to safeguard the common interests of all concerned and to present a unified front to any forces that are inimical to its well-being. While the plans under which the association will work have not yet been formulated in detail, enough has been revealed to indicate that this association will not be concerned with such matters as price fixing, coöperative advertising and educational and propaganda work. It will, nevertheless, function along the recognized best lines of trade association activity, and cannot help but aid not only the yarn producers, but the entire rayon industry as well.[8]

Fourteen yarn manufacturers (practically the entire industry) joined the association: American Viscose, Du Pont, Industrial, Tubize, American Glanzstoff, American Bemberg, Acme, American Enka, American Chatillon, Belamose, Delaware Rayon, New Bedford Rayon, A. M. Johnson Rayon Mills, and Skenandoa Rayon. The officers of the Association were as follows: President: Samuel A. Salvage, President of American Viscose Corporation; Vice-President: L. A. Yerkes, President of Du Pont Rayon Company; Executive Committee: S. R. Fuller, Chairman of the Board of American Glanzstoff Corporation; Hiram Rivitz, President of the Industrial Rayon Corporation; J. P. Wright, President of New Bedford and Delaware Rayon Corporations; and B. G. Slaughter, President of Tubize Artificial Silk Company of America. Counsel for the association was William C. Matthews.[9]

[5] Avram.

[6] C. J. Judkins, *Trade and Professional Associations of the United States,* Bureau of Foreign and Domestic Commerce, United States Department of Commerce (Washington, 1942).

[7] *Textile World,* August 2, 1930, pp. 41, 84.

[8] *Rayon Journal,* November 15, 1929, pp. 7–8.

[9] *Rayon Journal,* November 15, 1929, pp. 7–8.

Rayon Yarn Producers Group: The Rayon Yarn Producers Group was an outgrowth of the Rayon and Synthetic Yarn Association. It is described in *Trade and Professional Associations of the United States* as follows: C. H. LeRoy, secretary; number of members, under twenty; organized in 1933; staff, under three. Activities: chiefly coöperative advertising.[10]

The Textile Economics Bureau, Inc.: The Bureau compiles and disseminates production, shipments, stocks, prices, and other rayon data furnished on a voluntary basis by rayon producers. Data on rayon, other fibers, and general business activity are published monthly in the *Rayon Organon.* The Textile Economics Bureau, Inc. is an independent organization unaffiliated in any official capacity with rayon producers. Income is derived principally from individual rayon companies on a fee basis.

Collusive Agreement: On February 1, 1934 the Federal Trade Commission charged the ten largest viscose rayon producers with entering into a collusive agreement to maintain prices and restrict output from October 21, 1931 to May 23, 1932. A summary of the complaint, findings, and decision appears below:

Complaint, February 1, 1934;
Decision, July 3, 1937;
Allegation: violation of section 5 of Act of Congress approved September 26, 1914.[11]

Against: the Viscose Company, Du Pont Rayon Company, Inc., Tubize Chatillon Corporation, Industrial Rayon Corporation, American Glanzstoff Corporation, American Enka Corporation, Skenandoa Rayon Corporation, Delaware Rayon Company, Acme Rayon Corporation, the Belamose Corporation, all producers of viscose rayon yarn, and the partners of Price, Waterhouse and Company, organized as a firm of public accountants prior to 1931.

Charges:

(1) By agreement among themselves have fixed and maintained, and still fix and maintain, uniform prices for viscose yarn.
(2) Agreed to curtail and limit, and still curtail and limit, the supply of viscose yarn available.
(3) Hired the services of Price, Waterhouse and Company to detect any differences that may exist from time to time from the agreed to prices and production curtailment.
(4) Because the price of knitted cloth influences the price of viscose yarn, they have and still fix and maintain uniform prices of knitted cloth.
(5) Have sought and secured agreements from knitters not to sell knitted rayon cloth at a price below that set by the yarn producers.
(6) Have and still refuse to sell to knitters who will not agree to sell below the price set by the yarn producers.
(7) The Industrial Rayon Corporation, a corporation of strong financial resources and of large production capacity of viscose yarn, entered into the manu-

[10] Judkins, *Trade and Professional Associations.*
[11] Viscose Company *et al.,* F. T. C. *Decisions,* vol. XXV, Docket no. 2161.

facture and sale of knitted rayon cloth, so that all producers named above, through the Industrial Rayon Corporation, might punish price cutters of knitted rayon cloth by underselling them to take away their customers, and thus to force such knitters, if they would remain in business, to sell knitted rayon cloth at the prices fixed by the yarn producers.

The accounting firm knew of the agreement, combination, understanding, and conspiracy described above, and assisted in carrying them out.

The above companies account for virtually all of the viscose yarn produced in the United States and the knitting trades take about 45% of all viscose yarn.

Findings:

Respondents named above, who were in competition with one another prior to October 1931, did enter into an agreement, combination, understanding, and conspiracy, on October 21, 1931, fixed and maintained uniform prices to be exacted by them from the purchasers of viscose yarn, and carried out this agreement until May 23, 1932. During such time the agreement had a dangerous tendency to and actually hindered and prevented price competition in the sale of viscose yarn and cloth in interstate commerce. These practices were to the prejudice of the public and competitors and constitute unfair methods of competition in commerce within the intent and meaning of section 5 of an Act of Congress approved September 26, 1914 entitled "An Act to Create a Federal Trade Commission, to Define its Powers and Duties, and for Other Purposes."

Order:

To cease and desist, and report in writing in detail within sixty days after order how the order was complied with. The complaint against the several partners of Price, Waterhouse and Company is dismissed.

APPENDIX C
Methodology and Statistical Computations

A. Producers' Published Price Lists

Price lists of individual viscose rayon producers have been published in each issue of the *Rayon Journal* since July 1, 1926. In the early years the effective dates of such prices were seldom given but have appeared on substantially all lists since 1934. Rayon producers are supposed to notify the *Journal* of all price revisions as they become effective. If no new price list for a particular producer is received between publication dates by the *Journal,* the last price list received is assumed to be effective and is published.

In the computations presented in this study, where the producer who led a particular price change could not be established by other means, it was assumed that the producer whose price list bore the earliest revision date led the price change. In every instance where this assumption could be tested by comparing the price leader detected in this manner with the known price leader, it proved to be valid. When the published price lists of two producers bore the same effective date, but the producer first to announce the price change could not be established by other means, the two producers were assumed to have jointly led the price change. Since producers sometimes publish a price list bearing the same effective date as the price leader, even though they lagged behind the price leader by several days, such an assumption probably overstates by two or three the number of price changes jointly led by two producers. When more than two producers (usually four or five) published price lists bearing the same effective date and the producer first to announce the price change could not be determined, the price change was included among those for which no price leader could be identified. There were four such price changes in the rayon industry between July 1926 and June 1949.

For the 1926–1933 period, the eight years for which effective dates of individual company price lists were not usually published, the sequence

TABLE C-1

History of Viscose Rayon Yarn List Prices, 1925–1949

Date	Denier 50	75	100	125	150	300
1925: Feb. 1	—	$3.10	$2.90	$2.35	$2.00	$1.75
1926: July 1	—	2.75	2.55	2.00	1.65	1.50
Sept. 1	—	2.50	2.10	2.00	1.65	1.50
Nov. 1	—	2.30	1.90	1.70	1.45	1.25
1927: Mar. 16	—	2.45	2.05	1.75	1.50	1.30
Apr. 1	—	2.55	2.15	1.75	1.50	1.30
1929: Feb. 25	—	2.50	2.10	1.55	1.30	1.10
June 18	—	2.35	1.95	1.45	1.15	1.00
1930: May 1	$2.30	1.85	1.45	1.30	1.15	1.00
July 22	2.15	1.60	1.25	1.20	0.95	0.78
1931: Jan. 9	1.50	1.35	1.10	1.00	0.75	0.63
Oct. 23	1.35	1.20	1.00	0.90	0.75	0.63
1932: May 26	1.20	1.00	0.80	0.75	0.65	0.55
June 21	1.00	0.80	0.65	0.60	0.55	0.42
Aug. 22	1.00	0.90	0.75	0.60	0.55	0.42
Aug. 29	1.10	0.90	0.75	0.65	0.60	0.47
1933: Apr. 3	1.00	0.80	0.65	0.55	0.50	0.42
Apr. 26	1.10	0.87	0.72	0.60	0.55	0.45
June 20	1.15	0.92	0.77	0.65	0.60	0.50
July 27	1.25	1.00	0.85	0.72	0.65	0.55
1934: May 24	1.15	0.90	0.75	0.62	0.55	0.45
Dec. 13	1.15	0.90	0.78	0.65	0.58	0.47
Dec. 31	1.17	0.92	0.80	0.67	0.60	0.49
1935: Apr. 17	1.05	0.85	0.74	0.63	0.55	0.47
Aug. 8	1.07	0.87	0.76	0.65	0.57	0.48
Dec. 30	1.07	0.90	0.79	0.65	0.57	0.48
1936: June 15	1.07	0.90	0.79	0.66	0.60	0.49
1937: Apr. 12	1.09	0.93	0.82	0.68	0.63	0.50
Dec. 20	0.98	0.83	0.76	0.65	0.63	0.50
1938: Jan. 14	0.98	0.83	0.76	0.65	0.59	0.48
Jan. 21	0.93	0.77	0.71	0.60	0.54	0.46
May 20	0.80	0.71	0.65	0.56	0.49	0.44
July 29	0.83	0.74	0.68	0.59	0.51	0.46
1939: Sept. 20	0.86	0.76	0.70	0.61	0.53	0.48
Dec. 4	0.95	0.77	0.70	0.61	0.53	0.48
1940: Jan. 2	0.95	0.80	0.70	0.61	0.53	0.48
1941: July 1	1.00	0.80	0.70	0.63	0.53	0.48
Sept. 15	1.05	0.85	0.73	0.66	0.55	0.49
O.P.A. PRICES						
1946: Nov. 19	1.25	0.92	0.80	0.70	0.62	0.53
1947: Jan. 28	1.38[a]	1.00	0.86	0.78[a]	0.67	0.57
Dec. 15	1.45	1.07	0.94	—	0.74	0.61
1948: Aug. 9	1.48	1.10	0.97	—	0.77	0.62
1949: May 19	1.38	1.00	0.89	—	0.71	0.57

[a] Derived from cone prices. All other prices are for first quality skeins.
Source: Published price lists of the American Viscose Corporation.

of appearance of price lists could sometimes be used to determine the price leader. For example, if a comparison between a particular issue of the *Journal* and the previous issue showed a revised price list for one yarn producer but the old lists for all other producers, it was assumed that the company whose revised price list reached the *Journal* in time for publication led the price change. Obviously, such a method of detecting the price leader could be used only when a price revision occurred a few days before the date of the *Journal's* publication. Another limitation imposed by the omission of effective dates of published price lists before 1934 is that such data cannot be used in computing the average time lag behind the price leader. The limits to such lags could sometimes be established as from one to fifteen days (when the *Journal* was published semimonthly) and from one to thirty days (when the *Journal* was published monthly).

Published prices were also of some use in determining the price relationship among acetate yarn producers; however, continuous price data for none of the five acetate rayon companies are available. Moreover, trade publications were seldom as specific in their references to companies which led acetate rayon price changes as they were in the case of viscose rayon producers. When small acetate yarn producers initiated a price change it was so stated and, for the most part, whether or not the Celanese Corporation followed the price change was indicated. Since Celanese was the only large producer of acetate yarns over most of the period covered in this study, when it was stated in trade publications that "the large producer of acetate yarn initiated the recent price change," a term frequently employed, it was assumed that the reference was to the Celanese Corporation. No price leader could be indentified for eight of the twenty-two yarn price changes which occurred between 1931 and 1949. A history of published list prices for viscose yarn appears in Table C-1.

B. Seasonal Indexes for Rayon Yarn Deliveries

The sensitivity of rayon prices to seasonal fluctuations in demand was tested in this study by tabulating price increases and decreases according to how they occurred with respect to seasonal bulges and slumps. The monthly season indexes employed in the analysis were computed by the statistical staff of the Textile Economic Bureau, Incorporated, and appear in various issues of the *Rayon Organon*.[1] In the tabulation presented in Chapter 7, it was assumed that the monthly seasonal indexes for 1936 and 1937 were applicable through 1941, although monthly seasonal indexes were not published in the *Rayon Organon* after 1937. Rayon prices

[1] For the actual method of computation see *Rayon Organon*, October 1933, pp. 140–141.

remained unchanged from September 15, 1941 to November 12, 1946, and no postwar seasonal pattern has appeared in the deliveries series. Hence, the September 1941 price change was the last to be included in the tabulation.

C. Price Trend

The trend in 150-denier viscose rayon prices was obtained by fitting to the average annual price series (1919–1935) by the method of least squares a curve of the type

$$\log y = a + bx$$

in which

$$y = \text{price in cents per pound}$$
$$x = \text{deviation in years from 1927}$$

Solving for the constants,

$$a = 2.177730$$
$$b = 0.059662$$

The equation of the desired curve is, therefore,

$$\log y = 2.17773–0.059662x$$

with origin at 1927.

D. Production Trend

The trend in the rayon yarn production series has been represented by a Gompertz curve in a number of statistics textbooks. The ordinates of trend employed in this study appear in Table F of *Statistical Methods* by Fredrick C. Mills.[2]

E. Investment, Profits, and Rate of Return

The compilation of an investment and profit series for the rayon industry is made difficult by several factors in addition to the questionable reliability of accounting statements for purposes of economic analysis: (1) Some producers, notably Du Pont, Celanese, and Eastman Kodak, do not publish separate financial statements for each of their industrial activities. (2) As stated in several places in this study, rayon has changed considerably since about 1935. A narrow economic definition of rayon would preclude such new products as staple fiber; yet, published investment and profit data relate to all products produced by rayon yarn producers. (3) No financial records are available for several small firms

[2] Mills, *Statistical Methods Applied to Economics and Business* (New York, 1938), p. 674.

which have frequently undergone reorganization, or have failed before publishing accounting statements.

The investment and rate of return series which appear throughout the study are series compiled by the United States Federal Trade Commission[3] with some slight adjustments and extensions. The Commission computed investment in the rayon industry for eight companies for which continuous data up to 1938 were available. Annual balance sheet investment for each company at the end of the year was adjusted to more nearly

TABLE C-2

Average Annual Investment and Rate of Return for the Domestic Rayon Industry, 1915–1948

Year	Total Average Annual Investment	Rate of Return	Year	Total Average Annual Investment	Rate of Return
	(000 omitted)	%		(000 omitted)	%
1915	$ 7,802.5	26.32	1932	$235,853.9	1.47
1916	8,515.1	109.19	1933	251,713.7	12.16
1917	14,115.3	95.96	1934	260,436.7	6.88
1918	21,493.2	69.49	1935	265,784.2	6.74
1919	30,452.9	97.02	1936	277,307.9	11.47
1920	40,718.6	64.21	1937	292,064.7	12.14
1921	51,223.4	41.99	1938	309,216.2	2.52
1922	65,994.0	50.12	1939	305,588.8	N.A.
1923	89,088.7	43.15	1940	308,850.1	8.60[a]
1924	110,610.0	26.73	1941	323,860.9	N.A.
1925	143,738.9	30.60	1942	321,989.6	N.A.
1926	163,081.3	20.14	1943	320,689.3	N.A.
1927	170,554.2	25.76	1944	331,314.8	N.A.
1928	208,883.1	24.49	1945	362,413.2	N.A.
1929	241,467.7	18.05	1946	388,207.6	N.A.
1930	259,951.7	4.96	1947	444,543.3	18.70[a]
1931	247,534.6	3.35	1948	—	21.40[a]

[a] Rate of return after Federal income taxes for seven companies including the four largest companies. Rate of return for other years computed before Federal income tax payments. See Federal Trade Commission, *Investments, Profits, and Rates of Return for Selected Industries* (1941), Table 1; and 1949 mimeographed release, *Rates of Return for 528 Identical Companies in 25 Selected Manufacturing Industries, 1940, 1947 and 1948*, p. 12.

reflect actual investment in the rayon business by eliminating investment in government and other securities, surpluses arising from reappraisal of assets, and so forth. Similarly, net profits before taxes were adjusted for other income, other expenses, and like revenue items to obtain only the net revenue arising from rayon production. Average investment, computed from investment at the beginning and end of each year, was divided into net profit to obtain the rate of return for each company. The sum of the average investments for all companies was divided into

[3] F. T. C., *Investments, Profits, and Rates of Return for Selected Industries.*

total profit to obtain the rate of return for the industry. The Federal Trade Commission's investment series was adjusted as follows: (1) Average annual investment in the rayon industry for all rayon producers not included in the Commission's study but for which records were available was added to annual average investment for the eight producers in order to make the series more complete. (2) The adjusted series was then extended through 1947 (see Table C-2). The series slightly understates actual investment since no records are available for the rayon business of Eastman Kodak or for several small firms that failed before reaching the stage of commercial production. The rate of return series is the series published by the Federal Trade Commission. The Commission published no rate of return data for 1939 or for the period 1941–1946.

APPENDIX D
Tables

TABLE 1

Annual Production and Distribution of Domestic Rayon Yarn and Staple Fiber, All Processes, 1911–1948

(MILLIONS OF POUNDS)

	PRODUCTION									DISTRIBUTION							
	Filament Yarn			Staple Fiber			Total Rayon			Filament Yarn				Staple Fiber			
Year	Viscose and Cupra	Acetate	Total Yarn	Viscose	Acetate	Total Staple	Viscose and Cupra	Acetate	Grand Total	Domestic Shipments	Imports	Domestic Consumption	Producer Export	Domestic Shipments	Imports	Domestic Consumption	Total Domestic Consumption
1911	0.4		0.4				0.4		0.4	0.3	1.8	2.1					2.1
1912	1.1		1.1				1.1		1.1	1.1	1.8	2.9					2.9
1913	1.8		1.8				1.8		1.8	1.6	2.4	4.0					4.0
1914	2.4		2.4				2.4		2.4	2.4	2.7	5.1					5.1
1915	3.9		3.9				3.9		3.9	4.1	2.5	6.6					6.6
1916	5.8		5.8				5.8		5.8	5.7	.9	6.6					6.6
1917	6.5		6.5				6.5		6.5	6.4	.4	6.8					6.8
1918	5.8		5.8				5.8		5.8	5.8	.2	6.0					6.0
1919	8.2	0.1	8.3				8.2	0.1	8.3	8.2	1.1	9.3					9.3
1920	10.0	0.1	10.1				10.0	0.1	10.1	7.2	1.5	8.7					8.7
1921	14.9	0.1	15.0				14.9	0.1	15.0	16.5	3.3	19.8					19.8
1922	24.0	0.1	24.1				24.0	0.1	24.1	22.6	2.1	24.7					24.7
1923	34.8	0.1	34.9				34.8	0.1	34.9	29.5	3.0	32.5					32.5
1924	36.2	0.1	36.3				36.2	0.1	36.3	40.3	1.9	42.2					42.2
1925	49.4	1.6	51.0				49.4	1.6	51.0	52.8	5.4	58.2	0.1				58.2
1926	60.1	2.6	62.7				60.1	2.6	62.7	51.3	9.3	60.6	0.4				60.6
1927	70.4	5.1	75.5				70.4	5.1	75.5	85.0	15.0	100.0	0.4				100.0
1928	91.2	6.0	97.2	0.2		0.2	91.4	6.0	97.4	88.0	12.1	100.1	0.2	0.2	0.2	0.4	100.5
1929	113.0	8.4	121.4	0.5		0.5	113.5	8.4	121.9	116.4	15.1	131.5	0.2	0.5	1.4	1.9	133.4
1930	117.5	9.8	127.3	0.4		0.4	117.9	9.8	127.7	111.6	6.3	117.9	0.3	0.4	0.5	0.9	118.8
1931	135.2	15.6	150.8	0.9		0.9	136.1	15.6	151.7	155.5	1.8	157.3	0.3	0.9	0.7	1.6	158.9
1932	116.4	18.3	134.7	1.1		1.1	117.5	18.3	135.8	151.8	0.2	152.0	0.7	1.1	2.2	3.3	155.3
1933	172.4	41.1	213.5	2.1		2.1	174.5	41.1	215.6	210.9	0.9	211.8	1.1	2.1	3.3	5.4	217.2
1934	170.3	38.0	208.3	2.2	—	2.2	172.5	38.0	210.5	194.7	0.1	194.8	2.5	1.9	0.2	2.1	196.9
1935	202.0	55.5	257.5	4.3	0.3	4.6	206.3	55.8	262.1	252.7	—	252.7	2.2	4.9	1.5	6.4	259.1
1936	214.9	62.7	277.6	9.8	2.5	12.3	224.7	65.2	289.9	297.3	0.3	297.6	1.8	12.1	12.7	24.8	322.4
1937	238.2	82.4	320.6	16.6	3.6	19.9	254.8	86.0	340.8	266.2	0.9	267.1	1.1	17.0	20.6	37.6	304.7
1938	181.5	76.1	257.6	26.4	3.5	29.9	207.9	79.6	287.5	273.8	0.3	274.1	1.4	32.1	23.2	55.3	329.4
1939	231.3	97.3	328.6	45.3	6.0	51.3	276.6	103.3	379.9	359.6	0.2	359.8	1.9	51.6	47.4	99.0	458.8
1940	257.1	133.0	390.1	70.6	10.5	81.1	327.7	143.5	471.2	388.7	—	388.7	0.9	75.6	17.7	93.3	482.0
1941	287.5	163.7	451.2	105.3	16.7	122.0	392.8	180.4	573.2	452.4	—	452.4	1.3	127.7	11.7	139.4	591.8
1942	310.5	168.8	479.3	127.6	25.7	153.3	438.1	194.5	632.6	468.8	—	468.8	5.6	151.8	0.2	152.0	620.8
1943	338.5	162.6	501.1	129.6	32.4	162.0	468.1	195.0	663.1	494.2	—	494.2	9.5	161.9	—	161.9	656.1
1944	383.5	171.7	555.2	128.4	40.3	168.7	511.9	212.0	723.9	539.1	0	539.1	16.3	165.7	—	165.7	704.8
1945	448.8	174.9	623.7	129.1	39.3	168.4	577.9	214.2	792.1	602.4	—	602.4	20.0	165.1	—	165.1	767.5
1946	491.2	186.3	677.5	132.7	43.7	176.4	623.9	230.0	853.9	666.4	0.1	666.5	12.5	175.1	33.9	209.0	875.5
1947	525.2	221.5	746.7	168.2	60.2	228.4	693.4	281.7	975.1	729.0	0.2	729.2	16.8	222.5	36.4	258.9	988.1
1948	562.3	293.8	856.1	184.5	83.7	268.2	746.8	377.5	1,124.3	836.5	10.2	846.7	16.2	264.2	38.1	302.3	1,149.0

Source: *Rayon Organon*

TABLE 2

Per Cent of Capacity Operations for the Domestic Rayon Industry 1930–1940[a]

	1930	1931	1932	1933	1934	1935	1936	1937	1938	1939	1940
Jan.	82	60–75	75–80	100	100	—	—	100	60	—	—
Feb.	75	65–75	75–80	95	100	—	—	100	60	—	—
Mar.	—	80–85	60–70	75	—[c]	—	—	100	60	—[c]	—
Apr.	70	75–100	65	70	—[c]	—	—	100	60	—[c]	—
May	70	90–100	50	85–90	—[c]	—	—	100	—	—[c]	—
June	—	90–100	40	100	—[c]	—	100	100	—	—	—
July	50–70	90–100	—[b]	100	—[c]	—	100	100	—	—	85–88
Aug.	45–70	90–100	50	100	—[c]	—	100	100	—	—	—
Sept.	75	90–100	90	100	—[c]	—	100	100	—	100	—
Oct.	80–100	80–100	100	100	85–90	100	100	100	—	100	100
Nov.	75–85	80	100	100	—	—	100	85	—	100	100
Dec.	50–65	75–80	100	100	—	—	100	75	100	100	100

Source: *Rayon Organon*, *Rayon Journal*, *Textile World*, other trade publications, and various newspapers.

[a] The rayon industry operated at virtually 100 per cent capacity from 1940 to March 1949.

[b] Most plants reported complete shutdowns.

[c] Production reported as slightly curtailed; exact per cent of capacity operations data not available.

TABLE 3

Monthly Viscose Yarn Production in the United States 1930–1949

(MILLIONS OF POUNDS)

Year	Jan.	Feb.	Mar.	Apr.	May	June	July	Aug.	Sept.	Oct.	Nov.	Dec.
1930	12.72	11.21	11.11	10.12	9.75	8.63	8.86	8.24	9.53	9.33	9.92	8.01
1931	9.62	9.53	10.24	10.33	11.12	11.62	12.13	12.93	13.12	13.44	11.03	10.02
1932	11.57	10.46	10.17	9.38	9.15	4.84	2.55	5.98	11.11	12.83	13.70	14.72
1933	15.11	13.26	14.09	10.78	13.13	14.59	14.41	15.67	15.16	15.80	15.59	14.82
1934	15.12	14.75	16.36	13.87	13.50	12.37	12.92	14.72	12.60	14.84	15.03	14.09
1935	16.69	16.00	16.98	15.70	17.14	15.36	16.46	17.99	17.02	18.68	17.13	16.92
1936	18.34	17.41	17.28	16.77	16.94	17.61	18.19	18.47	18.28	18.72	17.57	19.21
1937	19.91	18.62	20.73	20.11	19.79	20.20	20.69	21.48	20.38	21.35	18.64	16.35
1938	13.77	13.90	15.91	12.67	12.34	12.31	11.88	16.17	18.08	18.56	18.39	17.47
1939	18.77	17.90	19.80	17.79	17.03	16.75	17.89	20.80	19.92	21.68	21.90	20.88
1940	22.02	20.80	21.19	21.41	22.07	20.89	19.78	21.83	19.91	23.74	22.43	21.09
1941	24.31	21.48	22.60	22.54	24.86	23.53	24.75	24.74	24.66	26.83	24.13	24.93
1942	26.84	23.74	26.04	25.94	25.74	26.04	25.64	25.74	25.54	26.64	25.54	27.04
1943	25.52	24.92	28.82	28.02	28.22	28.62	27.72	28.82	29.12	30.42	29.32	29.12
1944	30.45	30.25	32.65	29.95	32.65	31.35	29.15	32.65	31.75	33.75	35.25	33.65
1945	36.85	33.15	38.05	37.15	39.65	37.65	36.25	36.75	35.65	40.35	39.75	37.45
1946	41.62	38.62	42.52	42.42	40.82	35.62	39.62	43.22	41.42	45.42	42.82	37.92
1947	45.92	41.02	43.62	44.02	44.12	42.82	44.02	44.02	43.42	46.72	43.42	42.02
1948	47.32	42.02	47.12	45.42	46.42	47.02	47.62	48.52	45.62	47.32	47.42	47.72
1949	47.80	44.60	48.70	42.90	43.30	42.20	—	—	—	—	—	—

Note: Production obtained by adding domestic producers' exports to domestic producers' deliveries in the United States and adjusting the result by the amount of inventory change. Monthly export data not available after 1941; hence, the small amount of annual exports was assumed to have been spread evenly throughout each year.

TABLE 4

Monthly Acetate Yarn Production in the United States 1930–1949

(MILLIONS OF POUNDS)

Year	Jan.	Feb.	Mar.	Apr.	May	June	July	Aug.	Sept.	Oct.	Nov.	Dec.
1930	0.6	0.8	0.5	0.6	0.8	0.7	0.9	0.9	1.0	1.0	0.6	1.4
1931	1.2	1.3	1.2	1.3	1.5	1.4	0.8	1.2	1.4	1.5	1.5	1.3
1932	1.1	1.1	0.9	1.0	0.9	0.9	1.5	1.7	1.8	2.2	2.5	2.7
1933	3.3	3.5	3.8	3.5	3.3	3.3	3.6	3.6	3.4	3.4	3.1	3.0
1934	2.717	2.417	2.717	2.617	2.617	2.717	3.117	3.317	3.417	4.017	4.117	4.317
1935	4.317	4.117	3.917	4.317	4.117	4.117	4.617	4.817	4.917	5.217	5.417	5.617
1936	5.525	5.325	5.225	5.125	5.125	4.925	5.125	5.625	6.325	6.325	4.225	3.825
1937	6.317	6.217	6.917	6.617	7.417	7.217	7.217	7.617	7.417	7.317	6.817	5.017
1938	3.142	4.242	5.742	5.142	5.842	5.042	6.742	8.142	8.642	8.142	7.242	8.042
1939	8.750	8.050	8.750	7.950	7.350	7.750	7.750	4.750	7.050	9.550	9.850	9.850
1940	10.408	10.508	10.908	11.008	11.108	11.008	10.608	11.108	9.508	11.708	12.308	12.508
1941	13.633	11.433	13.133	13.733	14.133	13.833	14.133	13.233	13.433	15.633	13.633	13.833
1942	15.825	12.325	14.125	13.425	13.825	13.425	14.225	13.825	13.825	14.625	14.225	15.125
1943	13.375	13.175	14.475	14.075	14.475	11.575	12.875	13.675	12.975	14.175	13.975	13.775
1944	13.708	14.208	15.108	14.208	14.708	14.408	13.508	14.108	13.908	15.208	14.508	14.208
1945	14.916	13.016	14.916	13.816	15.016	14.416	14.116	14.916	14.316	15.816	15.116	14.516
1946	16.124	14.324	16.024	15.324	16.424	15.824	14.824	14.824	14.524	15.824	16.224	16.024
1947	19.075	16.275	17.875	18.175	17.475	13.075	20.075	19.175	19.675	20.875	19.975	19.875
1948	23.730	20.330	22.830	27.330	24.030	24.820	25.920	25.420	25.220	25.920	26.420	27.320
1949	26.700	24.000	21.700	16.300	14.400	14.700	—	—	—	—	—	—

Note: Production obtained by adding domestic producers' exports to domestic producers' deliveries in the United States and adjusting the result by the amount of inventory change. Monthly export data not available after 1941; hence, the small amount of annual exports was assumed to have been spread evenly throughout each year.

BIBLIOGRAPHY

I. Books and Articles

1. Avram, Mois, *The Rayon Industry* (New York: D. Van Nostrand Company, 1927; rev. ed., 1929).
2. Boulding, Kenneth E., *Economic Analysis* (New York: Harper and Bros., 1948, rev. ed.).
3. Burns, Arthur F., and Wesley C. Mitchell, *Measuring Business Cycles* (New York: National Bureau of Economic Research, 1946).
4. Chamberlin, E. H., *The Theory of Monopolistic Competition* (5th ed.; Cambridge: Harvard University Press, 1946).
5. Clark, J. M., "Toward a Concept of Workable Competition," *American Economic Review* (June 1940), p. 241.
6. *Cost Behavior and Price Policy* (New York: National Bureau of Economic Research, Price Studies No. 4, 1943).
7. Crum, William L., *Corporate Size and Earning Power* (Cambridge: Harvard University Press, 1939).
8. Edwards, Corwin D., *Maintaining Competition* (New York: McGraw-Hill Book Company, 1948).
9. Foltzer, Joseph, *Artificial Silk and Its Manufacture* (London: I. Pitman, 1924), translated from the French by T. Woodhouse.
10. Gordon, R. A., *Business Leadership in the Large Corporation* (Washington: The Brookings Institution, 1945).
11. Hall, R. L. and C. J. Hitch, "Price Theory and Business Behavior," *Oxford Economic Papers,* no. 2 (1939), p. 12.
12. Jones, Edgar, "Price Leadership in the Rayon Industry," *Manchester School of Economic and Social Studies* (October 1941), p. 86.
13. Lester, Richard A. "Short Comings of Marginal Analysis for Wage-Employment Problems," *American Economic Review* (March 1946), p. 63.
14. Machlup, Fritz, "Marginal Analysis and Empirical Research," *American Economic Review* (September 1946), p. 519.
15. Markham, Jesse W., "Integration in the Textile Industry," *Harvard Business Review* (January 1950), p. 74.
16. Mason, Edward S., "Price and Production Policies of Large-Scale Enterprise," *American Economic Review* (March 1939), p. 61.
17. McLaughlin, Glenn C., and Stefan Robock, *Why Industry Moves South,* National Planning Association Committee of the South, Report no. 3 (June 1949).

18. Mills, F. C., *Statistical Methods Applied to Economics and Business* (rev. ed.; New York: Henry Holt and Company, 1938).
19. Nichol, A. J., *Partial Monopoly and Price Leadership* (Philadelphia: Smith Edwards Co., 1930).
20. Schumpeter, Joseph A., *Capitalism, Socialism and Democracy* (New York: Harper and Bros., 1942).
21. Schwarz, E. W. K., and H. R. Mauersberger, *Rayon and Synthetic Yarn Handbook* (New York: Rayon Publishing Co., 1934; rev. ed., 1936).
22. ———, *Rayon and Staple Fiber Handbook* (New York: Rayon Publishing Co., 1939).
23. Stigler, George J., "Extent and Bases of Monopoly," *American Economic Review* (June 1942), p. 1.
24. ———, "The Kinky Oligopoly Demand Curve and Rigid Prices," *Journal of Political Economy* (October 1947), p. 432.
25. ———, "Notes on the Theory of Duopoly," *Journal of Political Economy* (August 1940), p. 521.
26. ———, "Production and Distribution in the Short Run," *Journal of Political Economy* (June 1939), p. 305.
27. Stocking, George W., and Myron W. Watkins, *Cartels in Action* (New York: The Twentieth Century Fund, 1946).
28. *Textile Markets* (New York: National Bureau of Economic Research, 1939).
29. Wallace, Donald H., *Market Control in the Aluminum Industry* (Cambridge: Harvard University Press, 1937).
30. Wheeler, Edward, *The Manufacture of Artificial Silk, with Special Reference to the Viscose Process* (New York: D. Van Nostrand Company, 1931).

II. Publications of the United States Government

Bureau of the Census

31. *Census of Manufactures,* rayon and allied products section, odd years, 1927 to 1947.
32. *Facts for Industry, Census of Pulp Mills and of Paper and Paperboard Mills* (1945).

Department of Agriculture

33. Evans, R. B., *Trends in the Consumption of Fibers, 1892–1937* (1940).
34. *Hearings on the Study of Agricultural and Economic Problems of the Cotton Belt,* before special subcommittee on cotton of the Committee on Agriculture, House of Representatives, 80th Congress, First Session (July 7 and 8, 1947).
35. Howell, L. D., *Marketing and Manufacturing Margins for Textiles,* Technical Bulletin no. 891 (March 1945).
36. *Report on Development and Use of Rayon* (1942).
37. *Weekly Cotton Linters Review,* Production and Marketing Administration (March 29, April 12, July 3, 1946).

Department of Labor, Bureau of Labor Statistics

38. *Monthly Labor Review,* employment, hours of labor, average hourly earnings and payrolls in the rayon and allied products industry, 1930 through 1949 issues.

39. *Productivity and Unit Labor Cost in Selected Manufacturing Industries, 1919–1940* (1942).
40. *Productivity and Unit Labor Cost in Selected Manufacturing Industries, 1939–1945*, mimeographed release (1946).
41. *Wages and Hours in the Rayon Industry*, bulletins no. 546, 568, 806, and no. 41 (second series).

Department of Commerce, Bureau of Foreign and Domestic Commerce

42. Judkins, C. J., *Trade and Professional Associations of the United States* (1942).
43. *Survey of Current Business*, monthly issues and special supplements, 1923–1949.

Federal Trade Commission

44. *Federal Trade Commission Decisions, Findings, Orders, and Stipulations*, vol. 25, Viscose Company, *et al.*, Docket no. 2161.
45. *Hearings* of the Federal Trade Commission v. Viscose Company *et al.*, 1934–1937, Record and Exhibits, Smith and Hulze, Washington, official reporters.
46. *Investments, Profits and Rates of Return for Selected Industries*, a special report before the Temporary National Economic Committee Congressional Committee, Washington, 1941.
47. *Rates of Return for 528 Identical Companies in 25 Selected Manufacturing Industries, 1940, 1947 and 1948*, mimeographed release (December 1949).

Tariff Commission

48. *The Rayon Industry* (1944).

Temporary National Economic Committee

49. Thorp, Willard, *et al.*, *The Structure of Industry*, Monograph no. 27.
50. Wilcox, Clair, *Competition and Monopoly in American Industry*, Monograph no. 21.

III. Newspapers and Trade Journals

51. *American Silk and Rayon Journal* (1915–1948).
52. *Barron's, The National Business and Financial Weekly* (May 29, 1939).
53. *Chemical and Metallurgical Engineering* (January 1946).
54. *Daily News Record* (March 7, 1928; April 25, 1946; January 23, 24, and February 6, 1950).
55. *Engineer*, Lockwood, Greene & Co., Inc. (November 1927).
56. *Financial News* (London: February 6, 1928).
57. *Fortune* (December 1934, July 1937, and September 1946).
58. *International Textile Apparel Analysis* (February 24, 1934, and September 28, 1935).
59. *Moody's Manual of Industrial Investments* (1930–1949).
60. *New York Times*, financial section (March 5, 1949).
61. *Rayon Journal* (1925–1950).
62. *Rayon Organon* (1929–1950).
63. *Silk and Rayon Digest* (1923–1947).

64. *Silk, Rayon and Other Synthetic Fibers* (1926–1947).
65. *Textile World* (1929–1950).

IV. Pamphlets, Manuscripts, and Special Reports

66. Axe, E. W., and Company, *Cotton and Rayon Textile Companies,* research department (New York, 1946).
67. ———, *Rayon Common Stocks* (New York, 1946).
68. Baker, Weeks, and Harden, *Strength of the Textile Industry* (New York, March 1948).
69. Celanese Corporation of America, *Notes on the Chemical Fiber Industry,* no. 2 in a series of informative bulletins to stockholders (January 1948).
70. Lockwood Greene Engineers, Inc., a confidential report which sets forth engineering estimates of cost of construction of rayon plants of various sizes relative to a proposed rayon plant in India. The report was directed by Mr. S. B. Lincoln. The information was obtained through Mr. H. E. Cousins, Vice-President of Lockwood Greene Engineers, Inc.
71. Metropolitan Life Insurance Corporation, *Rayon, A New Influence in the Textile Industry,* a special bulletin (1928).
72. *Report of the Japanese Cellulose Industry Reporters, Ltd.* (January 1935).
73. Vandermuelen, Daniel, "Inter-Textile Competition" (MS), an unpublished study of the textile market in the possession of Professor Vandermuelen, Claremont College, California.
74. Variation in Unit Cost with Size of Plant and with Per Cent of Installed Capacity Operated; confidential information submitted to the author by a large multi-plant rayon producer.

INDEX

Bei Fragen zur Produktsicherheit wenden Sie sich bitte an:
If you have any questions regarding product safety,
please contact:

Walter de Gruyter GmbH
Genthiner Straße 13
10785 Berlin
productsafety@degruyterbrill.com